Spiritual Masters

Series

World Wisdom
The Library of Perennial Philosophy

The Library of Perennial Philosophy is dedicated to the exposition of the timeless Truth underlying the diverse religions. This Truth, often referred to as the Sophia Perennis—or Perennial Wisdom—finds its expression in the revealed Scriptures as well as the writings of the great sages and the artistic creations of the traditional worlds.

The Original Gospel of Rāmakrishna appears as one of our selections in the Spiritual Masters: East and West series.

Spiritual Masters: East & West Series

This series presents the writings of great spiritual masters of the past and present from both East and West. Carefully selected essential writings of these sages are combined with biographical information, glossaries of technical terms, historical maps, and pictorial and photographic art in order to communicate a sense of their respective spiritual climates.

Shrī Rāmakrishna seated in ecstasy (*samādhi*) on the veranda of the Rādhākānta Temple, Dakshineshwar, 1883/1884. When Rāmakrishna saw a print of this photograph, he is said to have remarked: “This depicts a high yogic state. In times to come, it will be worshiped in every home.”

The Original Gospel of Rāmakrishna

Based on M.'s English Text, Abridged

Revised by
Swāmī Abhedānanda

&

Edited and Abridged by
Joseph A. Fitzgerald

Foreword by
Alexander Lipski

&

Biographical Introduction by
Swāmī Vivekānanda

World Wisdom

Niranjanam Nityam anantarūpam,
Bhaktānukampā dhritavigraham vai;
Ishāvatāram Paramesham Īdyam,
Tam Rāmakrishnam Shirashā Namāmah.

Salutations to Bhagavān Shrī Rāmakrishna, the perfect embodiment of the Eternal Truth which manifests itself in various forms to help mankind, and the Incarnation of the Supreme Lord who is worshiped by all.

Harī Om Tat Sat

The Original Gospel of Rāmakrishna:
Based on M.'s English Text, Abridged,

Cover:
Shrī Rāmakrishna standing in ecstasy (*samādhi*), supported by his nephew Hridāya. Photo taken at the home of Keshab Chandra Sen in Calcutta, September 21, 1879.

Library of Congress Cataloging-in-Publication Data

Ramakrishna, 1836-1886.
[Ramakrishna kathmrita. English. Selections]
The original gospel of Ramakrishna : based on M.'s English text, abridged / revised by Swami Abhednanda & edited and abridged by Joseph A. Fitzgerald ; foreword by Alexander Lipski & biographical introduction by Swami Viveknanda.
p. cm. -- (Library of perennial philosophy. Spiritual masters--East and West series)
Originally published in Bengali in 2 v. with title: Ramakrishna kathmrita. Calcutta, 1902-1903. Transcribed in the form of diary notes and translated into English by Mahendranath Gupta.
"The Gospel of Ramakrishna was first published in book form in 1907 in both an Indian and American edition, the latter of which, called the 'authorized edition,' is reproduced here in an abridged form"--Editor's Pref.
Includes bibliographical references and index.
ISBN 978-1-935493-97-6 (pbk. : alk. paper)
I. M, 1854-1932. II. Abhedananda, Swami, 1866-1939. III. Fitzgerald, Joseph A., 1977- IV. Title.
BL1280.292.R36A275213 2011
294.5'55092--dc23

2011040433

Printed on acid-free paper in the United States of America

For information address World Wisdom, Inc.
P.O. Box 2682, Bloomington, Indiana 47402-2682
www.worldwisdom.com

Contents

Foreword

Normally the term "Gospel," i.e. the Good News, refers to the words and deeds of Jesus. It is here deliberately used in reference to the teachings of Rāmakrishna, the spiritual giant of modern Hinduism.

Born in 1836 to Orthodox *brāhmin* parents, he had his first ecstatic experiences at the age of six. He gradually practiced different Hindu spiritual teachings including eventually *Vedānta*, which proved to him that the ultimate reality, i.e. *Brahman*, is beyond time, space, and causality. At the same time he realized that all religions, not just Hinduism, lead to the ultimate truth, and that anyone who wholeheartedly seeks God will attain his goal. God can be found anywhere. One need not go to the holy city of Benares. Benares is wherever you are. He told a disciple: "Cry to God with a yearning heart and then you will see Him. People will shed a jugful of tears . . . for the sake of money; but who sheds a tear for God? . . . The rosy light of the dawn comes before the rising sun; likewise a longing and yearning heart is the sign of God-vision that comes after." The proof of this statement was provided by Rāmakrishna whenever his disciples saw him in ecstasy. They concluded how deep the faith and devotion of their Master must be! It truly inspired his many followers.

Rāmakrishna welcomed equally Hindus, Muslims, Sikhs, and Christians to his spiritual abode, and he taught by example that he had risen above Hindu caste prejudices by cleaning the home of an untouchable. At the age of 50, August 15, 1886, Rāmakrishna relinquished his body. But his teachings were brought to the west by his greatest disciple, Swāmī Vivekānanda, when he addressed the Parliament of Religions in Chicago in 1893. Rightly Mahātmā Gandhi wrote: "Rāmakrishna's life enables us to see God face to face."

Alexander Lipski
California State University
Long Beach

Editor's Preface

The book known in English as *The Gospel of Rāmakrishna* chronicles the final four years of the life of Shrī Rāmakrishna (1836-1886), the Paramahamsa of Dakshineshwar. Through this precious record of events—observed and set down by one of his householder disciples, Mahendranāth Gupta—we are as if transported back in time to a small room in the northwest corner of a temple-compound that lies on the eastern bank of the river Ganges where it flows past the village of Dakshineshwar, about four miles north of Calcutta, Bengāl. There we are seated at the Paramahamsa's feet, listening to parables and sayings that Mahātmā Gandhi describes as "pages from the Book of Life." Gandhi also states—and the experience of countless men and women confirms it—that these words will most surely "leave on the reader an impression which he cannot resist."[1]

The recorder of the *Gospel*, seeking no worldly acclaim, signed his name simply as "M.," adding at times the epithet, "a son of the Lord and disciple." He was in his nature ideally suited to his role, combining as he did a phenomenal power of recollection with a rare sensitivity of soul. His Master, moreover, subtly aided him in the task he was to fulfill. From time to time Rāmakrishna would ask M. to repeat some point he had previously explained, and would correct him if he made a mistake. At other times, he would wait to begin an important discourse until M. was present. M., for his part, took detailed notes of each encounter with the Master—notes which later proved invaluable once M. decided, after Rāmakrishna's passing, to write an account of his life. The result was such that after hearing M.'s work read to her, the Holy Mother, Rāmakrishna's widow, exclaimed: "I felt as if it was he, the Master, who was saying all that."

M. wrote his underlying work, the *Shrī Shrī Rāmakrishna Kathāmrita*, or "Words of Nectar of Shrī Rāmakrishna," in his and the Master's native tongue of Bengāli. As a school-teacher in British-ruled India, M. also spoke and wrote in English, into which

1 Mohandas K. Gandhi, "Foreword," *Life of Sri Ramakrishna: Compiled from Various Authentic Sources* (Calcutta: Advaita Ashrama, 1924).

he was the first to translate selections from his *Kathāmrita*. His translation began to appear in 1897 as a series of "Leaves from the Gospel of the Lord Sree Rāmakrishna," published by two English language Indian journals.[2] Strange to say, it was only after this publication of the *Gospel* that the *Kathāmrita* itself began to appear in installments in various Bengāli language journals. For the following forty some years, until shortly before his death in 1932, M. continued to expand on the *Kathāmrita*, the full version of which runs to five volumes. He approached the writing of the *Kathāmrita*, not as a project to be hurriedly completed, but as a kind of spiritual exercise; on days that he would write, he would abstain from food but for one meal of boiled rice and clarified butter (*ghee*), and would dedicate several hours of the day to meditation.

The Gospel of Rāmakrishna was first published in book form in 1907 in both an Indian and American edition,[3] the latter of which, called the "Authorized Edition," is reproduced here in an abridged form.[4] The text of this edition is based on M.'s previously published "Leaves," as revised and expanded upon by Swāmī Abhedānanda, one of the direct monastic disciples of Rāmakrishna. The Bengāli *Kathāmrita* has since been re-translated several times, though never again by individuals who had benefited, as had M. and Abhedānanda, from intimate personal contact with the great soul whose words and deeds the book relates. Today, nonetheless, the most widely read translation is one made in the 1940s by Swāmī Nikhilānanda, a monk in the Rāmakrishna Order, who was the

2 *The Brahmavādin* (Madras) published one installment in its mid October issue and a second in its mid November issue, while *The Dawn* (Calcutta) published one installment in its December issue.

3 Respectively, *Gospel of Srī Rāmakrishna (According to M., a son of the Lord and disciple) or The Ideal Man for India and for the World*, Part I (Madras: The Brahmavadin Office, 1907) and *The Gospel of Ramakrishna* (New York: The Vedanta Society, 1907).

4 In order to enhance readability, the present edition eliminates some, usually repetitive, passages; other editorial changes include the re-arrangement or elimination of headings, the re-arrangement, elimination, or addition of notes, the altering of spelling, capitalization, and punctuation, the addition or substitution of a few words or phrases, and the preparation of a new glossary and index.

first to translate all five volumes of the *Kathāmrita* into English.[5] Nikhilānanda's work retains the now standard English title that M. first adopted, *The Gospel of Rāmakrishna*. The "Authorized Edition" of the *Gospel*, meanwhile, has suffered a lengthy period of relative neglect—outside of a slightly revised Indian edition, and recent archival facsimile reprints; it has not been offered to the public for more than sixty years.

To read multiple translations of the *Kathāmrita* may help one to comprehend more fully its meaning, just as to hear multiple descriptions of an unfamiliar temple may help one to picture more completely its design. At the same time, it cannot be denied that among descriptions of a temple, one made by the temple-builder himself will be of particular interest. Thus, it is our great honor to present once again that classic work based on M.'s own translation of his *Kathāmrita*—the original *Gospel of Rāmakrishna*.

In addition to the *Gospel*, which is centered on Shrī Rāmakrishna's final years, there exist numerous written accounts of the full course of his life. Among the earliest and most important of these biographical works is one written by the beloved disciple Narendranāth Gupta, known after his Master's passing as Swāmī Vivekānanda.[6] We believe this simple sketch usefully introduces the *Gospel* and serves also to illustrate Frithjof Schuon's conclusion that:

5 Nikhilānanda later created an abridged, though still lengthy, edition of his translation.

6 The biography is an edited version of a letter Vivekānanda wrote to Max Müller, published in Müller's *Rāmakrishna: His Life and Sayings* (New York: Charles Scribner's Sons, 1899), pp. 30-59; it is supplemented in a few places with material taken from a lecture Vivekānanda gave in New York, and elsewhere, published as *My Master* (New York: Baker & Taylor, 1901).

It should be noted that an appreciation of the value of this work does not oblige one to accept *en masse* the varied theses Vivekānanda propounded in his doctrinal works. For an evaluation of Vivekānanda's life, thought, and legacy, see Frithjof Schuon's chapter "*Vedānta*" in *Spiritual Perspectives and Human Facts* (Bloomington, IN: World Wisdom, 2007), pp. 120-129.

> There is something in Rāmakrishna that seems to defy every category: he was like the living symbol of the inward unity of religions; he was in fact the first saint to wish to enter into foreign spiritual forms, and in this consisted his exceptional and in a sense universal mission—something allying him to the prophets without making him a prophet in the strict sense of the word; in our times of confusion, distress, and doubt, he was the saintly "verifier" of forms and the "revealer" as it were of their single truth.[7]

In the Paramahamsa's death-bed words of self-witness: "He who was Rāma, who was Krishna, Buddha, Christ, and Chaitanya, has now become Rāmakrishna."[8] Blessed are we who may read of the "good news" of his life!

Joseph A. Fitzgerald

7 Schuon, *Spiritual Perspectives and Human Facts*, p. 122.

8 Intra p. 198.

Preface to the 1907 Edition

This is the authorized English edition of the *Gospel of Rāmakrishna*. For the first time in the history of the world's Great Saviors, the exact words of the Master were recorded *verbatim* by one of his devoted disciples. These words were originally spoken in the Bengāli language of India. They were taken down in the form of diary notes by a householder disciple, "M." At the request of Shrī Rāmakrishna's *sannyāsī* disciples, however, these notes were published in Calcutta during 1902-1903 A.D., in Bengāli, in two volumes, entitled *Rāmakrishna Kathāmrita*.

At that time M. wrote to me letters authorizing me to edit and publish the English translation of his notes, and sent me the manuscript in English which he himself translated, together with a true copy of a personal letter which Swāmī Vivekānanda wrote to him:

Dehra Dun, November 24th, 1897

My dear Master Mahasaya:

Many thanks for your second leaflet. It is indeed wonderful. The move is quite original, and never the life of a great teacher was brought before the public untarnished by the writer's mind as you are doing. The language also is beyond all praise. So fresh, so pointed, and withal so plain and easy.

I cannot express in adequate terms how I have enjoyed them. I am really in a transport when I read them. Strange, isn't it? Our teacher and Lord was so original and each one of us will have to be original or nothing. I now understand why none of us attempted his life before. It has been reserved for you, this great work. He is with you evidently. With all love and *namaskār*.

Vivekānanda

P.S.—Socratic dialogues are of Plato all over. You are entirely hidden. Moreover, the dramatic part is infinitely beautiful. Everybody likes it—here or in the west.

This letter of Swāmī Vivekānanda shows that the words of the Master were accurately recorded by M.

At the request of M. I have edited and remodeled the larger portion of his English manuscript; while the remaining portions I have translated directly from the Bengāli edition of his notes. The marginal headings, footnotes, and index, as well as the division of the *Gospel* into fourteen chapters, were added by me. I have endeavored to make every word of this edition as literal, simple, and colloquial as possible.

Some repetitions are purposely kept to show how the Master used the same illustrations on different occasions during the course of his eloquent conversations.

The completed work is now offered to the western world with the sincere hope that the sublime teachings of Shrī Rāmakrishna may open the spiritual sight of seekers after Truth, and bring peace and freedom to all souls struggling for realization.

Swāmī Abhedānanda
New York,
December 15, 1907

Biographical Introduction

Rāmakrishna, we are told, was born in the village of Kāmārpukur, in the Hooghly District, situated about four miles to the west of the Jahānābad subdivision, and thirty-two miles south of Burdwan. His life on earth began on the 20th of February, 1833,[1] and ended the 16th of August, 1886, 1 a.m. The village in which he was born was inhabited chiefly by people of the lower castes, mostly blacksmiths with some sprinkling of carpenters, cowherds, husbandmen, and oilmen. His father was the head of the only brāhminic family settled in the village. Though very poor, he would rather starve than stray from the strictest path of brāhminical orthodoxy. The original name given to his child was Gadādhara, a name of Vishnu, which means one who holds the club, and it was given him, we are told, on account of a prophetic dream of his father, to whom, while on a pilgrimage to Gaya, Vishnu appeared, telling him that he, the deity, would be born as his son. It was later in life that he began to be called Rāmakrishna. We are told, and we could hardly have expected anything else, that his father, whose name was Khudirām Chattopādhyāya, was a great lover of God, a man pure in mind, handsome of figure, straightforward and independent. Rumor says that he possessed supernatural powers, particularly what is called *vāk-siddhi*, power of speech, which means that everything he told, good or bad, of anybody, would always come to pass. He was highly reverenced by all the people of his village, who stood up whenever they saw him coming, and saluted him, nay who would never talk frivolity in his presence.

It could hardly have been otherwise than that his mother also, Chandrā Devī, was a pattern of simplicity and kindness. We are told that Mathur Bābu, the rich and devoted disciple of her son, came to her once and pressed her to accept a present of a few thousand *rupees*, but to his astonishment she declined the offer.

The father proved his independence while still living at Dere, on his own ancestral property. The *zamindār* (landlord) of the vil-

1 Editor's Note: Later research indicates that Rāmakrishna was more likely born on February 18th, 1836.

lage wanted him to appear as a witness on his side, threatening him with confiscation of his property and expulsion from his village, if he refused. Khudirām refused, left his village, and migrated to Kāmārpur, a village two or three miles east of Dere. There, through the help of some true friends, he managed to make a poor living, and yet he was always profusely generous to the poor and hospitable to everybody, living chiefly in the company of religious men, performing every kind of worship, and trying to realize religion to its fullest extent.

His son Rāmakrishna, we are told, had something in him which attracted everybody and made people love him, as if he were of their own kith and kin, even at the first appearance. The young child used to repeat the whole of the religious operas and dramas, the acting, the music, and everything, after hearing them once. He had a very good musical voice and a taste for music. He was a very good judge of the merits and defects of the statues or images of gods or goddesses, and his judgment was held as final by the old people of the village, even from his childhood. He could draw and make images of gods himself. One of the broken stone images of Shrī Krishna, which he repaired in later days, is still to be seen in the temple of Dakshineshwar of Rānī Rāshmani, about four miles to the north of Calcutta. After hearing a religious drama, e.g. the doings of Shrī Krishna, he would gather his playmates, teach them the different parts, and enact it in the fields, under the trees. Sometimes he would build an image of the god Shiva, and worship it with his companions. At the age of six he was well versed in the *Purānas*, likewise in the *Rāmāyana*, the *Mahābhārata*, and the *Shrīmad Bhāgavatam*, by hearing them from the *kathaks*, a class of men who preach and read these *Purānas* for the enlightenment of the uneducated masses all over India.

The pilgrim road to Purī passes through the outskirts of the village where he lived, and very often a whole host of ascetics and religious men would come and take shelter in the *dharmasālā* or pilgrim-house, built by the Lāhā family, the *zamindār* of the village. Rāmakrishna used to go there very often, talk to them on religious subjects, mark their habits, and hear their tales of travel.

It is the custom in India to gather all the learned *pandits* or professors of the neighborhood at a funeral ceremony. In one of these gatherings in the house of the Lāhā family, a question arose about some intricate points of theology, and the professors could not come to a conclusion. The boy Rāmakrishna went to them and decided it quickly with his simple language, and all present were astonished.

Before he reached his teens, he was walking in the fields one day. The sky was very clear and blue, and he saw a flight of white cranes moving along it. The contrast of colors was so very beautiful and dazzling to his imagination, and produced such thoughts in him, that he fell down in a trance.

He was the youngest child of a family of three sons and two daughters. His eldest brother, Rāmkumār Chattopādhyāya, was a very learned professor of the old school. He had his own school at Calcutta. At the age of sixteen Rāmakrishna, having been invested by his own father with the sacred brāhminic thread, was taken to this school, but what was his disgust to find that after all their high talk on being and non-being, on *Brahman* and *māyā*, on how the soul is liberated by the realization of *Ātman*, they would never dream of practicing these precepts in their own lives, but run after lust and gold, after name and fame. He told his brother plainly he would never care for that kind of learning, the sole aim of which was to gain a few pieces of silver, or a few maunds of rice and vegetables. He yearned to learn something which would raise him above all these, and give him as a recompense God Himself. From that time he kept aloof from the school.

The temple of the goddess Kālī at Dakshineshwar, about five miles to the north of Calcutta, was established in 1853 A.D. It stands on the side of the Ganges, and is one of the finest temples in India. The temple deeds were drawn in the name of the *guru*, or spiritual director of Rānī Rāshmani, for she being of a lower caste, none of the higher castes would come to the temple and take food there if she drew the deeds in her own name. The eldest brother of Shrī Rāmakrishna was appointed as priest to the temple. The two brothers came on the day when the temple was first opened and established, but such were the caste prejudices of Rāmakrishna at that time that he protested vehemently against his brother's taking service under a *shūdra* woman, or one of the lowest caste, and would not take any cooked food in the temple precincts, because it was forbidden in the *Shāstras*. So, amidst all the rejoicings of the day, in which some fifteen to twenty thousand people were sumptuously entertained, he was the only man who kept his fast. At night he went to the grocer's close by, took a pice-worth of fried paddy, and returned to Calcutta. But after a week his love for his brother made him return again, and at his entreaty he consented to live there, on condition, however, that he should be allowed to cook his own meals by the side of the Ganges, which is the holiest place according to the Hindus. A few months afterwards his brother became incapable of conducting the services through illness, and requested Rāmakrishna to take charge of the duties. He consented at last, and became a recognized worshipper of the goddess Kālī.

Sincere as he always was, he could do nothing from mercenary motives, nor did he ever do anything which he did not thoroughly believe. He now began to look upon the image of the goddess Kālī as his Mother and the Mother of the universe. He believed it to be living and breathing and taking food out of his hand. After the regular forms of worship he would sit there for hours and hours, singing hymns and talking and praying to her as a child to his mother, till he lost all consciousness of the outward world. Sometimes he would weep for hours, and would not be comforted, because he could not see his Mother as perfectly as he wished. People became divided in their opinions regarding him. Some held the young priest to be mad, and some took him to be a great lover of God, and all this outward madness as the manifestation of that love. His mother and brothers, thinking that his imagination would calm down when he had a young wife and a family of his own to look after, took him to his native village and married him to the daughter of Rāmachandra Mukhopādhyāya, who was then five years of age, Sāradā Devī by name. It is said when his mother and brothers were looking after a suitable bride for him, he himself told them that the daughter of such and such a man was destined to be joined to him in marriage, and that she was endowed with all the qualities of a goddess or *devī*, and they went and found the bride.

After his marriage he returned to Calcutta and took upon himself the charges of the temple again, but instead of toning down, his fervor and devotion increased a thousand-fold. His whole soul, as it were, melted into one flood of tears, and he appealed to the goddess to have mercy on him and reveal herself to him. No mother ever shed such burning tears over the death-bed of her only child.

Crowds assembled round him and tried to console him, when the blowing of the conch-shells proclaimed the death of another day, and he gave vent to his sorrow, saying, "Mother, oh my mother, another day has gone, and still I have not found thee." People thought he was mad, or that he was suffering from some acute pain, for how was it possible for them, devoted as they were to lust and gold, to name and fame, to imagine that a man could love his God or Goddess Mother with as much intensity as they loved their wives and children? The son-in-law of Rānī Rāshmani, Mathur Bābu, who had always had a love for this young *brāhmin* took him to the best physicians in Calcutta to get him cured of his madness. But all their skill was of no avail. Only one physician of Dacca told them that this man was a great *yogī* or ascetic, and that all their pharmacopeia was useless for curing his disease, if indeed it were a disease at all. So his friends gave him up as lost.

Meanwhile he increased in love and devotion day by day. One day as he was feeling his separation from Devī very keenly, and thinking of putting an end to himself as he could not bear his loneliness any longer, he lost all outward sensation, and saw his Mother (Kālī) in a vision. These visions came to him again and again, and then he became calmer. Sometimes he doubted whether these visions were really true, and then he would say, "I would believe them true, if such and such a thing happened," and it would invariably happen, even at the very hour he expected.

These visions grew more and more, and his trances became longer and longer in duration, till everyone saw it was no longer possible for him to perform his daily course of duties. For instance, it is prescribed in the *Shāstras* that a man should put a flower over his own head and think of himself as the very god or goddess he is going to worship, and Rāmakrishna, as he put the flower, and thought himself as identified with his Mother, would get entranced, and would remain in that state for hours. Then again, from time to time, he would entirely lose his own identity, so much so as to appropriate to himself the offerings brought for the goddess. Sometimes forgetting to adorn the image, he would adorn himself with the flowers. Mathur at first objected to this, but shortly afterwards, it is said, he saw the body of Rāmakrishna transfigured into that of the god Shiva, and from that day forward he looked upon him as God Himself, and addressed him always as Father whenever he spoke to him. He appointed the nephew of Rāmakrishna to conduct the regular services, and left him free to do whatever he liked.

The ardent soul of Rāmakrishna could not remain quiet with these frequent visions, but ran eagerly to attain perfection and realization of God in all His different aspects. He thus began the twelve years of unheard-of *tapasyā*, or ascetic exercises. Looking back to these years of self-torture in his later days, he said that a great religious tornado, as it were, raged within him during these years and made everything topsy-turvy. He had no idea then that it lasted for so long a time. He never had a wink of sound sleep during these years, could not even doze, but his eyes would remain always open and fixed. He thought sometimes that he was seriously ill, and holding a looking-glass before him, he put his finger within the sockets of the eye, that the lids might close, but they would not. In his despair he cried out, "Mother, oh! my mother, is this the result of calling upon thee and believing in thee?" And anon a sweet voice would come, and a sweeter smiling face, and said, "My son! how could you hope to realize the highest truth, if you don't give up the love of your body and of your little self?" "A torrent of spiritual light," he said, "would come then, deluging my mind and urging me forward. I used to tell my Mother, 'Mother! I could never learn from these erring men; but I will learn from thee, and thee alone,' and the same voice would say, 'Yea, my son!'" "I did not once," he continued, "look to the preservation of my body. My hair grew till it became matted, and I had no idea of it. My nephew, Hridāya, used to bring me some food daily, and some days succeeded and some days did not succeed in forcing a few mouthfuls down my throat, though I had no idea of it. Sometimes I used to go to the closet of the servants and sweepers and clean it with my own hands, and prayed, 'Mother! destroy in me all idea that I am great, and that I am a *brāhmin*, and that they are low and pariahs, for who are they but Thou in so many forms?'"

"Sometimes," he said, "I would sit by the Ganges, with some gold and silver coins and a heap of rubbish by my side, and taking some coins in my right hand and a handful of rubbish in the left, I would tell my soul, 'My soul! this is what the world calls money, impressed with the queen's face. It has the power of bringing you rice and vegetables, of feeding the poor, of building houses, and doing all that the world calls great, but it can never help thee to realize the ever-existent knowledge and bliss, the *Brahman*. Regard it, therefore, as rubbish.' Then mixing the coins and the rubbish in my hands, while repeating all the time, 'money is rubbish, money is rubbish,' I lost all perception of difference between the two in my mind, and threw them both into the Ganges. No wonder people took me for mad." About this time Mathur, who was very devoted to him, one day put a shawl fringed with gold round him, which cost about 1,500 *rupees*. At first he seemed to be pleased with it. But what was the astonishment of Mathur when the next moment Rāmakrishna threw it on the ground, trampled and spat on it, and began to cleanse the floor of the room with it, saying, "It increases vanity, but it can never help to realize the ever-Existent Knowledge and Bliss (*Sat-Chit-Ānanda*), and therefore is no better than a piece of torn rag."

"About this time," he said, "I felt such a burning sensation all over my body; I used to stand in the waters of the Ganges, with my body immersed up to the shoulders and a wet towel over my head all through the day, for it was insufferable. Then a *brāhmin* lady came and cured me of it in three days. She smeared my body with sandalwood paste and put garlands on my neck, and the pain vanished in three days."

Now this *brāhmin* lady was, we are told, an extraordinary Bengāli woman. She was versed in the philosophies and mythologies of India, and could recite book after book from memory. She could hold her ground in argument with the best *pandits* of the country. Tall and graceful, she combined in herself all the physical and intellectual qualities that would raise any man or woman high above ordinary mortals. She had a fine voice and was well versed in music. She had given up the world, practiced *yoga* (asceticism), attained to some wonderful yogic powers, and was roaming all over India in the red garb of a *sannyāsī*. Nobody knew anything of her birth or family or name even, and nobody could induce her to say anything about them. She was as if some goddess had come to this earth to help men to perfection, moved by the sorrows and sins of this wicked world. She seemed to have known full well that she was destined to help three particular personages, who were very advanced in attaining perfection. Rāmakrishna had been informed by his Divine Mother that she would come and teach him the certain way to attain perfection. He recognized her at once, and she recognized him and said, "I have found out the other two, and have been searching for thee for a long, long time, and today I have found thee."

All people were astonished at the wonderful learning of this *brāhmin* lady, but they could not understand how she could sympathize and place even above herself this half-crazed Rāmakrishna they took him for. To prove that he was not mad, the lady mentioned some Vaishnava scriptures, got the manuscripts from some learned *pandits*, and quoted passage after passage, showing that all these physical manifestations come to an ardent lover of God. It was recorded in these books that all these states physical and mental did happen to the great religious reformer of Bengāl, Shrī Chaitanya, four hundred years back, and the remedies were given, too, by which he overcame them. For instance, this burning sensation, as if all the body were in flames, from which Shrī Rāmakrishna was suffering at the time, was mentioned in these Vaishnava scriptures as having happened to the shepherdess of Braja, to the stainless Shrī Rādhā, the beloved of Krishna, centuries before, and again in later times to Shrī Chaitanya, when both of them felt deeply the pain of separation from their Beloved (God). In both these cases relief came by smearing the body with sandalwood paste and wearing garlands of sweet-scented flowers. The lady held it to be no real disease, but a state of physical disturbance, which would come to all who arrive at that stage of *bhakti*, or love of God. She applied the same remedies for three days, and the trouble passed away.

The lady lived there for some years, and made her friend practice all the different sorts of *yoga* which make a man complete master of his body and mind, render his passions subservient to his reason, and produce a thorough and deep concentration of thought, and, above all, the fearless and unbiased disposition which is essential to everybody who desires to know the truth and the whole truth.

About this time Rāmakrishna began to practice *yoga*, or the physical discipline, which makes the body strong and enduring. He began by regulating his breath, and went through the eight-fold methods prescribed by Patanjali. His teachers were astonished at the short time in which he came to the realization and attained the end of all these ascetic practices. One night, when he was practicing *yoga*, he was very much frightened at two strings of clotted blood coming out of his mouth. The temple services were then in the hands of one of his cousins, Haladhārī, a man of great learning and purity and possessed of certain psychical powers, such as *vāksiddhi*, power of speech. A few days before, Rāmakrishna had offended him by pointing out to him certain defects of his character, so much so that his cousin cursed him and said that blood should come out of his mouth. So Rāmakrishna was frightened, but a great *yogī* who was living there at the time came to his help, and after inquiring into his case assured him that it was very good that the blood had come out that way. It was because he had to teach many men, and to do good to them, that he was not permitted to enter into that *samādhi* (ecstasy) from which nobody returns. He explained to him that when a man has attained to the perfection of this *yoga* his blood rushes to his brain, and he becomes absorbed in *samādhi*, perceives his identity with the Supreme Self, and never returns any more to speak of his religious experiences to others. Only a few returned, namely, those who by the will of God were born to be the great teachers of mankind. In their case the blood rushes to the brain, and they feel the identity for some time, but after that the blood flows out again and they are able to teach.

By this time Rāmakrishna had learnt all that the *brāhmin* lady could teach, but he was still hankering after higher truths, when a *jnāni* (a true philosopher) came and initiated him into the truths of the *Vedānta*. This was a *sannyāsī* named Totāpurī, tall, muscular, and powerful. He had taken the vow of the order from his very boyhood, and after a hard struggle had succeeded in realizing the highest truths of the *Vedānta*. He wore no clothes whatever, and never rested under a roof. When the doors of palaces might have been opened to him if he had only wished, he passed the night always under a tree or the blue canopy of the heavens, even in winter and in the rainy season, never remaining more than three days in any place, and never caring to ask for food from anybody. Free as the wind, he was roaming all over the country, teaching and exhorting wherever he could find a sincere soul, and helping them to attain to that perfection which he had himself reached. He was a living illustration of the truth that *Vedānta*, when properly realized, can become a practical rule of life. On seeing Shrī Rāmakrishna sitting on the border of the Ganges, he at once recognized in him a great *yogī* and a perfectly-prepared ground for the reception of the seeds of the highest truths of religion. He addressed him at once and said, "My son! Do you want to learn the way to perfect freedom? Come, then, and I will teach it to you." Rāmakrishna, who never did anything without first asking his Mother (the goddess Kālī), said that he did not know what he should do, but he would go and ask his Mother. He came back in a few minutes and told the *sannyāsī* that he was ready. Totāpurī made him take the vow, and told him how he was to meditate and how to realize unity. After three days of practice he attained to the highest, the *nirvikalpa* stage of *samādhi*, where there is no longer any perception of the subject or of the object. The *sannyāsī* was perfectly bewildered at the rapid progress of his protégé, and said, "My boy! what I realized after forty years of hard struggle, you have arrived at in three days. I dare not call you my disciple; henceforth I will address you as my friend." And such was the love of this holy man for Shrī Rāmakrishna that he stayed with him for eleven months, and in his turn learnt many things from his own disciple.

There is a story told of the *sannyāsī*. He always kept a fire and regarded it as very holy. One day as he was sitting by this fire and talking to Shrī Rāmakrishna, a man came and lighted his pipe out of the same fire. The *sannyāsī* felt enraged at this sacrilege, when a gentle scolding came from his disciple, who said, "Is this the way that you look upon everything as *Brahman*? Is not the man himself *Brahman* as well as the fire? What is high and what is low in the sight of a *jnāni*?" The *sannyāsī* was brought to his senses, and said, "Brother, you are right. From this day forth you shall never find me angry again," and he kept his word. He could never understand, however, Rāmakrishna's love for his Mother (the goddess Kālī). He would talk of it as mere superstition, and ridicule it, when Rāmakrishna made him understand that in the Absolute there is no thou, nor I, nor God, nay, that it is beyond all speech or thought. As long, however, as there is the least grain of relativity left, the Absolute is within thought and speech and within the limits of the mind, which mind is subservient to the universal mind and consciousness; and this omniscient, universal consciousness was to him his Mother and God.

After the departure of Totāpurī, Rāmakrishna himself tried to remain always in union with the Absolute *Brahman* and in the *nirvikalpa* state. Looking back to this period of his life in his later days, he said, "I remained for six months in that state of perfect union which people seldom reach, and if they reach it, they cannot return to their individual consciousness again. Their bodies and minds could never bear it. But this my body is made up of *sattva* particles (pure elements) and can bear much strain. In those days I was quite unconscious of the outer world. My body would have died for want of nourishment, but for a *sādhu* (an advanced religious ascetic) who came at that time and stayed there for three days for my sake. He recognized my state of *samādhi*, and took much interest to preserve this body, while I was unconscious of its very existence. He used to bring some food every day, and when all methods failed to restore sensation or consciousness to this body of mine, he would even strike me with a heavy club, so that the pain might bring me back to consciousness. Sometimes he succeeded in awakening a sort of partial consciousness in me, and he would immediately force down one or two mouthfuls of food before I was lost again in deep *samādhi*. Some days when he could not produce any response, even after a severe beating, he was very sorrowful."

After six months the body gave way under these severe irregularities, and Rāmakrishna was laid up with dysentery. This disease, he said, did much in bringing him back to consciousness, slowly and gently, in a month or two. When the native physicians had cured him, his deep religious zeal took another turn. He began to practice and realize the Vaishnava ideal of love for God. This love, according to the Vaishnavas, becomes manifested practically in any one of the following relations—the relation of a servant to his master, of a friend to his friend, of a child to his parents, or vice versa, and a wife to her husband. The highest point of love is reached when the human soul can love his God as a wife loves her husband. The shepherdess of Braja had this sort of love towards the Divine Krishna, and there was no thought of any carnal relationship. No man, they say, can understand this love of Shrī Rādhā and Shrī Krishna until he is perfectly free from all carnal desires. They even prohibit ordinary men to read the books which treat of this love of Rādhā and Krishna, because they are still under the sway of passion. Rāmakrishna, in order to realize this love, dressed himself in women's attire for several days, thought of himself as a woman, and at last succeeded in gaining his ideal. He saw the beautiful form of Shrī Krishna in a trance, and was satisfied.

After having thus devoted himself to Vaishnavism, he practiced in turn many other religions prevalent in India always arriving at an understanding of their highest purposes in an incredibly short time. Whenever he wished to learn and practice the doctrines of any faith, he always found a good and learned man of that faith coming to him and advising him how to do it. He found a Mohammedan saint and placed himself under him; he underwent the disciplines prescribed by him, and to his astonishment found that when faithfully carried out, these devotional methods led him to the same goal he had already attained. He gathered similar experience from following the true religion of Jesus the Christ. He had seen Jesus in a vision, and for three days he could think of nothing and speak of nothing but Jesus and His love. He went to all the sects he could find, and whatever he took up he went into with his whole heart. He did exactly as he was told, and in every instance he arrived at the same result. Thus from actual experience, he came to know that the goal of every religion is the same, that each is trying to teach the same thing, the difference being largely in method and still more in language.

During all these years he forgot entirely that he had been married, which was not unnatural for one who had lost all idea of the existence even of his own body. The girl had in the meantime attained the age of seventeen or eighteen. She had heard rumors that her husband had become mad, and was in deep grief. Then again she heard that he had become a great religious man. She determined therefore to find him and to learn her fate from himself. Having obtained permission from her mother, she walked all the way, about thirty or forty miles, to the Dakshineshwar temple. Rāmakrishna received her very kindly, but told her that the old Rāmakrishna was dead, and that the new one could never look upon any woman as his wife. He said that even then he saw his Mother, the Goddess Kālī, in her, and however much he might try he could never see anything else. He addressed her as his Mother, worshipped her with flowers and incense, asked her blessings, as a child does from his mother, and then became lost in a deep trance. The wife, who was fully worthy of such a hero, told him she wanted nothing from him as her husband, but that he would teach her how to realize God, and allow her to remain near him and cook his meals and do what little she could for his health and comfort. From that day forward she lived within the temple compound, and began to practice whatever her husband taught her. Mathur offered her the sum of 10,000 *rupees*, but she declined, saying that her husband had attained perfection by renouncing gold and all pleasures, and she did not care for any, as she was determined to follow him. She is living still, revered by all for her purity and strength of character, helping others of her sex to religion and perfection, looking upon her husband as an Incarnation of God Himself, and trying to forward the work her husband began.[2]

Though Rāmakrishna had no proper education, he had such a wonderful memory that he never forgot what he once heard. In his later days he had a desire to hear the *Adhyātma Rāmāyana*, and he requested one of his disciples to read it to him in the original verse. As he was hearing, another of his disciples came and asked him whether he was understanding the original verses. He said he had heard the book before, with an explanation of it, and therefore knew all of it, but he wanted to hear it again because the book was so beautiful, and he repeated at once the purport of some of the verses which followed, and which were about to be read.

He had attained to great yogic powers, but he never cared to display these marvelous powers to anybody. He told his disciples that all these powers would come to a man as he advanced, but he warned them never to take any heed of the opinions of men. They had not to please men, but to try to attain the highest perfection, that is, unity with *Brahman*. The power of working miracles was rather a hindrance in the way to perfection, inasmuch as it diverted the attention of man from his highest goal. But persons who went to him have found abundant proofs of his possessing such powers as thought-reading, predicting future events, seeing things at a distance, and healing a disease by simply willing. The one great power of which he made most use, and which was by far the most wonderful, was that he was able to change a man's thoughts by simply touching his body. In some this touch produced immediate *samādhi*, in which they saw visions of gods and goddesses, and

2 Editor's Note: This was written sometime around 1899; Rāmakrishna's wife, Sāradā Devī, died on July 20th, 1920.

lost for some hours all sensation of the outward world. In others it produced no outward changes, but they felt that their thoughts had received a new direction and a new impetus, by which they could easily travel in the path of progress in religion. The carnally minded, for instance, would feel that their thoughts never ran after carnal pleasures afterwards, the miser would find that he did not love his gold, and so on.

About that time Mathur and his family went on a pilgrimage, and took Rāmakrishna with them. They visited all the sacred places of the Hindus as far as Brindāvan, and Rāmakrishna took the opportunity not only of seeing the temples, but of forming acquaintances with all the religious men, and with the *sannyāsīs* who were living in these places. These *sādhus* assigned to him a very high position, and regarded him not only as a *Brāhma-jnāni*, but as a great religious teacher (*āchārya*), nay, as an Incarnation of God Himself. At Brindāvan he was so much struck by the natural scenery and associations of the place, that he nearly made up his mind to reside there for ever. But the memory of his old mother made him return home. On his way back he was so much struck by the poverty of a village near Vaidyanāth, that he wept bitterly, and would not go from the place without seeing them happy. So Mathur fed the whole village for several days, gave proper clothing and some money to each of the villagers, and departed with Rāmakrishna contented.

"When the rose is blown, and sheds its fragrance all around, the bees come of themselves. The bees seek the full-blown rose, and not the rose the bees." This saying of Shrī Rāmakrishna has been verified often and often in his own life. Numbers of earnest men, of all sects and creeds, began to flock to him to receive instruction and to drink the waters of life. From day-dawn to night-fall he had no leisure to eat or drink, so engaged was he in teaching, exhorting, and ministering to the wants of these hungry and thirsty millions. Men possessed of wonderful *yoga* powers and great learning came to learn from this illiterate Paramahamsa of Dakshineshwar, and in their turn acknowledged him as their spiritual director (*guru*), touched as they were by the wonderful purity, the childlike simplicity, the perfect unselfishness, and by the simple language in which he propounded the highest truths of religion and philosophy. At night, too, he had no rest, for some of the more earnest would remain and spend the night with him. He then forgot his sleep, and talked to them incessantly about *bhakti* (devotion) or *jnāna* (knowledge) and his own experiences, and how he arrived at them. Though this incessant labor began at last to tell upon him, yet he would not rest. In the meanwhile the crowds of men and women began to increase daily, and he went on as before. When pressed to take rest, he would say, "I would suffer willingly all sorts of bodily pains, and death also, a hundred thousand times, if by so doing I could bring one single soul to freedom and salvation."

In the beginning of 1885 he suffered from what is known as "the clergyman's throat," which by-and-by developed into cancer. He was removed to Calcutta, and the best physicians were engaged, who advised him to keep the strictest silence; but the advice was to no effect. Crowds of men and women gathered wherever he went, and waited patiently to hear a single word from his mouth, and he, out of compassion for them, would not remain silent. Many a time he would be lost in a *samādhi*, losing all consciousness of his body and of his disease, and coming back he would talk incessantly as before. Even when the passage of his throat became so constricted that he could not swallow even liquid food, he would never stop his efforts. Once a man asked him, "Sir, you are a great *yogī*. Why do you not put your mind a little on your body and cure your disease?" At first he did not answer, but when the question had been repeated, he gently said, "My friend, I thought you were a sage, but you talk like other men of the world. This mind has been given to the Lord. Do you mean to say that I should take it back and put it upon the body which is but a mere cage of the soul?"

He was undaunted and remained as cheerful as ever, till on August 16, 1886, at 10 o'clock in the night, he entered into *samādhi*, from which he never returned. His disciples took it at first to be an ordinary *samādhi*, such as he used to have every day, during which the best doctors even could not find any pulsation or beating of the heart; but, alas, they were mistaken.

He was a wonderful mixture of God and man. In his ordinary state he would talk of himself as servant of all men and women. He looked upon them all as God. He himself would never be addressed as *guru*, or teacher. Never would he claim for himself any high position. He would touch the ground reverently where his disciples had trodden. But every now and then strange fits of God-consciousness came upon him. He then became changed into a different being altogether. He then spoke of himself as being able to do and know everything. He spoke as if he had the power of giving anything to anybody. He would speak of himself as the same soul that had been born before as Rāma, as Krishna, as Jesus, or as Buddha, born again as Rāmakrishna. He told Mathur, long before anybody knew him, that he had many disciples who would come to him shortly, and he knew all of them. He said that he was free from all eternity, and the practices and struggles after religion which he went through were only meant to show the people the way to salvation. He had done all for them alone. He would say he was a *nitya-mukta*, or eternally free, and an Incarnation of God Himself. "The fruit of the pumpkin," he said, "comes out first, and then the flowers; so it is with the *nitya-muktas*, or those who are free from all eternity, but come down for the good of others."

Swāmī Vivekānanda

The Original Gospel of Rāmakrishna

Based on M.'s English Text, Abridged

CHAPTER 1

Shrī Rāmakrishna at the Temple of Dakshineshwar

Where Rāmakrishna Lived

Bhagavān[1] Shrī Rāmakrishna lived for many years in Rānī Rāshmani's celebrated temple garden on the eastern bank of the Ganges in the village of Dakshineshwar about four miles north of Calcutta. This temple with the garden attached was dedicated by its foundress (Rānī Rāshmani) to the Divine Mother (Kālī). In the northwest corner of the spacious temple-compound is a small room which faces on the west the waters of the sacred river Ganges. This room with its holy surroundings was consecrated as the dwelling-place for many years of Bhagavān Shrī Rāmakrishna, whose divine presence made the spot holier and more sacred. It was from this retired corner that the rays of his divine glory, emanating from his God-intoxicated soul, dazzled the eyes of the seekers after Truth and attracted them to him as a blazing fire attracts moths from all quarters. Hundreds of educated men and women were drawn towards this superhuman personality to listen with the deepest reverence to the words of wisdom uttered by one who had realized God and who lived in constant communion with the Divine Mother of the universe.

Mahendra's Visit to the Temple

One Sunday in the month of March, 1882, Mahendra, hearing from a friend about this divine man, was so deeply impressed that he came to the temple garden to pay him a respectful visit. It was the day of a special religious festival and people had gathered in great numbers in Shrī Rāmakrishna's room and on the veranda. The Bhagavān was seated on a raised platform, and on the floor around him were Kedār, Shuresh, Rāma, Manomohan, Bijoy, and many

1 "*Bhagavān*" is a Sanskrit title meaning "The Blessed Lord." When the word is used without the accent on "a" of the last syllable it signifies the vocative case used in addressing a savior.

other devotees. They gazed up into his radiant face and drank the nectar of the living words of divine wisdom that fell from his hallowed lips. With a smiling face Shrī Rāmakrishna was speaking to them of the power of the Lord's holy name and true *bhakti* (devotion) as the means of attaining God-vision. Addressing Bijoy,[2] he asked: "What do you say is the means of attaining to God?"

Bijoy: "Bhagavan, by the repetition of His holy name. In this age the holy name of the Lord has saving powers."

Power of the Lord's Holy Name

Bhagavān: "Yes, the holy name has saving powers, but there must be earnest longing with it. Without earnest longing of the heart no one can see God by mere repetition of His name. One may repeat His name, but if one's mind be attached to lust and wealth, that will not help much. When a man is bitten by a scorpion or a tarantula, mere repetition of a *mantram* will not do; a special remedy is necessary."

Bijoy: "If that be the case, Bhagavan, then how did Ajāmila,[3] who was the greatest of sinners and committed all sorts of crimes, obtain salvation by repeating the name of the Lord at the time of his death?"

Rāmakrishna: "Perhaps in the previous incarnations Ajāmila was righteous and performed a great many good deeds. Besides, it is said that he practiced asceticism later in this life. It may also be said that at the last moment of his life the repetition of the holy name purified his heart and therefore he attained salvation. When an elephant is washed, immediately he throws dust and dirt over himself; but if he is kept in a clean stall after his bath, then he cannot cover himself with dirt. By the power of the holy name a man may be purified, but he may once more commit sinful acts because his mind is weak. He cannot promise that he will never sin again.

2 Bijoy was the first name of Bijoy Krishna Goshwami, the celebrated preacher, lecturer, writer, and spiritual teacher (*āchārya*) of the Brāhmo Samāj in Calcutta. For Brāhmo Samāj, see note 4, p. 5.

3 Ajāmila was the name of a sinner who received salvation by repeating the name of the Lord (which was also the name of his son) at the last moment of his life. The story of his life is given in the *Purānas* and is well known to the Hindus.

The water of the Ganges may wash away past sins, but there is a saying that sins perch like birds on the top of trees. When a man comes out of the Ganges and stands under a tree, the sins drop over his shoulders and seize upon him; these old sins ride him, as it were. Therefore, repeat the holy name of the Lord, but at the same time pray to Him that you may have true love and devotion for Him, and that your love for wealth, fame, and the pleasures of the body may decrease because they are transitory, they last only until tomorrow."

All Religions Lead to God

"When there is true devotion and love, one can reach God by any of the sectarian religions. The Vaishnavas, the worshippers of Krishna, will attain God in the same way as the Shāktas, the worshippers of the Divine Mother (*Shakti*), or the followers of *Vedānta*. Those who belong to the Brāhmo Samāj,[4] the Mohammedans, and the Christians, will also realize God through their respective religions. If you follow any of these paths with intense devotion, you will reach Him. If there be any mistake in the path chosen, He will correct the mistake in the long run. The man who wishes to see Jagannāth[5] may go towards the south instead of towards the north, but someone will sooner or later direct him in the right way and he will surely visit Jagannāth in the end. The one thing necessary for realization is whole-hearted and whole-souled devotion to God."

Many Names of One God

"Vaishnavas, Mohammedans, Christians, and Hindus are all longing for the same God; but they do not know that He who is Krishna is also Shiva, Divine Mother, Christ, and Allah. God is one, but He has many names. The substance is one, but is worshipped under

4 Brāhmo Samāj is the name of the Hindu unitarian church founded by Rājā Rāmmohan Roy in 1830 A.D. It has now various branches in India. The original organization is now known as the Ādi Samāj. Keshab Chandra Sen was the founder of the sect called "New Dispensation," while Shivanāth Shāstri was the founder of the Shādhāran Brāhmo Samāj.

5 Jagannāth literally means the "Lord of the universe." The great temple of Jagannāth is in Pūri, or Jagannāth Pūri, as it is often called.

different names according to the time, place, and nationality of His worshippers. All the different scriptures of the world speak of the same God. He who is described in the *Vedas* as Absolute Existence-Intelligence-Bliss or *Brahman*, is also described in the *Tantras*[6] as Shiva, in the *Purānas*[7] as Krishna, in the Koran as Allah, and in the Bible as Christ. Yet the various sects quarrel with one another. The worshippers of Krishna, for instance, say that nothing can be achieved without worshipping Krishna; those who are devoted to the Divine Mother think that the worship of the Divine Mother is the only way to salvation; similarly, the Christians say that no one can reach heaven except through Christ; he is the only way and Christianity is the only religion, all other religions are false."

Bigotry is Not Right

"This is narrow-mindedness. 'My religion is true while that of others is false'—this kind of belief is not right. It is not our business to correct the errors of other religions. He who has created the world will correct them in time. Our duty is in some way or other to realize Him. God can be reached through many paths; each of these sectarian religions points out a path which ultimately leads to Divinity. Yes, all religions are paths, but the paths are not God. I have seen all sects and all paths. I do not care for them any more. People belonging to these sects quarrel so much! After trying all religions, I have realized that God is the Whole and I am His part; that He is the Lord and I am His servant; again I realize, He is I; I am He."

God Personal and Impersonal

"People dispute amongst themselves, saying: 'God is personal with form. He cannot be impersonal and formless'—like the Vaishnavas who find fault with those who worship the Impersonal *Brahman*. When realization comes, then all these questions are settled. He who has seen God can tell exactly what He is like. As Kabīr[8] said:

6 *Tantras* are sacred writings of the Shaiva and Shākta sects among the Hindus.

7 *Purānas* are the sacred scriptures of the Hindus next in authority to the *Vedas*. There are eighteen great *Purānas* and many smaller *Purānas*.

8 Kabīr was a Hindu saint who lived between 1440 and 1518 A.D. Rising from the

'God with form is my Mother, God without form is my Father. Whom shall I blame, whom shall I praise? The balance is even.' He is with form, yet He is formless. He is personal, yet He is impersonal, and who can say what other aspects He may have!"

Parable of the Elephant and the Blind Men

"Four blind men went to see an elephant. One touched a leg of the elephant and said: 'The elephant is like a pillar.' The second touched the trunk and said: 'The elephant is like a thick club.' The third touched the belly and said: 'The elephant is like a huge jar.' The fourth touched the ears and said: 'The elephant is like a big winnowing-basket.' Then they began to dispute among themselves as to the figure of the elephant. A passer-by, seeing them thus quarrelling, asked them what it was about. They told him everything and begged him to settle the dispute. The man replied: 'None of you has seen the elephant. The elephant is not like a pillar, its legs are like pillars. It is not like a big water-jar, its belly is like a water-jar. It is not like a winnowing-basket, its ears are like winnowing-baskets. It is not like a stout club, its trunk is like a club. The elephant is like the combination of all these.' In the same manner do those sectarians quarrel who have seen only one aspect of the Deity. He alone who has seen God in all His aspects can settle all disputes."

Parable of the Chameleon

"Again: Two persons were hotly disputing as to the color of a chameleon. One said: 'The chameleon on that palm-tree is of a red color.' The other, contradicting him, replied: 'You are mistaken, the chameleon is not red but blue.' Not being able to settle the matter by argument, both went to the person who always lived under that tree and had watched the chameleon in all its phases of color. One of them asked him: 'Sir, is not the chameleon on that tree red?' The person replied: 'Yes, sir.' The other disputant said: 'What do

low caste of a weaver he became the founder of a Vaishnava sect called after his name "Kabīr Panth." His teachings were so broad and universal that they were accepted by the Mohammedans as well as the Hindus of all castes. Even now there are thousands among the lower classes of the Hindus who regard him as their spiritual master.

you say? It is not red, it is blue.' The person again humbly replied: 'Yes, sir.' The person knew that the chameleon is an animal which constantly changes color; thus it was that he said 'yes' to both these conflicting statements. The *Sat-Chit-Ānanda* (the Absolute Existence-Intelligence-Bliss) likewise has many forms. The devotee who has seen God in one aspect only, knows Him in that aspect alone. But he who has seen Him in manifold aspects is alone in a position to say with authority: 'All these forms are of one God and God is multiform.' He is formless and with form, and many are His forms which no one knows."

Relation Between God Personal and Impersonal

"As in the ocean intense cold will freeze a portion of the water into ice which may float in various forms on the water, similarly intense devotion (*bhakti*) may condense a portion of Divinity and make it appear in different forms. The Personal God with form exists for the sake of His *bhaktas* (dualistic devotees). When the sun of wisdom rises, the block of ice melts and becomes water once more; above, below, and on every side the Infinite Being pervades. Therefore there is a prayer in the scriptures: 'O Lord, Thou art personal with form. Thou art also impersonal and formless. Thou hast manifested Thyself in a human form and hast lived in our midst, but in the *Vedas* Thou art described as beyond speech and mind, unspeakable, imperceptible, and unthinkable.' But it can be said that for a certain class of *bhaktas* He is eternally personal and always with form. There are places where the ice never melts, it becomes crystallized."

Evening at the Temple

Night had fallen and the priests were waving the lights before the shrines to the accompaniment of bells, cymbals, and drums. From the southern end of the garden was wafted the sweet music played by the temple musicians upon flutes and other instruments—the music being carried far over the Ganges until it was lost. The breeze blowing from the south was gentle and fragrant with the sweet odor of many flowers. The moon was rising and the garden was soon bathed in its soft silvery light. It seemed as if nature as well as man was rejoicing and holding herself in readiness for the sacred ceremony of the *āratī* (evening service).

One by one the disciples began to take their leave. Mahendra and his friend, who had been visiting the different temples, now wended their way back through the grand quadrangle to Shrī Rāmakrishna's chamber. Coming up to the door of the room, they noticed that it was closed. Near the door stood a maid-servant named Brindā. Mahendra spoke to her, saying: "Well, my good woman, is the holy man in?"

Brindā: "Yes, he is in his room."

Mahendra: "I suppose he has many books to read and study?"

Brindā: "Oh dear, no; not a single one. Everything, even the highest truths, is spoken by his tongue. His words are all inspired."

Mahendra: "Indeed! Is he now going through the evening service? May we go in? Will you kindly tell him of our anxiety to see him?"

Brindā: "Why, you may go in, my children. Go in and take your seats before him."

Thereupon they entered the room. No other people were there. Bhagavān Shrī Rāmakrishna was alone, seated as in the afternoon on the platform beside his bed. Incense was burning and the doors were closed. Mahendra saluted the Bhagavān with folded hands. A mat was pointed out on the floor. At his word Mahendra and his friend took their seats upon it. The Bhagavān asked him: "What is your name? Where do you live? What are you? What has brought you to Barāhanagar[9]?"

Mahendra answered each of these questions, but he noticed that in the course of the conversation Shrī Rāmakrishna's mind was fixed upon some other object, on which he was meditating. He was only half-conscious of the physical plane. Mahendra learned afterwards that this was the state of *samādhi* or God-consciousness which invariably came over him every day during the evening service. Very often in this state he would become absolutely unconscious of the external world. Mahendra, observing his abstraction, said to Shrī Rāmakrishna: "I am afraid, Bhagavan, that thou wouldst prefer to go through the evening service (*sandhyā*) alone. In that case we will not disturb thee any more, but will call some other time."

9 Barāhanagar is a suburb of Calcutta.

Shrī Rāmakrishna replied: "Oh no, you need not be in a hurry."

But he was silent again for a time. He then opened his lips and said: "*Sandhyā*? Evening service? It is not that."

A short while after, Mahendra saluted the Bhagavān, who in turn bade him goodbye, saying: "Come again."

Chapter 2

Shrī Rāmakrishna with His Disciples at the Temple

The Bhagavān was in his room seated in his usual place on the small platform beside his bed. It was Sunday and the room was filled with a large number of devotees. Among them was a young college student only nineteen years of age named Narendra, who afterwards became the world-renowned Swāmī Vivekānanda. Everyone noticed even at that time that he was a sincere and earnest seeker after Truth and that his mind was above all worldly concerns.

The Bhagavān was discoursing on worldly people who ridicule the worshippers of God. Especially addressing Narendra, he asked: "What do you say, Narendra? Worldly men will speak all manner of things against godly people, but they should act like the elephant. When an elephant passes through a public road, dogs run after him and bark at him; but the elephant turns a deaf ear to their barking and goes on his own way. Suppose, my boy, people should speak ill of you behind your back, what would you think of them?"

Narendra: "I would look upon them as a lot of barking dogs."

God Dwells in All

The Bhagavān laughed and said: "No, my friend, do not go so far as that. You should love everyone; no one is a stranger; God dwells in all beings; without Him nothing can exist. When Prahlāda[1] realized Him, the Lord asked him to crave a boon. Prahlāda replied: 'When I have seen Thee, what other boon do I need?' The Lord asked him again. He then prayed: 'If Thou wishest to grant me a boon, do Thou forgive those who have persecuted me.' Prahlāda meant that by persecuting him they had persecuted the Lord dwelling within him. Know that God resides in all things animate and inan-

1 Prahlāda was a great *bhakta* who, from his childhood, showed his extreme faith, love, and devotion for the Supreme Lord of the universe. He is the ideal *bhakta* among the Hindus. His life is described in the *Purānas*.

imate. Hence everything is an object of worship, be it men, beasts or birds, plants or minerals. In our relation with men all that we can do is to take heed to ourselves that we mix with good people and avoid bad company. It is true, however, that God resides in bad people also, yes, even in a tiger; but surely it does not follow that we should embrace a tiger. It may be asked: 'Why should we run away from a tiger when God is dwelling in that form?' To this the answer is that God abiding in our hearts directs us to run away from the tiger. Why should we not obey His will?"

Parable of the Disciple and the Mad Elephant

"In a certain forest there lived a sage who had a number of disciples. He taught his disciples the truth: 'God dwells in all things. Knowing this, you should bend your knee before every object.' One day a disciple went out into the forest for wood. On his way he saw a man riding a mad elephant and shouting: 'Get out of the way, get out of the way! This is a mad elephant.' The disciple, instead of running away, remembered his master's teaching and began to reason: 'God is in the elephant as well as in me. God cannot be hurt by God, so why should I run away?' Thus thinking, he stood where he was and saluted the elephant as he came nearer. The driver (*māhut*) kept on shouting: 'Get out of the way!' but the disciple would not move, until he was snatched up by the mad elephant and dashed to one side. The poor boy, bruised and bleeding, lay on the ground unconscious. The sage, hearing of the accident, came with his other disciples to carry him home. When after some time the unfortunate pupil recovered consciousness, he described what had happened. The sage replied: 'My boy, it is true that God is manifest in everything. But if He is in the elephant, is He not equally manifest in the driver (*māhut*)? Tell me why you did not pay heed to the warning of the driver?'"

God in Everything

The Bhagavān continued: "In the sacred scriptures it is written, 'God dwells in water'; but some water can be used for divine service, or for drinking purposes, some for bathing or washing, while dirty water cannot be touched even. In the same manner, although God resides in all human beings, still there are good men and bad men, there are lovers of God and those who do not love God. We should recognize Divinity in all, but we should not mix with bad people or with those who do not love God. Our relation with them must not be very close. It is wise to avoid the company of such people."

Narendra: "What attitude should we hold when wicked people come to disturb our peace or do actually offend us?"

Resistance of Evil

Bhagavān: "A person living in society should have a little *tamas* (the spirit of resisting evil) for purposes of self-protection. But this is necessary only for outward show, its object being to prevent the wicked from doing harm to you. At the same time you should not do actual injury to another on the ground that he has done injury to you."

Parable of the Snake and the Holy Man

"There was a large venomous snake in a field. No one dared to go that way. One day a holy man (*mahātmā*) passed by that road and the serpent ran after the sage to bite him. But when the snake approached the holy man, he lost all his ferocity and was overpowered by the gentleness of the *yogī*. Seeing him, the sage said: 'Well, my friend, think you to bite me?' The snake was abashed and made no reply. At this the sage continued: 'Hearken, friend; do not injure anyone in future.' The snake bowed and nodded assent. The sage went his way, and the snake entered his hole and thenceforward began to live a life of innocence, without attempting to harm anyone. In a few days all the neighborhood concluded that the snake had lost his venom and was no longer dangerous; so everyone began to tease him. They pelted him with stones or dragged him mercilessly by the tail, and there was no end to his troubles. Fortunately the sage again passed that way, and seeing the bruised and battered condition of the snake, was very much moved and inquired into the cause. 'Holy sir,' the snake replied, 'this is because I do not injure anyone after your advice. But alas! they are so merciless!' The sage smilingly said: 'My friend, I simply advised you not to bite anyone; but I did not tell you not to frighten others. Although you should not bite any living creatures, still you should keep people at a distance by hissing at them.'" And Shrī Rāmakrishna added: "There is no harm in 'hissing' at wicked men and at your enemies, showing that you can protect yourself and know how to resist evil. Only you must be careful not to pour your venom into the blood of your enemy. Resist not evil by causing evil in return."

One of the devotees present said: "But when a person is annoyed with me, Bhagavan, I feel unhappy. I feel that I have not been able to love everyone equally."

Love for All

Rāmakrishna: "When you feel that way, you should have a talk with that person and try to make peace with him. If you fail after such attempts, then you need not give it further thought. Take refuge with the Lord. Think upon Him. Do not let your mind be disturbed by any other thing."

Devotee: "Christ and Chaitanya[2] have both taught us to love all mankind."

A True Devotee Always Calm

Rāmakrishna: "You should love everyone because God dwells in all beings. But to wicked people you should bow down at a distance. (To Bijoy, smiling) Is it true that people blame you because you mix with those who believe in a Personal God with form? A true devotee of God should possess absolute calmness and never be disturbed by the opinions of others. Like a blacksmith's anvil, he will endure all blows and persecutions and yet remain firm in his faith and always the same. Wicked people may say many things about you and blame you; but if you long for God, you should endure with patience."

Company of the Wicked

"One can think on God even dwelling in the midst of wicked people. The sages of ancient times, who lived in forests, could meditate on God although surrounded by tigers, bears, and other wild

2 Chaitanya (1486-1534 A.D.), the founder of a sect of the Vaishnavas, is regarded in India as the Incarnation of Krishna.

beasts. The nature of the wicked is like that of a tiger or bear. They attack the innocent and injure them. You should be especially cautious in coming in contact with the following: First, the wealthy. A person who possesses wealth and many attendants can easily do harm to another if he so desires. You should be very guarded in speaking with him; sometimes it may even be necessary to agree with him in his opinion. Second, a dog. When a dog barks at you, you must not run, but talk to him and quiet him. Third, a bull. When a bull chases you, you should always pacify him by talking to him. Fourth, a drunkard. If you make him angry, he will call you names and swear at you. You should address him as a dear relative, then he will be happy and obliging.

"When wicked people come to see me, I am very careful. The character of some of them is like that of a snake. They may bite you unawares. It may take a long time and much discrimination to recover from the effects of that bite. Or you may get so angry at them that you will wish to take revenge. It is necessary, however, to keep occasionally the company of holy men. Through such association right discrimination will come."

Four Classes of Individual Souls

"There are four classes of *jīvas*, or individual souls: First, *baddha*, the bound; second, *mumukshu*, the seeker after freedom; third, *mukta*, the emancipated; and fourth, *nitya-mukta*, the eternally free. This world is like a net, the soul is the fish, and the Lord of the phenomenal world is the fisherman. When a fisherman draws in his net, some of the fish try to escape by rending the net, that is, they struggle for freedom. So are the souls of the second class, the *mumukshus*, the seekers after freedom. But among the fish that struggle, only a few escape. Similarly, a few souls only attain to freedom and they belong to the third class, the *muktas*. There are some fish, however, that are naturally cautious and never fall into the net. Such are the souls of the fourth class, the *nitya-muktas*, who are never caught in the net of the phenomenal world, but who remain eternally free, like Nārada[3] and others like him. Most of the

3 In the Hindu scriptures Nārada is described as the ideal lover of God. He communed with the Lord under all conditions. The Lord Vishnu selected him as his most beloved messenger.

fish, however, fall into the net and have not the sense to know that they are going to die there. When caught, they try to run away and hide in the mud at the bottom by swimming with the net. They make no effort to get out of the net, but go deeper and deeper into the mud. These may be compared to the souls who are bound fast in the world. They are caught in the net, but they delude themselves by thinking that they are happy. They remain attached to worldliness. They plunge into the mire of worldly evils and are content, while those who are seeking after freedom or who are emancipated do not like worldliness and do not care for sense-pleasures."

Bound Souls

"Those who are thus caught in the net of the world are the *baddhas*, or bound souls. No one can awaken them. They do not come to their senses even after receiving blow upon blow of misery, sorrow, and indescribable suffering. The camel loves thorny bushes, and although his mouth bleeds when he eats them, still he does not cease to love them dearly and no one can keep him away from them. The bound souls may meet with great grief and misfortune, but after a few days they are just as they were before. Although they may occasionally feel that the world is unreal, they can neither give it up nor can they fix their minds on the Reality of the universe. I once saw a relative of Keshab Chandra Sen, who was quite old, still playing cards as if the time for meditating on God had not come for him.

"There is another sign of a *baddha*, or worldly soul. If you remove him from the world and put him in a better place, he will pine away and die. He will work like a slave to support his family, and he will not hesitate to tell lies, to deceive, or to flatter in order to earn his livelihood. He looks upon those who worship God or who meditate on the Lord of the universe as insane. He never finds time or opportunity to think of spiritual subjects. Even at the hour of death he will think and talk of worldly things. Whatever thought is strongest in the minds of worldly people comes out at the time of death. If they become delirious, they rave of nothing but material objects. They may go to places of worship, but so long as their minds are attached to the world, worldly thoughts will rise at the last moment. As a parrot may be taught to utter the Lord's holy name, but when attacked by a cat, screams and gives its natural cry; so they may repeat the holy name of the Lord, but when attacked by death, the natural tendency of their minds will predominate. It is said in the *Bhagavad Gītā* that the future is determined by the thought that is uppermost at the moment of death, and in the *Purānas* there is a story that King Bharata was born as a deer because when he died, his mind was fixed on the thought of a deer. He who passes away thinking of God and meditating on Him, does not come back to this world."

A devotee: "Bhagavan, will a man who thinks of God, but who does not meditate on Him at the time of death, be born again?"

Concentration and Meditation

Shrī Rāmakrishna: "An ordinary soul who has no faith in God may think of Him for a time, but easily forgets Him again and becomes attached to the world. If, however, he concentrates his mind upon God at the last moment of his life, his heart and soul become purified and remain so even after death. People suffer so much because they have no faith in God. In order to be able to think of God at the time of death, we must prepare our mind by constant practice. The practice of meditation on God will create a tendency of mind to think of Him spontaneously even at the last moment."

A devotee: "Bhagavan, what condition of mind is necessary for a worldly person to attain to freedom?"

Dispassion

Rāmakrishna: "If by the grace of the Lord strong dispassion for worldly things arises in his mind, then such a person becomes free from all earthly attachment. What is this *strong* dispassion? Let me tell you. Ordinary dispassion makes the mind think of the Lord occasionally, but there is no longing in the heart. Strong dispassion, on the contrary, makes the mind dwell constantly on the Lord with the same intense longing as a mother feels for her only child. He who has strong dispassion does not want anything but the Lord. He looks at the world as a deep well and is always fearful lest he may fall into it. Earthly relations seem to him very distant. He does not seek their company. His whole heart and soul yearn for God. He does not think of his family, nor does he think of the morrow. He also possesses great spiritual force."

Parable of the Farmer and the Canal

"Let me explain this to you by a parable: In a certain place there had been a long drought. The farmers were irrigating their fields by canals, bringing water from a long distance. One farmer had great determination and force of character. One morning he made up his mind that he would continue to dig his canal until he had connected it with the river and brought the water to his field. He was so busy with digging that he lost account of time. The hour for luncheon came and passed. His wife called him to come home, wash, and eat. 'The luncheon is getting cold. Leave your work until tomorrow,' she urged. At first he paid no heed to her words, but when she repeated her request, he bade her go home and not disturb him any more. 'You have no sense,' he said, 'with this terrible drought we cannot grow anything. There will be no food for the children, the whole family will die of starvation. I have resolved that this very day I shall bring the water of the river to my field; then I shall think of washing and eating.' Hearing this, his wife ran home. The farmer worked hard the whole day and towards evening he joined the canal to the river and sat on one side with great delight as he saw the stream of water running into his field. His mind was then peaceful and happy. He went home and called his wife, saying: 'Now give me a little oil and fill my pipe,' and he washed, ate a hearty dinner, and enjoyed a sound sleep. This kind of determination and firmness of purpose must be at the back of strong dispassion. Another farmer who was trying to bring water to his field was likewise called by his wife at the hour of the noonday meal. 'It is getting late, come home, and wash and eat,' she said, and at once he dropped his spade and replied: 'My dear, when you ask me to go, I must go.' So his field remained dry. As a farmer cannot irrigate his field, so a devotee cannot attain to God without firm determination.

"When God is attained through such strong dispassion, all worldly attachment fades away. A householder may then live with his family, but he becomes unattached and there is no more danger for him. If there be two magnets, one very large and the other very small, which do you suppose will attract a piece of iron? The larger one of course. God is the greatest magnet. Compared to Him the attraction of the world is small and powerless."

A devotee: "Bhagavan, why are we so bound to the world that we cannot see God?"

Sense of "I"

Rāmakrishna: "The sense of 'I' in us is the greatest obstacle in the path of God-vision. It covers the Truth. When 'I' is dead, all troubles cease. If by the mercy of the Lord one realizes 'I am a non-doer,' instantly that man becomes emancipated in this life. This sense of 'I' is like a thick cloud. As a small cloud can hide the glorious sun, so this cloud of 'I' hides the glory of the Eternal Sun. If the cloud is dispersed by the mercy of a *guru*, or spiritual master, the glory of the Infinite becomes visible. When Rāma, the Divine Incarnation in a human form,[4] was walking in the forest, Lakshmana (the individual soul), who was at a short distance, could not see Him because Sītā or *māyā*, or the sense of 'I,' was standing between. Look at me. I cover my face with this handkerchief and you cannot see me; still my face is there. So God is the nearest of all, but because of the sense of 'I' you do not see Him. The soul in its true nature is Absolute Existence, Intelligence, and Bliss, but on account of *māyā* or the sense of 'I,' it has forgotten its real Self and has become entangled in the meshes of the various limitations of mind and body."

Money is Power

"Each attribute limits the soul and modifies its nature. He who dresses smartly will naturally sing love-songs, play cards, and carry a cane, and such things will appeal to him. If you have a pencil in your hand, you will unconsciously scribble on anything; such is the power of the pencil. Money has great power. When a man becomes wealthy his nature is entirely changed. He is a different being. A poor *brāhmin*, for instance, used to come here. He was very humble. He lived on the other side of the Ganges. One day as I was landing from a boat, I saw him sitting at the riverside. Seeing me, he shouted in a disrespectful tone, 'Hello! is it you, my good

4 The word Rāma refers to the divine hero described in the Hindu epic called the *Rāmāyana*. It is also a name which the Hindu *bhaktas* use for the Supreme Lord of the universe.

fellow?' Immediately I understood by his manner that he had got hold of some money, otherwise he would not dare to address me thus. A toad had a *rupee* in its hole. An elephant was coming that way and passed over the hole. The toad was very angry; it came out and was about to kick the elephant, saying: 'How darest thou pass over me?' Such is the power of wealth! It makes one so egotistic."

Seven Stages of Spiritual Evolution

"This sense of 'I,' however, vanishes at the approach of divine wisdom, which leads to super-consciousness (*samādhi*) and eventually to God-consciousness. But it is very difficult to acquire this divine wisdom. It is said in the *Vedas* that when the mind reaches the seventh stage of spiritual evolution, the soul enters into *samādhi* and instantly its sense of 'I' disappears. The mind naturally dwells in the first three stages, the realm of worldly tendencies and animal propensities, and becomes attached to lust and wealth. When the mind dwells in the purified heart, spiritual light is perceived by the soul. At that time the soul exclaims: 'What is this! What is this!' When it rises near the throat and remains there, the devotee loves to hear and speak of God. When the mind rises still higher, near the space between the eyebrows, it beholds the vision of the Infinite Being whose nature is Absolute Existence-Intelligence-Bliss. The soul then desires to touch and embrace that Being, but fails. As a light within a lantern can be seen but cannot be touched from outside, so the soul beholds the vision but cannot lay hold on it, cannot enter into it, cannot become one with it. In the seventh stage, however, the mind is bereft of the sense of 'I,' enters into God-consciousness and realizes its oneness with the Infinite."

Devotee: "Bhagavan, what happens after reaching the seventh stage when divine wisdom comes? What does the man see?"

Rāmakrishna: "It cannot be described by words. In the seventh stage when the mind goes into its causal form, *samādhi* comes and what happens then no one can tell."

Difference Between Soul and God

"This sense of 'I' which makes one worldly and attached to lust and wealth is the cause of bondage. The difference between the Supreme and the individual soul is created by this sense of 'I' which stands between. If you hold a stick on the surface of a stream, the water will appear to be divided into two parts, but in reality the water is one. It appears as two because of the stick. The sense of 'I' may be compared to this stick. Remove this limiting adjunct and the current will be one and unbroken."

Devotee: "Bhagavan, if we cannot get rid of worldliness except by losing the sense of 'I' in *samādhi*, is it not better to follow the path of wisdom which leads to *samādhi*, since in the path of devotion the sense of 'I' still remains?"

Servant "I" of a Bhakta

Rāmakrishna: "Very few can get rid of the sense of 'I' through *samādhi*. It generally clings to us. We may discriminate a thousand times, but the sense of 'I' is bound to return again and again. You may cut the branches of a fig-tree today, but tomorrow you will see that new twigs are sprouting. If this sense of 'I' will not leave, then let it stay as the servant of God. 'O God! Thou art my Lord, I am Thy servant!' Think in this way: 'I am His servant, I am His *bhakta*, devotee.' There is no harm in this kind of 'I.' Sweet things cause dyspepsia and acidity, but crystallized sugar-candy is harmless. The path of wisdom is very difficult. It cannot be followed so long as the sense of 'I' is connected with the body. In this age the consciousness of the body and the sense of 'I' cannot be overcome easily. But in the path of devotion, through prayer and repetition of His holy name with extreme longing, God can he reached without fail."

Devotee: "Bhagavan, dost thou teach us to renounce the worldly 'I' and not the sense of the servant 'I'?"

Rāmakrishna: "Yes, the servant 'I' or 'I am the servant of God,' 'I am His devotee,' this egoism is not bad but on the contrary it helps us to realize God."

Devotee: "Bhagavan, does he who has the sense of the servant 'I' possess passion and anger?"

A Child's "I"

Rāmakrishna: "If this attitude of a servant be genuine and perfect, then passion and anger will drop off leaving only a scar in the mind. This 'I' of a *bhakta* or devotee does no harm to any living creature. It is like a sword which, after touching the Philosopher's Stone, is turned to gold. The sword retains the same form but it cannot cut or injure anyone. The dry leaves of the coconut-tree drop off in the wind, leaving a mark on the trunk; that mark proves that there was a leaf at one time. Similarly, the scar of the sense of 'I' remains in the mind of one who has realized God, but his whole nature is transformed into that of an innocent child. The child's sense of 'I' is not attached to worldly objects. He may like a thing at one moment, but the next moment he may dislike it. You can take from him an object of great value by giving him a doll worth a penny. To a child everyone is equal, there is none greater or smaller. Therefore a child has no sense of caste or creed. If his mother says: 'He is your brother,' however low his caste may be, the child will sit with him and eat with him without feeling dislike or difference of any kind."

True Devotion and Love

"Some *bhaktas* after attaining to *samādhi* or God-consciousness, when they return, retain the sense of 'I' as 'I am His servant, I am His devotee.' They do not lose the sense of 'I' entirely but keep a small portion of it to repeat the holy name of the Lord, to sing His praises, and to love and serve Him. Again, those who constantly practice this sense of 'servant I' eventually reach the Supreme Lord. This is the path of *bhakti* or devotion. But true devotion is very rare. True devotion leads to intense love for God; and when that intense love comes, the Divine Being is not very far. In that intense love the sense of worldliness is wiped out entirely and the whole heart and soul rest upon nothing but the Lord of the universe. Some are born with this intense love for God; it is natural with them. Its expression is to be found even in their childhood. At that tender age even, they cry for God. There are many examples of such born *bhaktas* like Prahlāda and others. Ordinary devotion which is confined by scriptural laws of sacrifice and worship is preparatory. As in hot weather one fans oneself for a breath of air so long as the breeze is not blowing, but when the breeze springs up, the fan is no longer needed; so when the breeze of intense love begins to blow in the soul, all devotional exercises like repetition of the name of the Lord, sacrifice, prayers, and asceticism become unnecessary. Devotion without intense love is the sign of unripe *bhakti*. When it ripens, it leads into divine love, which is perfect and which brings the highest realization."

A disciple: "Bhagavan, how can God be realized?"

God is Like a Magnet

Rāmakrishna: "God can be realized by the purified heart alone. Ordinarily the mind is stained with worldliness. The mind may be compared to a needle. If a needle be covered with thick mud, it is not attracted by the magnet; but when the mud is washed off, the magnet attracts it. Similarly, when the mind is covered with the mud of worldliness, it does not feel the attraction of the Lord; but whosoever repents, saying: 'O Lord, I shall never again commit such an act,' and sheds tears of true repentance, washes off all impurities and the magnet of the Lord then attracts the needle of the mind. Instantly super-consciousness comes and is followed by God-vision."

The Mercy of the Lord

"A man may make thousands of attempts, but nothing can be accomplished without the mercy of the Lord. Without His mercy no one can see Him. Nor is it an easy thing to obtain His mercy. The egotistic sense of 'I' which says: 'I am the doer,' must be abandoned entirely before the divine mercy can be felt. So long as there is a steward in charge of the storehouse, if any come to the master and beg him, saying: 'Master, wilt thou not come to the storehouse and give me this thing?' he will reply: 'The steward is there, what need have I to go?' In like manner, so long as the ego thinks of himself as the 'doer' and the master of the storehouse of the heart, the real Master does not enter there. The mercy of the Lord is the surest way of God-vision. He is the sun of wisdom. A single ray of this eternal sun illumines this world, and by that light we are conscious of ourselves and of one another and we acquire various kinds of knowledge. If He turns that light towards His own face, He becomes visible to His *bhakta* or devotee."

Illustration of a Bull's-Eye Lantern

"In the night the watchman goes from place to place holding in his hand the bull's-eye lantern. By its light he sees everyone's face and people see each other, but no one can see him. If anyone wishes to see the watchman, he must beg him to turn the light towards himself. Similarly, he who wishes to see the Lord must pray to Him thus: 'O Lord, in Thy mercy do Thou turn the light of Thy wisdom towards Thine own face that I may behold Thee.' If there be no light in a house, that is the sign of extreme poverty. Therefore one must light the lamp of wisdom within the heart. 'O mind, why dost thou not see the face of the Divine Mother by lighting the lamp of wisdom in the chamber of the soul!'"

Chapter 3

The Bhagavān with Certain of His Householder Disciples

One day in winter a certain householder disciple, who was a college professor, came to see the Bhagavān. Shrī Rāmakrishna was seated on the southern veranda of his room, and he was smiling. After a short conversation he asked: "Do you prefer to meditate on God with form or without form?" The disciple hesitated and answered. "I prefer to meditate upon God as the formless Being rather than as a Being with form."

God is Formless and with Form

The Bhagavān replied: "That is good. There is no harm in looking at Him from this or the other point of view. Yes, to think of Him as the formless Being is quite right. But do not go away with the idea that that alone is true and that all else is false. Meditating upon Him as a Being with form is equally right. You, however, must hold on to your particular conception of God until you have realized and seen God."

The disciple asked: "Bhagavan, one may believe that God is with form, but surely He is not in the earthen images that are worshipped?"

Shrī Rāmakrishna replied: "My dear sir, why do you say earthen images? The image of the Divine Being is made of the spirit."

The disciple could not understand the meaning of this, but answered: "Yet should it not be one's duty to make clear to those who worship images that God is not the same as the images and that at the time of worship they should think of God Himself and not of the image made of clay?"

Image Worship

The Bhagavān said: "The Lord of the universe teaches mankind. He who has made the sun and moon, men and brutes; He who has created things for them to live upon, parents to tend and rear them; He who has done so many things will surely do something to bring them to the light. The Lord dwells in the temple of the human body. He knows our innermost thoughts. If there is anything wrong in image worship, does He not know that all worship is meant for Him? He will be pleased to accept it knowing that it is for Him. Why should you worry yourself about things which are beyond your reach? Try to realize God and love Him. This is your first duty.

"You speak of images made of clay. Well, there often comes a necessity for worshipping such images and symbols. In *Vedānta* it is said, the Absolute Existence-Intelligence-Bliss pervades the universe and manifests Itself through all forms. What harm is done by worshipping the Absolute through images and symbols? We see little girls with their dolls. How long do they play with them? So long as they are not married. After marriage they put away those dolls. Similarly, one needs images and symbols so long as God is not realized in His true form. It is God Himself who has provided these various forms of worship. The Master of the universe has done all this to suit different men in different stages of spiritual growth and knowledge. The mother so arranges the food for her children that each one gets what is best for him. Suppose a mother has five children with one fish to cook for all. She will make different dishes of it that she may give to each just what suits him—the rich *polāo* (dish with rice) for one, soup for another, fried fish for a third, fish with sour tamarind for a fourth, and so on, exactly according to the power of digestion of each. Do you now understand?"

The disciple replied: "Yes, Bhagavan, now I do. But, revered sir, how can one fix one's mind on God?"

How to Fix One's Mind on God

Shrī Rāmakrishna: "To that end one must always sing forth the holy name of God and talk without ceasing of His glory and attributes. Then one must seek the company of holy men. One must from time to time visit the Lord's devotees or those who have given up attachment to the things of the world for the sake of the Lord. It is, however, difficult to fix one's mind upon God in the midst of worldly cares and anxieties; hence the necessity of going into solitude now and again with a view to meditating on Him."

Solitude Necessary

"In the first stage of one's spiritual life one cannot do without solitude. When plants are young, they stand in need of fences around them for their protection; otherwise goats and cattle will destroy them. The depth of the heart, the retired corner, and the forest are the three places for meditation. One should also practice discrimination. One should discriminate between the Real and the unreal, between matter and Spirit. It is thus that one will shake off one's love for the things of the world and attachment to sensual pleasures, wealth, fame, and power."

Avadhuta and a Kite

Then turning to Bijoy, who had come in, the Bhagavān continued: "Shivanāth, the leader of the Brāhmo Samāj, has great cares, he has to edit a newspaper and do various other works. In attending to worldly affairs, one naturally loses peace of mind and is overwhelmed with worries and anxieties. It is said in the *Bhāgavatam* that Avadhuta[1] had twenty-four *gurus* (spiritual guides). The kite was one of them. In a certain place some fishermen were catching fish, a kite swooped down and snatched a fish. Seeing the kite with the fish in his claws, hundreds of crows flew after him and began to caw, making a great noise. In whatever direction the kite flew, the crows followed. When he flew to the south, they pursued him; when he flew to the north, they were after him, and he found no peace in any direction. At last the kite dropped the fish. Then the crows flew after the fish and the kite rested calmly on the branch of a high tree. He thought within himself: 'That fish was the cause of all this trouble. Now that I no longer have it, I am happy and in perfect peace.' The Avadhuta learned from this kite that as long as a man is attached to worldly objects, so long he has toil, cares, anxiety, unrest, and unhappiness. When attachment is gone, all works end, and then comes peace. But work without attachment is good; it does not bring unrest."

1 "Avadhuta" is a Sanskrit title which is given to one who has become the absolute master of nature and who has realized God. Such a great soul was Dattātreya. In the *Purānas* he is called Avadhuta. He was also the author of the *Avadhuta Gītā*, a famous work on *Advaita Vedānta*.

Avadhuta and a Bee

"It is very difficult, however, to work and remain unattached. A few only can accomplish it. Those who have attained to God-consciousness, like the sage Nārada,[2] work for the good of humanity. Avadhuta had another *guru*—a bee. What trouble a bee takes to collect honey! But it is not for its own use; someone else comes and takes the honey from the comb. The Avadhuta learned from the bee that it is not wise to collect anything. Truly spiritual men should depend absolutely upon God and should not desire to possess anything. But this is not possible for householders. They will have to support their families and therefore they should gather and possess. A fowl does not gather into barns, but when it has a number of young ones, then it brings food for them in its bill."

Practice of Non-Attachment

"Perform all your duties with your mind always fixed on God. As for your parents, wife, and children, serve them as your own, but always remember they do not belong to you, that they are the children of God. You are also a child of God and your own people are those who love God. The tortoise moves about in the water in quest of food; where do you think her mind is? On the water's edge where her eggs are laid. In the same manner you may go about in the world, but take good care that your mind always rests upon the hallowed feet of the Lord."

Need of Solitude

"Suppose you have not acquired true love for the Lord. If in this state you enter the world, then you will surely get entangled. Misfortune, grief, misery, sorrow, suffering, and the various diseases of the body will disturb the balance of your mind; and the more you will throw yourself into the affairs of the world and trouble yourself about worldly matters, the more your attachment to the world will be increased. Rub your hand with oil if you desire to

2 In the Hindu scriptures Nārada is described as the ideal lover of God. He communed with the Lord under all conditions. The Lord Vishnu selected him as His most beloved messenger.

break open the jackfruit, else the milky gum of the fruit will stick to your hands. First rub your soul with the oil of love and devotion to the Lord, then you may come in contact with the affairs of the world. But to this end solitude is the one thing needful. If you want butter, you must curdle the milk and set it in a place where no one can disturb it; otherwise the curd will not stand. Then churn it and the butter will rise. Similarly the neophyte should sit in solitude and not be disturbed by worldly-minded people; then through the churning of the settled mind by the practice of meditation the butter of divine love will be acquired. If you give your mind to God in solitude, you will obtain the spirit of true renunciation and absolute devotion. If you give the same mind to the world, it will grow worldly and think of woman and gold.

"The world may be likened to water, and the mind to milk. Pure milk once mixed with water cannot be separated from it; but if it is first turned into butter and then placed in water, it can remain separate. Let the milk of your mind be turned into the butter of divine love by means of religious practices in solitude. The mind then will never get mixed with the water of worldliness, but will rise above and remain unattached to the world. Having attained true knowledge and devotion the mind will stand apart from the world."

Lust and Gold Unreal

"Along with this, practice discrimination. 'Lust and gold' are unreal; God is the one Reality. What uses has money? It can give one food, clothes, house, the luxuries and comforts of life, but it cannot bring spiritual perfection or God-vision. Therefore the acquisition of wealth should not be the highest end and aim of life. In this manner you should discriminate. Similarly by discrimination you will overcome your attachment to personal beauty. Think what the body of a beautiful woman is made of. Like all bodies it is of flesh and blood, skin and bones, fat and marrow, etc. The wonder is that man loses sight of God and gives his mind purely to such transitory objects of sense."

The disciple asked: "Bhagavan, is it possible to see God?"

Means of God-Vision

Shrī Rāmakrishna: "Certainly. The following are some of the means of seeing God: going from time to time into solitude; singing forth His name and His attributes; and discrimination."

The disciple: "Bhagavan, what state of mind leads to God-vision?"

Shrī Rāmakrishna: "Cry to God with a yearning heart and then you will see Him. People will shed a jugful of tears for the sake of their wife or children; they will be carried away by a stream of their own tears for the sake of money; but who sheds a tear for God? Cry for Him, not for show, but with a longing and yearning heart. The rosy light of the dawn comes before the rising sun; likewise a longing and yearning heart is the sign of God-vision that comes after."

How to Love God

"You can see God if your love for Him be as strong as the strength of these three attachments put together: namely, the attachment of a miser to his wealth, that of a mother to her new-born child, and that of a chaste wife to her husband.

"To see God one must love Him with the whole heart and soul. One must make one's prayers reach the Divine Mother. Absolute self-resignation to the will of the Divine Mother is the surest way to God-vision. As the kitten resigns itself to the will of its mother, so a devotee shall resign himself to the will of the Divine Mother. The kitten knows nothing more than to cry 'mew, mew,' and the mother-cat may keep her young one on the bare floor of the kitchen or on the downy bed of the householder. The kitten is always contented. Similarly the true devotee should always cry unto the Divine Mother and be contented with whatever She wishes to do with him.

"God-consciousness does not come so long as there are three things in the heart—shame, hatred, and fear. These three and the caste pride are the fetters of the soul. When these fetters are broken, freedom is attained. Bound by fetters is *jīva* (the ego), free from fetters is Shiva (God)."

Madness of Divine Love

"Every man has certain debts to pay—a debt to the Divine Spirit, a debt to the sages, debt to mother, to father, to the wife. No man can renounce everything without paying off these debts. But if his soul be intoxicated with divine love and become mad after God, then he is free from all duties and debts. Then who is his father, who is his mother, and who is his wife? He behaves like a madman who is free from all bondage and who has no duty to perform. Do you know what that madness of divine love is? In that state one forgets the world and becomes unconscious of one's own body which is so dear to one. Chaitanya Deva possessed this madness of ecstasy. He had neither hunger, nor thirst, nor sleep, nor consciousness of his physical form."

Pride

"Some people are proud of their wealth, their fame, and social position, but these things are transitory. None can take them away after death. It is not good to be proud of wealth. You may say, 'I am wealthy,' but then there are millionaires, multi-millionaires, and so on. In the evening fireflies think that they are lighting the world; but when the stars begin to shine, their pride is subdued. The stars in turn think that they are lighting the world, but when the moon shines, the stars are put to shame. The moon, too, believes that her light illumines everything; but lo! the dawn appears and the rising sun effaces the light of the moon. If wealthy people thought of these things, they would no longer be proud of their wealth."

A householder: "Revered sir, we are householders; please give us some further instructions."

Shrī Rāmakrishna: "First know God, then perform the duties of a householder."

Householder: "Revered sir, is this world unreal?"

The World Unreal

Shrī Rāmakrishna: "So long as a man does not realize God, so long it is real; because at that time he makes mistakes and through self-delusion says: 'me and mine.' Being fettered by this self-delusion, he drowns in the sea of lust and worldliness, and becomes so blinded by ignorance that he cannot see the way out. You yourself can notice how transitory the world is. Look at this house; how many people have come and gone; how many people have been born and have died in it! Now it exists, now it does not; it is ephemeral. Those whom you call your own will vanish when your eyes are closed. If you have no one in the household, still you are bound and cannot go anywhere because of some distant relative. The way is open, but the fish cannot escape from the net. The silkworm makes its own cocoon, but does not know how to get out and consequently dies in it."

How a Householder Should Live in the World

"A householder should take care of his children, but at the same time he should think of them as baby Krishna, or as children of God. Serve your father as God, and your mother as Divine Mother. After realizing God, if a man lives with his wife, he has no physical relation with her. Both live like *bhaktas* or true devotees. They talk of spiritual subjects and spend their time in thinking of God and in caring for His *bhaktas*. They serve God who dwells in all beings."

Householder: "But, revered sir, we do not find any such husbands and wives."

Rāmakrishna: "Yes, there are some, but they are very rare. Worldly people do not easily recognize them. But in order to live like this both must be spiritual. If both enjoy divine love, then such a life is possible; otherwise there will be no harmony, but discord and trouble between husband and wife. Perhaps the wife will complain, saying: 'Why did I marry this man? What pleasure does he give me? He simply sits quietly and thinks of God. He is losing his mind.'"

A devotee: "These are some of the obstacles; but there may be others. The children may be disobedient or may be diseased. Then, revered sir, what is to be done?"

Rāmakrishna: "It is very difficult for a householder to practice devotion. There are many obstacles. You all know them very well—disease, sorrow, poverty, disharmony with the wife, disobedience and evil tendencies in the children; but there is a way out of it. One should occasionally live in solitude and pray and struggle hard to attain to God."

A householder: "Revered sir, is it necessary to leave one's home?"

Rāmakrishna: "Not for good; but occasionally when you find opportunity, for a day or two, leaving behind responsibility, care, and anxiety. But during this time you should not mix with worldly people or think of worldly affairs. Either live alone, or in the company of some saint or holy man."

Householder: "Revered sir, how can we know or recognize a saint?"

How to Recognize a Saint

Rāmakrishna: "He is a saint whose heart, soul, and inner nature have turned towards God; he who has renounced woman and wealth. A saint does not look at women with the eye of desire; if he comes near a woman, he sees the Divine Mother in her and worships her. His thoughts are always on God and his words are of Him. He sees God everywhere and knows that by serving others, he serves Him. These are some of the outward signs of a saint."

Householder: "Revered sir, is it necessary to remain long in solitude?"

Rāmakrishna: "Until right discrimination is acquired."

Householder: "Revered sir, what is right discrimination?"

Right Discrimination

Rāmakrishna: "God is Truth, the world is untruth; this is discrimination. Truth means that which is unchangeable and permanent, and untruth is that which is changeable and transitory. He who has right discrimination knows that God alone is the Reality; all other things are unreal. When right discrimination comes, then rises intense desire to know God. As long as one loves untruth, such as the pleasures and comforts of the body, fame, honor, and wealth, so long one does not desire to know God, the Truth. Right discrimination between Truth and untruth leads one to search after God."

Another householder devotee: "Bhagavan, we have heard that thou hast attained to ecstasy and God-consciousness; wilt thou please explain when and how such a state comes?"

Ecstasy

Rāmakrishna: "Ecstasy does not come to one who has not realized God. When a fish rises from deep water, it disturbs the surface of the water, and the larger the fish, the greater the disturbance. Therefore, a person in the state of ecstasy sometimes laughs, sometimes weeps, sometimes sings, sometimes dances, but one cannot remain in that state of ecstasy for a long time."

Householder devotee: "Bhagavan, we have heard that thou hast seen God. If this be true, please make us see Him also."

Work Necessary for God-Vision

Rāmakrishna: "Everything depends upon the will of the Lord. What can man do? One may repeat His holy name, but sometimes tears flow and sometimes not. At the time of meditation, one day you may have perfect concentration and another day you will not be able to fix your mind at all. Work is necessary for God-vision. Once I was passing by a pool, the surface of which was covered by a thick scum; I saw a poor man pushing the scum to one side to look at the water. This showed me that if you wish to see the water, you must push aside the scum. That act of pushing is like the work which removes all the impurities of the heart. Then God is visible. Concentration, meditation, repetition of the name of the Lord, charitable works, and self-sacrifice, these works will remove the scum of ignorance which covers the water of Divinity in the pool of the heart."

Mahima,[3] who had joined the group of devotees, exclaimed: "Oh yes, Bhagavan, such works are absolutely necessary. Tireless labor is needed to attain great results. How much we must study! Innumerable are the sciences, scriptures, and philosophies."

Book Knowledge and Realization

Rāmakrishna: "How much can you study? What results can you get by mere discrimination? First try to realize God. Have faith in the words of your *guru*, and perform some good work. If you have

3 Mahima was the first name of a *brāhmin zamindār* and a scholar who was known as Mahima Charan Chakravarti. He lived the life of a pure and spiritual householder and regarded Rāmakrishna as the greatest Hindu sage of the age.

not found a *guru*, a true spiritual master, earnestly pray to God. He will show you what He is like. What can you know by reading books? Before you enter a market-place, you can hear only a loud confused uproar; but when you go near, all confusion will vanish and you will distinguish what each one is calling. Before you reach the shore, you hear the roar of the waves; but when you come near, you see vessels, sea-gulls, birds, and you can count the waves. One cannot realize Divinity by reading books.

"There is a vast difference between book knowledge and realization. After realization all books, sciences, and scriptures seem to be like worthless straw. It is necessary first to make acquaintance with the landlord. Why are you so anxious to know beforehand how many houses, how many gardens, how many stocks and bonds he possesses? If you ask the servants, they will not tell you; nor will they notice you. But if you can once become acquainted with the landlord, by whatever means, you will learn about his possessions in a moment, and the servants then will bow down to you and honor you."

A devotee: "Bhagavan, how can one make acquaintance with the Landlord?"

Work and Grace

Rāmakrishna: "For that, I say, work is necessary. What is the use of sitting quietly and saying, 'God exists'? If you merely sit on the shore of a lake and say: 'There are fish in this lake,' will you catch any? Go and get the things necessary for fishing, get a rod and line and bait and throw some lure in the water. Then from the deep water the fish will rise and come nearer, and you will be able to see and catch them. You wish me to show you God while you sit quietly by, without making the least effort. How unreasonable! You would have me set the curds, churn the butter, and hold it before your mouths. You ask me to catch the fish and place it in your hands. How unreasonable! If a man desires to see the king in his palace, he will have to go to the palace and pass through all the gates; but if after entering the outermost gate he exclaims, 'Where is the king?' he will not find him. He must go on through the seven gates, then he will see the king."

Mahima: "Bhagavan, by what kind of work can God be attained?"

Rāmakrishna: "There is no difference in work. Do not think that this work will lead to God and that will not. Everything depends upon His grace. Whatever work you perform with sincerity and earnest longing will attract His grace and help towards realization. Through His grace the conditions for realization will become perfect. These conditions are association with the holy, right discrimination of the Real from the unreal, and the finding of the real *guru*, or true spiritual master. If your family depends upon you, perhaps your brother will assume its responsibility for you. Perhaps your wife will not hinder you in your spiritual life, but will rather help you; or perhaps you will not marry at all and will not be attached to the world in any way. When such conditions become absolutely favorable, the realization of God becomes easy."

Non-Attachment Necessary

"God cannot be attained so long as the mind is not absolutely free from all worldly attachment. A true sage is one who cannot hoard anything for himself. There is a saying: 'A fowl of the air and a true sage do not gather stores; they do not keep anything for the morrow.' As regards myself, I cannot keep anything even for my personal needs. At one time I thought of going to Benares, but afterwards I discovered that I had to carry clothes and take money with me, so it was impossible for me to go. (Turning to Mahima) But you are householders, you can have both this and that, both the world and the spiritual life."

Mahima: "Bhagavan, 'this' cannot remain long."

Rāmakrishna: "When I was practicing renunciation, one day I went to the Ganges near the *Panchavati*[4] and took up a handful of earth and a handful of coins; then I began to discriminate, saying that earth and gold are one and the same; earth is gold and gold is earth; and after realizing the sameness, I threw both into the river. I prayed to my Divine Mother, saying: 'O Mother, I do not desire material wealth or earthly prosperity, but only that Thou dwell within my heart.' When the mind renounces attachment to lust and wealth, it turns towards God and ultimately becomes at-

4 Five sacred trees planted in such a way as to form a grove to be used for contemplation.

tached to Him. Then that which was bound becomes free. To be turned away from God is bondage. The mind is like the needle of a scale and God is the central point of balance. When the weight of worldly attachment is in the heart, the scale drops to one side and the needle of the mind is deflected from the central point or God. The heavier the weight, the greater is the deflection. Why does a child cry after its birth? It thinks, as it were: 'I was enjoying divine communion, but now I have lost it. Where have I come and where is my God, where is my God?' For you (to Mahima) the renunciation should be in the mind only. You should remain in the world, but unattached to it."

Mahima: "Revered sir, can the world exist for the mind which is fixed on God?"

The Kingdom of God is Everywhere

Rāmakrishna: "Of course it will exist; otherwise where will it go? I see that wherever I remain, I am in the kingdom of God. Verily I say unto you, this world is the kingdom of God. Rāmachandra, the Divine Incarnation and the hero of the epic *Rāmāyana*, said to his father that he would renounce the world and go to a spiritual *guru* in order to attain spiritual wisdom. The father summoned the great sage Vashishta to reason with his son. Vashishta saw that Rāma had intense dispassion for the world; he then said to him: 'O Rāma, first discriminate with me, then renounce the world.' By right discrimination Rāma realized that God manifests Himself in the form of *jīva*, or the individual soul and the world. Everything lives and exists in and through His Being. Then Rāma kept silent.

"Some time ago the scholar Vaishnava Charan said that perfect knowledge of God is attained when one perceives Him in all human beings. I have now come to a stage of realization in which I see that God is walking in every human form and manifesting Himself alike through the sage and the sinner, the virtuous and the vicious. Therefore when I meet different people, I say to myself: 'God in the form of the saint, God in the form of the sinner, God in the form of the unrighteous and God in the form of the righteous.' He who has attained to such realization goes beyond good and evil, above virtue and vice, and realizes that the divine will is working everywhere."

Parable of the Monk and the Zamindār

"There was a Hindu monastery in a certain village. The monks of the monastery went out every day with begging bowls to gather food. One day, a monk, passing by, saw a *zamindār* (landlord) severely beating a poor man. The holy man, being very kind-hearted, entreated the *zamindār* to stop beating the man. The *zamindār*, blind with rage, immediately turned on the monk and poured upon him the venom of his anger. He beat him until he was knocked unconscious on the ground. Another man, seeing his condition, went to the monastery and told what had happened. His brother monks ran to the spot where the holy man was lying. They lifted him and brought him to the monastery and laid him in a room; but the holy man still remained unconscious for a long time. Sorrowful and anxious, his brothers fanned him, bathed his face, put milk into his mouth, and tried to nurse him back to life. Gradually they brought him back to consciousness. The holy man opened his eyes and looked at his fellow-brethren. One of them, desiring to know whether he could recognize his friends, asked him in a loud voice: 'Mahārāj,[5] dost thou recognize him who is feeding thee with milk?' The holy man answered in a feeble voice: 'Brother, he who beat me is now feeding me.'" And Rāmakrishna added: "But one cannot realize this oneness of the Spirit unless one has reached God-consciousness."

Resignation

"Live in the world like a dead leaf. As a dead leaf is carried by the wind into a house or on the roadside and has no choice of its own, so let the wind of divine will blow you wherever it chooses. Now it has placed you in the world, be contented. Again when it will carry you to a better place, be equally resigned. The Lord has kept you in the world, what can you do? Resign everything to Him, even your own dear self; then all trouble will be over. You will see then that He is doing everything; everywhere is the will of Rāma (God)."

5 "Mahārāj" is a Sanskrit title meaning literally "great king."

Parable of the Pious Weaver

"In a certain village there lived a weaver. He was very spiritual; everyone trusted and loved him. The weaver went to the market to sell his cloth. If a customer asked the price of it, he would say: 'By the will of Rāma the thread cost one *rupee*, by the will of Rāma the labor cost four *ānnās*, by the will of Rāma the profit is two *ānnās*, by the will of Rāma the price of the cloth as it stands is one *rupee* and six *ānnās*.' People had such confidence in him that they would immediately pay the price and take the cloth. This man was a true devotee. At night after dinner he would sit for a long time and meditate on God and repeat His holy name.

"Once it was late into the night; he could not sleep; he was sitting alone in the courtyard near the entrance, smoking. A gang of robbers was passing that way. They wanted a carrier, and seeing this man, they dragged him away with them. Then they broke into a house and stole a great many things, some of which they piled on the poor weaver's head. At this moment the watchman came up, the robbers ran away and the poor weaver with his load was caught. He had to spend that night in confinement. Next morning he was brought before the judge. The people of the village, hearing what had happened, came to see the weaver. They unanimously declared: 'My lord, this man has not stolen anything.' The judge then asked the weaver to describe what had occurred. The weaver said: 'My lord, by the will of Rāma, I was sitting in my courtyard; by the will of Rāma it was very late in the night; I, by the will of Rāma, was meditating upon God and repeating His holy name; when, by the will of Rāma, a band of robbers passed that way; by the will of Rāma they dragged me away with them; by the will of Rāma they broke into a house; by the will of Rāma they piled a load on my head; when, by the will of Rāma, the watchman came up and, by the will of Rāma, I was caught. Then, by the will of Rāma, I was kept in a prison, and this morning the will of Rāma has brought me before thee.' The judge, seeing the innocence and spirituality of the man, ordered him to be released. Coming out, the weaver said to his friends: 'The will of Rāma has released me.'

"Whether you live in the world or renounce it, everything depends upon the will of Rāma. Throwing your whole responsibility upon God, do your work in the world. If you cannot do this, what else can you do?"

Everything Depends on God's Will

"If a clerk be imprisoned, when the term of his sentence is over and he comes out, tell me, will he pass his time in dancing for joy over his release or resume his work as clerk? So when the householder is liberated from the prison of the world, will he spend his life in rejoicing over his liberation? He may continue to perform his duties as householder, if he so desires. He who has attained wisdom makes no distinction between this place and that place; to him all places are equal. He who has found God here has also found Him there. When the tail of a tadpole drops off, it can live both in water and on land. When the tail of ignorance drops off, man becomes free. He can then live both in God and in the world equally well."

The World is Like a Dream

"Those who follow monistic (*Advaita*) *Vedānta*, however, look upon this world as unreal, like a dream. According to them, the *Paramātman*, or the Over-Soul, is the witness of the three states of consciousness—waking, dream, and dreamless sleep. All these are ideas. The dream state is just as real as the waking state. Let me tell you a story."

Parable of the Farmer and His Only Child

"There was a farmer who was a monist; he had attained to some realization. He lived like any other farmer with his family, and he had a child. He and his wife had extreme love for this son, because he was their only child. The farmer himself was a very spiritual man. He was respected and loved by everyone in the village. Once he was working in the field, when suddenly a man brought the news of his son's severe illness. He went home, called physicians, took great care, but could not save the child's life. Everybody in the household was overwhelmed with grief, but the farmer looked as if nothing had happened. He consoled others by saying: 'What can be gained by mourning over the child?' The next day he went to the field as usual, and after finishing his work he came home and found his wife and the other members of the family still weeping and wailing and plunged in deep sorrow. The wife reproached him, saying: 'How heartless you are! You have not shed a single tear for your only child.' The farmer then calmly replied: 'Shall I tell you why I do not weep? Last night I had a wonderful dream. I saw that I was a king, and the father of eight beautiful children, and that I was enjoying all the pleasures and comforts of life. Suddenly I woke up and the dream passed away. Now I am in great confusion—whether I shall weep and wail for my eight children or for this only one.'

"The farmer was an *Advaita jnāni*, therefore he realized that the waking state was as unreal as the dream state, and that the one permanent reality was *Ātman*. But I accept all states as true—the state of *samādhi*, which is the fourth state, and again, the waking, dream, and dreamless sleep state. I accept *Brahman* the Absolute and *māyā*, *jīva*, and the world. If I do not take all, a portion will be missing and the weight will be less."

A devotee: "How could the weight be less?"

The Absolute and the Phenomenal

Rāmakrishna: "*Brahman* the Absolute is with the individual souls and the phenomenal world. First, when a person is discriminating by saying, 'not this, not this,' he leaves the individual ego and the phenomenal world aside; then after reaching the Absolute, when he returns, he realizes that the Absolute appears as the phenomenal world. In a wood-apple there are seeds, pulp, and the shell. When I take the pulp, I leave out the seeds and the shell; but when I speak of the weight of the wood-apple, the weight of the pulp alone would not be equal to it. You will have to weigh the pulp, seeds, shell, and everything. That which has pulp, has also seeds and shell. Similarly, that which is the Absolute has also all phenomena. Therefore I take both the Absolute Reality and the phenomenal reality. I do not blow away the phenomenal world by calling it a dream, because then the weight will be less."

Mahima: "This is a wonderful harmony. From the Absolute to the phenomenal and from the phenomenal to the Absolute."

Rāmakrishna: "Those who are *jnānis* (monists), look at the world as a dream, but the realistic *bhaktas* take every state as real. There are some cows who pick only certain tufts of grass and give very little milk; but there are other cows who eat all kinds of grass and give plenty of milk. The *jnānis* may be compared to the former, and the *bhaktas* to the latter. The highest of the *bhaktas* take both the Absolute and the phenomenal; therefore when they come down from the Absolute to the plane of relativity, they continue to enjoy the Absolute through the phenomenal. (To Mahima) You explain *Om* as containing three letters, *A-u-m*."

Mahima: "Revered sir, *A-u-m* means creation, preservation, and destruction."

Meaning of Om

Rāmakrishna: "But for me it is like the sound d-o-n-g of a big bell, which is at first audible, then inaudible, and ultimately melts away into infinite space. So the phenomenal melts away in the Absolute; the gross, subtle, and causal states lose themselves in the Great Cause, the Absolute; the waking, dream, and dreamless sleep states become merged in the fourth state, *samādhi*. When the bell sounds, it creates waves like those in the ocean when a heavy stone is thrown into it. From the Absolute, phenomena come out; from the same Absolute, which is the great First Cause, have also evolved the gross, subtle, and causal bodies; from the same Absolute, again, which is the fourth state, come the other three states of consciousness. The waves of the ocean are once more dissolved in the ocean. By this illustration of d-o-n-g I show that the eternal word *Om* is symbolic of the evolution and involution of phenomena from and into the Absolute. I have *seen* all these things. My Divine Mother has shown me that in the infinite ocean of the Absolute, waves rise and again merge into it. In that infinite spiritual space, millions of planets and worlds rise and are dissolved. I do not know what is written in your books; I have *seen* all this."

Chapter 4

Visit to the *Pandit* Vidyāsāgara

Shrī Rāmakrishna desired to meet Pandit Iswara Chandra Vidyāsāgara.[1] One afternoon he was seen coming in a carriage with some of his disciples all the way from Dakshineshwar, a distance of about six miles, to pay a visit to the *pandit* at Bādurbagan in Calcutta.

Rāmakrishna's Childlike Nature

The carriage, a short while after, drew up in front of the *pandit*'s house. Shrī Rāmakrishna alighted, supported by one of his disciples. Before reaching the staircase which led to the *pandit*'s study, which was also the drawing-room, the Bhagavān, putting his hand on his shirt, asked a disciple with some concern: "My shirt is unbuttoned; is it necessary to button it?" The disciple answered: "Do not trouble thyself, Lord; none will find fault with thee on that account." The Bhagavān, like a child, seemed to be satisfied and did not think about it again. The party was then led upstairs into a room where the *pandit* was seated in a chair facing the south. A table after the European fashion, with books and papers lying about on it, was before him, and he was talking with some of his friends. As the Bhagavān Shrī Rāmakrishna entered the room, the *pandit* rose to receive him. The Lord stood with his face to the west and with one hand resting upon the table. He looked upon the *pandit* intently as if he was an old acquaintance, and with a smile on his sweet, childlike, radiant face, lost all sense-consciousness, and went into the ecstatic *samādhi*.

After a while, taking his seat on a bench, the Bhagavān in his semiconscious state uttered: "I wish some water to drink." Thereupon Vidyāsāgara inquired of a disciple whether the Bhagavān

1 Pandit Ishwara Chandra Vidyāsāgara was the greatest Hindu scholar of his time in Calcutta. He was a true philanthropist, a patriot, an educationalist, and the founder of the Metropolitan Institution (present Vidyāsāgara College) in Calcutta. The word "*vidyāsāgara*" is a Sanskrit title which he acquired on account of his vast erudition. It means "ocean of knowledge."

would also like some delicious sweetmeats which he had just received from Burdwān.[2] Finding no objection, the *pandit* went into his inner apartments and returned with water and the sweetmeats. He placed them before the Lord. The disciples partook of the sweetmeats, but when they were offered to one young man, Vidyāsāgara said: "Oh, he is a child of this house; do not trouble about him." The Bhagavān then said, "Yes, this young man is good. He is like the river Falgu,[3] covered with dry sand, but if you dig a little you will find a strong invisible current underneath. He has a spiritual current inside, although he does not show it on the outside."

Rāmakrishna's Love of Humor

Then addressing Vidyāsāgara he continued: "Today I have at last reached the ocean (referring to the literal meaning of the word *vidyāsāgara*—the ocean of knowledge). So long I have seen only canals, lakes, or, at most, rivers, but now I see the ocean itself."

Vidyāsāgara: "Then, sir, thou art welcome to take some salt water from it."

Bhagavān: "No, my dear sir, why salt water? You are not the ocean of *avidyā* (ignorance), which leads away from God, but you are the ocean of milk, the ocean of *vidyā*, or true knowledge leading Godward."

Vidyāsāgara: "Revered sir, thou mayest say *that*."

Good Works and Compassion for All

Bhagavān: "Your *karma* proceeds from the *sattva* element of nature. From it rises compassion. Whatever work is done for the good of others is absolutely free from fault. It may be called *rājasika*, but it is the activity of *sattva*. There is no harm in such works. Shukadeva[4] and others like him had compassion for all. They worked

2 Burdwān, an old city in Bengāl, famous for delicious sweetmeats.

3 Falgu is the name of a sacred river near the holy city of Gayā in India. It was on the bank of this river that Buddha attained to the highest enlightenment. Its bed is covered with sand like a desert, but a strong current of pure water flows underneath.

4 Shukadeva was the son of Vyāsa, the author of the *Vedānta Sutras* and many

for humanity and helped mankind in the path of Divinity. You are giving free education and doing charitable works; that is good. He who performs good works through love, without seeking results, attains to God. But he who works for name, fame, or any other selfish purpose, remains bound. Further, I may say that you have already become *siddha* (perfected)."

Vidyāsāgara: "Sir, how is that?"

Bhagavān: "You know that *siddha*, or well-boiled potato, becomes soft and tender. Have you not become tender-hearted by your compassion for all?"

Vidyāsāgara: "But the paste of *kalai* (a kind of pulse) when boiled (*siddha*) becomes harder. Is it not so?"

Book-Learned Pandits Like Vultures

Bhagavān, laughing: "Yes, but you are not like that. Mere book-learned *pandits* (scholars) are hard-hearted. They do good neither to themselves nor to others. They are like vultures who soar high in the sky, but always search after carrion-pits. They may talk about divine truths, but their minds are attached to woman and wealth. Their attachment is to worldly things (*avidyā*). Compassion, devotion (*bhakti*), dispassion (*vairāgya*)—these are the manifestations of *vidyā*."

Vidyāsāgara was listening to the words of wisdom with whole attention, while the eyes of other gentlemen present were fixed upon the blissful face of Rāmakrishna radiant with divine glory.

Vidyā and Avidyā

The Bhagavān continued: "The Absolute *Brahman* is beyond the reach of *vidyā* (knowledge) as well as of *avidyā* (ignorance), which keeps one away from the realization of the Absolute.

"The Absolute *Brahman* is beyond the reach of *māyā*, while *māyā* is either *vidyā* or *avidyā*. *Vidyā-māyā* and *avidyā-māyā* both exist in this world. As there are knowledge (*jnāna*) and devotion (*bhakti*), so also there are lust and greed for wealth. Good and evil,

of the *Purānas*. He was born with the *Brahma jnāna*, or the knowledge of the Absolute. He, in his childhood, renounced the world with all its pleasures and attractions. He is regarded by the Hindus as the ideal *jnāni*, or knower of *Brahman*.

virtue and vice, are to be found in this world of relativity; but *Brahman* is unaffected by them. They exist in relation to *jīva* (individual ego), but cannot touch the Absolute *Brahman*."

Brahman Untouched by Good and Evil

"*Brahman* may be compared to the light of a lamp. As by the same light one may read the holy scriptures and another may forge a document, while the light remains unaffected by the good and evil deeds, so is the Absolute *Brahman* untouched by the good and evil of the world. He is like the sun who shines equally upon the virtuous and the wicked."

Brahman Indescribable

"If you ask, misery, sin, suffering, unhappiness—whose are these? I should answer, they are for the *jīva*. They do not affect the *Brahman*. Evil to *jīva* is not evil to *Brahman* any more than the venom in the fangs of a snake is poison to the snake. Others may die of snake-bite, but as the poison does not hurt the snake, so indeed is the existence of sin and evil in relation to *jīva* alone. Who can describe what the Absolute *Brahman* is? Whatever can be uttered by the mouth has become defiled as it were, like the leavings of food. The revealed scriptures, *Vedas*, *Tantras*, *Purānas*, and all holy books, have become defiled as it were, like leavings of food, for they have been uttered by human mouths. But there is one thing that is never defiled in this manner and that is the Absolute *Brahman*. No one has ever succeeded in describing the Absolute by words of mouth. *Brahman* is unspeakable, indescribable, unthinkable."

Vidyāsāgara, interrupting, said to his friends: "This is a grand idea. Today I have learned this truth, that the *Brahman* is the one substance that has never been defiled by the mouth."

Bhagavān: "Yes, that is so."

Parable of the Vedic Father and His Two Sons

"A certain father had two sons. To instruct them in the knowledge of *Brahman* he sent them to an *āchārya* (preceptor). After a few years they returned home and saluted their father. The father was anxious to know how far they had learned about *Brahman*, so he asked his eldest son: 'My dear son, you have studied all the scriptures and philosophies, tell me what is *Brahman* like?' The eldest son then tried to describe the Absolute *Brahman* by quoting various passages from the *Vedas*. The father kept silent.

"Turning to his younger son he asked the same question. The younger son did not answer in words, but remained motionless and communed with the *Brahman* in silence. The father then exclaimed: 'My dear child, thou hast approached the realization of the *Brahman*. Thy silence is a better answer than the recitation of a hundred texts of the *Vedas*, for *Brahman* is indescribable by words. It is indeed the Absolute Silence.' The knowledge of the Absolute *Brahman* is attained in the state of *samādhi*. Then all thoughts cease to rise and perfect silence prevails in the soul. Even the power of speech remains unmanifested. How can one describe *Brahman* by words of mouth?"

Parable of the Ant and the Mount of Sugar

"An ant went to a mount of sugar. The ant did not realize how high was the mountain, but ate a small particle of sugar and was satisfied. It carried home another particle in its mouth. On its way it thought: 'Next time I will carry the whole mountain.' Such, alas, is the thought of small minds. They think that they have known the Absolute, not realizing that *Brahman* is beyond the reach of mind and thought. However great the mind may be it cannot fully comprehend the Absolute *Brahman*. Shukadeva and other great spiritual teachers may be compared to large ants. They could carry in their mouths at utmost eight or ten grains from the mountain of sugar. It is as absurd to say that *Brahman* has been fully comprehended by a great man as it is absurd to say that the whole mountain of sugar was carried away by a large ant.

"What the *Vedas* and other scriptures have said about the Absolute is like the description of the ocean given by a man who saw the vast ocean. When asked what the ocean was like, he exclaimed in utter amazement: 'Oh! what I have seen; how vast is the expanse! How big are the waves! What a thundering roar!'

"Like unto this is the talk about the Absolute *Brahman*. The *Vedas* declare that *Brahman* is the ocean of the Absolute Existence, Intelligence, and Bliss. Shukadeva and other great spiritual teachers stood on the shore of that infinite ocean, saw it and touched its waters.

"Some believe that even those great souls did not go into the ocean, for whoever enters into that ocean of the *Brahman* does not return to this mundane existence."

Parable of a Salt Doll

"A doll made of salt once went to the ocean to measure its depth. It had a desire to tell others how deep was the ocean. Alas! Its desire was never satisfied. No sooner had it plunged into the ocean than it melted away and became one with the ocean. Who would bring the news regarding the depth? Similar is the condition of the *jīva* who enters into the infinite ocean of the Absolute *Brahman*."

Someone asked: "Bhagavan, is it true that the man who has entered into *samādhi*, or who has acquired *Brahma jnāna* does not speak?"

The Brahman is Silence

Rāmakrishna to Vidyāsāgara: "Yes, he who has realized *Brahman* becomes silent. Discussions and argumentations exist so long as the realization of the Absolute does not come. If you melt butter in a pan over fire, how long does it make a noise? So long as there is water in it. When the water is evaporated it ceases to make further noise. Again if you throw a piece of dough in that hot clarified butter (*ghee*) there will be noise until the cake is thoroughly fried. The soul of a seeker after *Brahman* may be compared to fresh butter. It is mixed with the water of egoism and worldliness. Discussions and argumentations (*vichāra*) of a seeker are like the noise caused during the process of purification by the fire of knowledge. As the water of egoism and worldliness is evaporated and the soul becomes purer, all noise of debates and discussions ceases and absolute silence reigns in the state of *samādhi*."

Egoism of a Saint

"Thus realizing the Absolute *Brahman* in silence, the soul comes down on the plane of relativity to help others and to teach mankind the highest wisdom of *Brahman*. Then he talks again and makes a noise again, as the hot *ghee* does when in contact with a piece of dough. Such a soul retains the sense of 'I' simply to help mankind. Shankarāchārya[5] and other spiritual teachers kept the purified sense of 'I' without which all teaching is impossible."

Sages Teach for the Good of Others

"The bee buzzes so long as it is outside the lotus and does not settle down in its heart to drink of the honey. As soon as it tastes the honey all buzzing is at an end. Similarly all noise of discussion ceases when the soul of the neophyte begins to drink the nectar of divine love in the lotus feet of the Almighty. Sometimes, however, the bee after being intoxicated by the honey makes a sweet humming sound. So the God-intoxicated soul sometimes speaks for the good of others.

"A pitcher makes a noise when it is being filled with water in a tank. But all noise stops as soon as the pitcher is full to the brim. The noise will be heard again if some water of the pitcher be poured into another pitcher."

Relation Between Guru and Disciples

"The question now arises, how we do explain the relation between a perfect *guru* and his disciples. The *guru* must talk in order to drive away the ignorance of his disciples. This kind of discrimination, however, does no harm. The boiling butter after it is clarified ceases to make any noise; but if the raw cake made of flour is thrown into it, it will produce much noise because of the water in the cake. The noise will continue until the cake is properly fried. The unfried may be compared to the disciple, and the boiling butter to the *guru*, the spiritual teacher. The sound of teaching is heard so long as the disciple is not perfectly enlightened."

5 Shankarāchārya was the greatest exponent of the *Vedānta* philosophy in India. He lived about the beginning of the eighth century of the Christian era. His commentaries on the *Upanishads*, the *Vedānta Sutras*, and on the *Bhagavad Gītā* have shown the profound depth of his philosophical reasoning. He became a *sannyāsī* when he was eight years old. He wrote his famous commentaries in Sanskrit at the age of twelve and finished his literary work when he was sixteen years old. Then for sixteen years he preached monistic *Vedānta*, and established monastic orders and monasteries in the four corners of India. He finished his glorious and eventful career when he reached the age of thirty-two. He is regarded in India as the Incarnation of Shiva and the embodiment of divine wisdom.

Non-Attachment

Shrī Rāmakrishna continued: "So long as the individual soul has the slightest attachment to the world of senses and desires it cannot attain to *Brahma jnāna*. He is a *jnāni* who relinquishes all worldly desires and sense-pleasures by saying, 'Not this, not this,' and then realizes the Supreme *Brahman* in *samādhi*.

"A *jnāni* knows that all phenomena of the universe which are subject to evolution, whether physical or mental, are within the realm of *māyā*; they are unreal and transitory like the objects of vision in a dream. Therefore as one climbs the stairway step by step until the roof is reached, so he rises above them step by step, saying 'not this,' until he reaches the Absolute *Brahman*, which is the roof of the phenomenal universe."

All Phenomena Unreal

"A *jnāni* goes so far as to realize that *Brahman* is the Absolute Reality and all phenomena unreal. A *vijnāni*, however, goes farther and realizes more. He sees that the roof and the steps are all made of the same substance. Few can stay long on the roof (the realm of the Absolute). All those who reach this state of *samādhi* must return to lower planes, just as no one can sing on '*ni*,' the highest note of the gamut, for a long time. The sense of 'I' drags one down. But when a *vijnāni* returns from *samādhi* to a lower plane of consciousness and perceives the world of relativity, he sees the *Brahman* everywhere, and that the same Absolute Being appears as *jīva* and all the phenomena of the universe. He realizes, 'I am *Brahman*,' 'I am He.'"

Jnāna Yoga and Bhakti Yoga

"There are various paths which lead to the realization of the Absolute *Brahman*. The path of a *jnāni* is as good as that of a *bhakta*. *Jnāna yoga* is true; so is *bhakti yoga*. There is another path of *bhakti* mixed with *jnāna* which is equally true. So long as the sense of 'I, me, mine' remains in the devotee, the path of *bhakti* is easier for him.

"A *vijnāni*, however, realizes the Absolute *Brahman* as the unchangeable Reality of the universe, firm and immutable like the Mount Sumeru. It is beyond all activity of *māyā*. He also sees that the world has evolved out of the three *gunas* (*sattva*, *rajas*, and *tamas*) of the *prakriti* or cosmic energy."

Māyā

"*Māyā* or *prakriti* consists of *vidyā* and *avidyā*. *Vidyā* is that energy which leads Godward. It manifests itself as discrimination (*viveka*), non-attachment (*vairāgya*), devotion and love of God (*bhakti, prema*). But *avidyā* leads to worldliness. This energy expresses itself as various passions, desires for wealth and honor, ambition, work with attachment, selfishness. All these *vidyā* and *avidyā* forces rise from the Divine Energy (*Shakti*) of the *Brahman*—they cannot affect the *Brahman*."

Vijnāni and Bhakta

"The *vijnāni* realizes that the same Absolute *Brahman* appears as the Personal God (*Īshvara*), that He who is beyond all attributes is also the Personal God with all attributes and blessed qualities. The *vijnāni* sees that *jīva*, phenomenal world, mind, intellect, *bhakti*, dispassion, knowledge—all these are the glory of the supreme Personal Deity. If these manifestations of the divine glory did not exist, who would have worshipped Him as the Lord of the universe? If a rich man does not possess wealth and property, but becomes bankrupt, nobody will call him rich. Do you not see how beautiful is this world? How many varieties of phenomena—the sun, moon, stars, various kinds of animals and vegetables, things large and small, good and bad, some men with great powers, others with few."

Vidyāsāgara: "Is it then true, revered sir, that God has given to some greater powers than to others? Is the Lord partial?"

Unity in Diversity

Bhagavān: "The Lord dwells as the All-Pervading Being (*Vibhu*) equally within all living creatures great or small, nay, even in the smallest ant or animalcule. The difference lies in the manifestation of powers (*shakti*), otherwise how will it be possible for one strong man to defeat ten men in a hand-to-hand fight, while a weakling will run away from the presence of an ordinary mortal?

"If there were no difference in powers, why should people respect and honor you? You have no monstrosity, like two horns on your forehead, that people will come to see you out of curiosity. You have more compassion, more wisdom than others, therefore people come to see you and pay respects to you. Do you not think so?"

Book-Learning

"There is nothing in mere book-learning. One should study books simply to find out the ways by which He (the Absolute *Brahman*) can be realized. A holy man had a manuscript with him. Someone asked what it contained. The saint opened it and showed that on every page was written the sacred formula '*Om Rāma*,' the holy name of the Lord.

"Chaitanya Deva, when travelling on a pilgrimage in the Deccan (Southern India), saw in one place a man reading aloud the texts of the *Bhagavad Gītā*. At a little distance another man, with unrestrainable tears running down his cheeks, was listening. Chaitanya Deva asked him whether he understood the meaning of the text. The poor man replied: 'My Lord, I do not understand one word of what the *pandit* is reading.' Chaitanya Deva questioned him: 'Why are you weeping, then?' The devotee answered: 'I see the chariot of Arjuna, and the blessed Lord Krishna is speaking before him. This divine vision brings tears of love to my eyes.'"

Sense of "I"

Shrī Rāmakrishna continued: "You may ask why does a *vijnāni* prefer to have *bhakti* (love and devotion)? The answer is: Because it is difficult for one to be free from the sense of 'I.' In the state of *nirvikalpa samādhi*,[6] it may vanish for the time being, but it comes back again; while for ordinary individuals it is almost impossible to eliminate this sense of 'I, me, and mine.' However, many times you may cut off the branches of the *asvattha* tree, so long as the root is alive new branches will sprout; similarly you may try to get rid of the sense of 'I,' but so long as the root is alive it will sprout up again and again. Even after acquiring *Brahma jnāna* the emancipated soul is forced back to the plane of this '*aham*,' the sense of 'I.'

"If you dream of a tiger you will tremble in every limb and your heart will throb violently. When you wake up you may realize that it was a mere dream, but still your heart will go on palpitating all the same. Similarly the sense of 'I' remains even after the

6 *Nirvikalpa samādhi* is described in the *rājā yoga* as the highest state of *samādhi* in which the soul rises above the sense of "I" and the plane of all thoughts, ideas, and emotions, and reaches the realm of the Absolute.

realization of the Absolute. Thus, if the sense of 'I' is the cause of all troubles and it is impossible to be free from it, let it stay on as 'I,' the servant of the Lord.

"Rāmachandra (God-Incarnate) once asked his great devotee Hanumān:[7] 'My son, in what relation do you regard me?' The devotee replied: 'When I think of myself as embodied, I am Thy servant and Thou art the Lord. When I think of myself as the *jīva* (ego), I am Thy part and Thou art the universal whole; but when I think of myself as the *Ātman*, I am one with Thee. Then I realize 'I am Thou and Thou art I.'"

Ajnāna and Jnāna

"'I' and 'mine'—these two are the signs of *ajnāna*, ignorance. My house, my wealth, my learning, my glory, all these are mine—this idea proceeds from ignorance of one's true Self, but *jnāna* or divine knowledge means that state where *jīva* realizes: 'O Lord, Thou art the Master of all; house, family, children, friends, relatives, nay, whatever exists in the universe belongs to Thee.' 'Whatever is mine is Thine.' 'Nothing belongs to me'—such ideas rise from true knowledge.

"It is good for everyone to remember that after death nothing of this world will remain with us. We have come here simply to perform certain *karma* and gain some experience. Just as country people come to a big city like Calcutta to do some work, so we have come to fulfill our desires according to the tendencies with which we were born."

Parable of the Rich Man and His Sircar

"A rich man has given the charge of his beautiful garden to his *sircar* (steward). When visitors come to see the garden the *sircar* waits on them attentively. He shows them the beautiful parts of the garden with luxurious fruit-trees, flower-beds, palace-like buildings, lakes, etc., saying: 'These are, gentlemen, our mango-trees. This is our orchard; this is our lake; how beautiful are our flowers!

7 Hanumān was a great devotee of Rāma, who, by the power of his absolute faith in the Lord, jumped across the ocean from India to Lankā (Ceylon). He is regarded by the Hindus as the ideal *bhakta* of India.

Here you see is our drawing-room with most expensive furniture, fine paintings by the best artists—all these belong to us.' The same *sircar* may be found fault with and dismissed by his master at any time with peremptory order to leave the garden at once. He will not be allowed sufficient time to pack up his trunk and take his own baggage with him. Such is the miserable plight of those who lay claim upon things which do not in reality belong to them. Everything belongs to the Lord. It is ridiculous for man to say, 'I am *kartā*' (the doer), 'All these things are mine.'"

The Lord Smiles on Two Occasions

"On two occasions the Lord cannot help smiling: A person is taken seriously ill and is about to die. The physician says to the mother of the patient: 'Mother, there is no cause for fear. I shall save your son's life.' The physician forgets that the will of the Lord is at the root of every event of life and death. The Lord then smiles, thinking: 'How foolish this man must be who boasts of saving the life of his patient when the latter is dying under My will.' The Lord smiles again when two brothers are engaged in partitioning their estate. They take a measuring-tape and, putting it out across the land, say: 'This portion is mine, and that is yours.' The Lord smiles, thinking: 'The whole universe belongs to Me, but these foolish brothers say: "This portion is mine and that is yours."'"

The Omnipotence of Faith

"The Absolute *Brahman* cannot be known by reasoning. Be His servant and, taking refuge with Him, pray to Him with earnestness and sincerity. He will surely reveal Himself unto you. Book-learning or intellectual discussions cannot reveal the Divinity. Reason cannot go far enough and must stop short of the goal. Faith will work wonders."

The Parable of the Brāhmin Priest and His Boy

"There was a certain *brāhmin* priest who served in a household chapel. Once he went away leaving the charge of the service to his son. He told the boy to place the daily offering of food before the Deity and see that He ate it. The boy, following the instructions of his father, placed the offering before the image and silently waited.

But the image neither spoke nor ate. The boy watched for a long time. He had firm faith that the Deity would come down from the altar, take the seat before the offering and eat it. Then he prayed: 'O Lord, come and eat. It is getting very late; I cannot wait any longer.' But the Lord did not speak. Then the boy began to cry, saying: 'Lord, my father told me to see that Thou didst eat the offering. Why dost Thou not come? Thou comest to my father and eatest his offering. What have I done that Thou dost not come to me and eat my offering?' He cried bitterly and for a long time. Then as he looked up at the seat, he saw the Deity in a human form eating the offering. When the service was ended and the boy came out, the members of the household said to him, 'If the service is over, bring out the offering.' The boy replied: 'Yes, but the Lord has eaten everything.' In amazement they asked: 'What did you say?' With absolute innocence the boy repeated: 'Why, the Lord has eaten all that I offered.' Then they entered the chapel and were dumbfounded at the sight of the empty dishes. Such is the power of true faith and true yearning!"

The Bhagavān sang:

The Name of the Lord

1. O my Divine Mother, if I die with Thy hallowed name (Durgā, Durgā) on my lips.
Then in the end, O giver of all bliss, shall it be seen whether
Thou savest Thy poor child drowning in the ocean of sin.

2. I might have slain a cow or a *brāhmin* or an unborn child!
I might be a drunkard, nay more, the slayer of a woman!
But of all these dire sins I have not the slightest fear.
Through faith in Thy holy name I can reach the highest bliss of *Brahman*.

"Yes, faith is at the root of all spiritual progress. Thou canst do without all other things, only thou must have faith. Have but faith in the Lord and thou shalt become at once free from the vilest, the blackest, of all sins.

"The one thing needed is faith and *bhakti*—love, devotion, prayerfulness, self-surrender. It is exceedingly difficult, especially in this age, for a man with his limited faculties to come to my Mother through *vichāra* (discrimination of the real *Brahman* from the unreal phenomenal universe), unaided by the Divine Person. Verily has Prasād, the 'Sweet Psalmist' of Bengāl, laid stress on this difficulty in his well-known song."

The Bhagavān sang:

The Divine Mother and the Absolute Brahman

1. Like a madman, O mind, what seekest thou in the dark room?
He (Divine Being) cometh in deep meditation; without that, who can approach Him?

2. The moon of desire still shineth in thy secret chamber.
First bring it under control with all thy might. It will hide itself at the dawn of divine wisdom.

3. Holding this as the ideal, the great *yogī* practiceth meditation for ages. When realization cometh it attracts the soul as a magnet draws unto itself a piece of iron.

4. Thou shalt not find It in the six schools of philosophy, in the *Vedas*, *Tantras*, or in the holy scriptures. It loveth the sweetness of true devotion (*bhakti*) and abideth in the body with everlasting bliss.

5. Prasād says: O mind, shall I disclose in public (*chātar*) the true nature of that which I worship as my Divine Mother? Guess and understand it from these hints.

There was a deep silence at the close of this song, which had been listened to with rapt attention. Everyone was moved.

Rāmakrishna's Samādhi

At the end of this song the Bhagavān was once more found to be in that indescribable state of *samādhi*. His sweet divine voice became still. His eyes remained fixed and steadfast. But his spiritual eye was feasting on the beatific vision of the divine glory. There was left just enough of self-consciousness to bring the soul face to face with the Divine Mother. This blessed vision the Bhagavān enjoyed for a long time. His face was radiant with celestial light and expressed by sweet smiles the unbounded happiness which he was enjoying within himself, and in his semiconscious state he uttered these words:

Brahman Impersonal and Personal

"That which is the Absolute, impersonal beyond all attributes (*nirguna*), is also the same as the Personal God who is with all attributes and blessed qualities. The Absolute *Brahman* again is inseparable from the Divine Energy (*Shakti*).

"The term '*Brahman*' refers to that aspect of Divinity which is impersonal and which is beyond all activity. But when we think of Him as creating, preserving, and destroying all phenomena, then we call Him the Personal God, Divine Mother or Kālī."

Brahman and Shakti are One

"In reality there is no distinction between '*Brahman*,' or the Impersonal Absolute, and '*Shakti*,' the Divine Mother. The *Brahman* and the *Shakti* are one just as fire and its burning power are one. As by the word fire we understand its power of burning, so by the latter we know that it is the same as fire. By realizing the one both are realized.

"They are one just as much as milk and its whiteness are one. We cannot conceive of the milk without its whiteness. They are one just as a gem and its brightness are one. We cannot conceive of a gem without the brightness. They are one just as the serpent and its sinuous motion are one. We cannot conceive of the serpent without the serpentine movements. He who knows what light is has the knowledge of darkness also. He who has the conception of the phenomenal world must have also some conception of the Absolute Noumenon. He who knows the *Shakti*, or the personal aspect of the Absolute Being, knows also the Impersonal *Brahman*. Again, he who has realized the Absolute Noumenon has also realized the phenomenon. He who has realized *Brahman* has also realized the Personal God or Divine Mother (*Shakti*)."

The Power of the Divine Mother

"This Divine Mother bestows the highest knowledge of the *Brahman* (*Brahma jnāna*) by bringing Her devotee into the state of *samādhi*. She it is who brings him down on the plane of sense-consciousness and allows him to retain the sense of 'I' and 'me.'

"By the power of my Divine Mother all mortals (*jīvas*) possess the sense of 'I' and 'mine.' She again reveals to the soul of one who is in *samādhi*, that all living beings, nay, the whole universe, is but the manifestation of the Divine Energy. It is She who makes one reach the *Brahma jnāna*, the highest knowledge of the Absolute, and She again makes another Her beloved devotee who surrenders himself to Her omnipotent will. This truth is the great secret of all secrets. Therefore the Psalmist says: 'Shall I disclose it in the *chātar* (market place)?'"

To Vidyāsāgara, smiling: "Oh, you are a *pandit*, a great scholar, you must know all this. When I sing the praise of my Divine Mother I refer to the same Absolute *Brahman*. The term 'mother' is very sweet. Therefore I like to call Him 'Mother.' We must learn to love the Personal God (*Īshvara*). Through love He can be easily attained. Love, devotion, and faith are the most valuable. Listen to another song."

The Bhagavān sang again:

Love for the Divine Mother

1. Ecstasy dawneth when I meditate upon my Divine Mother. As is the ardor of thought so is the attainment; but the root must be perfect faith.

2. If the mind diveth into the sea of bliss at the feet of my Mother, then is there no further need of worship, rituals, sacrifice, or repetition of the Lord's name.

3. The devotee of the Divine Mother is free even in this life and doth enjoy everlasting bliss.

The Lord, the Ocean of Immortality

"He who can dive into the sea of bliss becomes immortal. The Lord is described in the *Vedas* as the ocean of immortal bliss. Whosoever enters into it becomes free from death. Some people have a wrong idea that too much meditation upon the Absolute will unbalance the mind. No one becomes unbalanced by meditating upon the Absolute.

"Devotional exercises, rituals, ceremonials, sacrifices, or the pouring of oblations into the sacred fire—such works are needless when true love for the Lord comes in the heart of the devotee. A fan is needed so long as there is no breeze. So when the breeze of the divine love blows all ritualistic works become unnecessary."

Selfless Works Purify the Heart

Referring to Vidyāsāgara, the Bhagavān continued: "The works which you are doing are good works. If you can perform them without seeking their result and without thinking that you are the 'doer,' then it will be still better. The highest result of works done in this selfless manner is the attainment of true love for God. Such works purify the heart and bring God-consciousness in the end. But as your love for the Lord becomes more and more intense, your religious works will become less and less. A married woman diligently performs the household duties, but she is not allowed to do any heavy work when she is about to give birth to her child. You are doing charitable works and other works for the good of humanity. In reality, however, they are of great help to yourself. They will purify your heart and bring unselfish love for God. Man has no power to do good to the world; the Lord doth everything. He who hath made the sun and the moon, He who hath given affection in the hearts of parents, He who hath bestowed compassion upon the great souls, He who hath brought unselfish love and devotion in the hearts of saints and sages, doth everything for the good of His world; who else hath the power to perform any good act? Whosoever performeth good works without holding any desire for their fruits will do good for himself.

"There is gold inside, under the cover of earth. You have not discovered it yet. If you once realize this secret treasure your worldly duties will vanish and you will not care for other works, just as a mother loves nothing better than to fondle and kiss her new-born baby. Go onward and do not stop in one place. The goal is the realization of God. By His grace His true devotee can see Him and can talk with Him just as I am talking with you."

Absolute silence prevailed when the blessed Lord spoke these words with fire and eloquence. Everyone's heart was moved by that divine love which was flowing with mighty force within the soul of Bhagavān Shrī Rāmakrishna.

Rāmakrishna Leaves Vidyāsāgara

At about eight in the evening it was announced that the carriage was ready to take Shrī Rāmakrishna back to Dakshineshwar. The Bhagavān became absent-minded for a while; perhaps his mind was fixed upon the Divine Mother, or perhaps he was asking Her blessing upon his kind host. The Bhagavān then rose to bid him farewell and Vidyāsāgara, with a lighted candle in his hand, led the way down the stairs and through the compound of his house to the gate. Outside the gate a carriage was waiting. An unexpected sight greeted the eyes of the party as they came out. It was a man who might have been a little under forty standing before the gate with folded hands. He was dressed in white and wore a white turban on his head. He had a fair complexion and expressive eyes and a smile was on his face. No sooner did he see the Bhagavān than he fell at his feet with his head touching the ground.

The Bhagavān said: "Is it you, Balarām? How is it that I find you here?"

Balarām[8] replied, smiling: "O revered sir, I have been waiting for some time here at the gate to see thee."

Bhagavān: "Why did you not come in?"

Balarām: "I came late, so I would not interrupt thee, but thought it better to stay here."

The Bhagavān then stepped into the carriage with his companions.

Vidyāsāgara asked a disciple: "Shall I see the carriage hire is paid?"

8 Balarām Bose was a Hindu *zamindār* in Calcutta. He was a true householder disciple of Rāmakrishna. His house was blessed many a time by the visit of Rāmakrishna and his beloved disciples. His whole family regarded Rāmakrishna as the Divine Incarnation in a human form. See Chapter 12.

The disciple replied: "No, sir, you need not trouble yourself. It has already been paid by a friend."

The *pandit* then folded his hands and bent his head and body to make his *pranāma* (salutation) to the Bhagavān. All assembled about the carriage did the same. The little group at the gate, with the venerable Vidyāsāgara at their head still holding the lighted candle in his hand, stood for a while looking in the direction of the carriage, wondering who this God-intoxicated man might be, so wise yet so childlike, so full of joy, so sweet, so godly! Verily a light come down to set ablaze the dry bones of a workaday world! Embodied love, like the dew of heaven falling on the dry thirsty heart of man! A voice came crying unto sunken, self-weary man, 'Thou must be born again and love!' A healer from another clime of this strange disease of modern life! A man among men, eager to solve for them the enigma of the universe.

Chapter 5

Day on the River with Keshab Chandra Sen

It was the day of the festival of Lakshmī.[1] Shrī Rāmakrishna was seated in his room talking with Bijoy and Haralal, when a gentleman entered and announced that Keshab Sen[2] had come on board a steamer which had just landed and was lying at anchor before the *ghāt* (landing-place with steps). A short while after Keshab's disciples came in and bowed down before the Bhagavān, saying: "Keshab Bābu has sent us to thee with the request that thou wilt kindly join him, if it so please thy Holiness." Shrī Rāmakrishna consented and, accompanied by several of his devotees, was taken by Keshab's disciples to the steamer.

Rāmakrishna Goes on Board the Steamer

As the small boat which carried the Bhagavān came alongside, everybody was eager to have a glimpse of the blessed Master and crowded to the gangway. Keshab was anxious to see that he got on board in safety. Mahendra, who had been there for some time, looked at him and noticed that he was in *samādhi* and as motionless as a statue. It was with great difficulty that he was brought back to sense-consciousness once more in order to be taken into the cabin on the upper deck. The state of divine ecstasy had not entirely left him even then. He leaned on a disciple as he was led to the cabin. His body moved mechanically, but his mind was fixed

1 Lakshmī, the goddess of fortune and prosperity.

2 Keshab Chandra Sen was the third great Brāhmo Samāj leader after Rājā Rāmmohan Roy. He was born in 1838 and died in 1884 A.D. In 1858 he became a member of the Ādi Brāhmo Samāj. In 1866 he founded a new branch under the namc of Bhāratavarshiya Brāhmo Samāj, which was afterwards known as the church of the "New Dispensation." In 1870 he went to England to propagate his mission. He was an eloquent preacher and orator. He accepted a great many of the teachings of Rāmakrishna and regarded him as one who had constant communion with *Brahman*.

on God. When he had entered the cabin, Keshab and others bowed at his feet. But what little sense-consciousness remained now began to leave him.

Inside the cabin were a bench, a table, and a few chairs. The Bhagavān was seated on one of the chairs; Keshab also took a chair and Bijoy, another. Other devotees, most of them Brāhmos, sat on the bare floor. The cabin being a small one, many remained standing at the door or at the windows looking in eagerly. The Bhagavān was absolutely devoid of outer consciousness. Everybody was watching his face. Keshab noticed that so large a number of people had come together in the cabin that the Bhagavān was in need of air. The devotees all gazed with fixed eyes. After a time the Bhagavān came down from his *samādhi*, but the consciousness of the divine presence was as intense as before. He talked to the Mother of the universe in words that were scarcely articulate, saying: "O Mother, why hast Thou brought me here? They are hedged around and are not free! Is it indeed possible for me to save them out of their prison house?"

Pahāri Bābā of Gāzipur

A Brāhmo said to the Bhagavān: "Sir, these gentlemen have been fortunate enough to see Pahāri Bābā[3] at Gāzipur. The Bābā is another holy man like thy revered self." Shrī Rāmakrishna had not yet recovered the power of speech. His heart was full and he could not speak, but only smiled on the good man who talked of the Bābā. The Brāhmo continued: "Sir, Pahāri Bābā has thy photograph, which he has put up in his room."

Devotee's Heart the Temple of the Lord

The Bhagavān smiled again, pointing to his body with his finger and in a subdued tone said: "A pillow-case! It is nothing but a pillow-case. But there is one thing to be borne in mind: the heart of

3 Pahāri Bābā was a great Vaishnava saint who lived for many years in an underground cave near Gāzipur. The name "Pahāri," which literally means "one who lives on air," was given to him because he could live for months without eating or drinking anything. "Bābā" is a Sanskrit title, which literally means "father," given on account of great wisdom or age. He was regarded by all as the greatest Vaishnava saint of the age.

the devotee is the temple of the Lord. It is indeed a fact that the Lord is more or less manifest in all things, but He is manifest in a special sense in the heart of a devotee (*bhakta*). Thus a *zamindār* may be met at any of the houses of which he is the owner, yet people will say that he is usually to be seen in some particular drawing-room. The heart of the devotee is the Lord's drawing-room. If one wishes to meet the Lord, one would better seek an audience in the drawing-room."

Various Aspects of the Brahman

"The same Being whom the followers of non-dualistic (*Advaita*) *Vedānta* call *Brahman*, the Absolute, is called *Ātman* (Self) by the *yogīs*, and *Bhagavān*, or the Personal God with divine attributes, by the devotees, or *bhaktas* (lovers of God). The high-caste *brāhmin* is always the same person; but when he worships the Lord, he is called a priest; and when the same man is employed in the kitchen, he is called a cook."

Discrimination of an Advaitin

"The follower of monistic (*Advaita*) *Vedānta*, who seeks to realize the Absolute *Brahman*, discriminates, saying: 'Not this, not this.' That is, the Absolute is not this, not that, not any finite object, not the individual soul, not the external world. When, as the result of this kind of reasoning, the heart ceases to be moved by desires; when, in fact, the mind is merged in superconsciousness, then the *Brāhma jnāna* is reached. One who has truly attained to this *Brāhma jnāna* realizes that *Brahman* the Absolute alone is real, and the world is unreal, and that all names and forms are like dreams. What *Brahman* is cannot be described by word of mouth, nor can one even say that He is personal. Such is the point of view of a non-dualist."

Bhakta's Attitude

"The dualist devotees and lovers of the Personal God (*bhaktas*), on the contrary, accept all states as real. Unlike the non-dualists, they look upon the waking state as a reality and they do not hold that the external world is like a dream. They say that the external world is the glory of the Lord. The heavens, stars, moon, mountains, oceans, men, birds, and beasts, all these He has created. He manifests His glory by these. He is both within and without. He dwells in our hearts. The most advanced *bhaktas* say that the Lord Himself manifests as the twenty-four categories of the *Sānkhya*[4] philosophy, that He appears as the individual soul and the external world.

"A *bhakta* wishes to enjoy communion with his Lord and not to become one with Him. His desire is not to become sugar, but to taste of it. Do you know what are the innermost thoughts and feelings of a true devotee? He says: 'O Lord! Thou art the Master, I am Thy servant. Thou art my Mother, and I am Thy child'; or again: 'Thou art my Child and I am Thy father or Thy mother'; or thus: 'Thou art the Whole and I am Thy part.' The dualistic devotee does not wish to say, 'I am *Brahman*.'"

Rājā Yogī

"A *rājā yogī* also seeks to realize the Universal Being. His object is to bring the finite human soul into communion with the Infinite Spirit. He tries first to collect his mind which is scattered in the world of senses, and then seeks to fix it on the Universal Spirit; hence the necessity of meditating on Him in solitude and in a posture which causes no distraction."

Different Aspects of God

"But all these various ideals are of one and the same *Brahman*, the difference being only in the names. It is the same Being whom men call by the name of the Absolute (*Brahman*), the Universal Spirit, the Impersonal God, or the Personal God with divine attributes."

The steamer had already started and was on its way to Calcutta. Many there were who looked on Shrī Rāmakrishna with eyes that did not move, and who drank the nectar of the words that dropped from his hallowed lips. They did not perceive that the steamer was in motion. The temple garden of Kālī had faded from sight. Be-

4 One of the six schools of classical Indian philosophy.

neath were the sacred waters which reflected the blue firmament above, but the murmur of the waves fell unheeded on the ears of the devotees. The magic of the blessed vision had thrown a charm over them. They beheld before them a wonderful being, a God-in-Man and a Man-in-God, with smiles playing on his sweet face, radiant with the joy of the Lord, and with eyes enhanced in beauty by the collyrium of divine love.

Relation Between Brahman and Shakti

Shrī Rāmakrishna: "The followers of *Advaita Vedānta* maintain that creation, preservation, and dissolution, the individual ego, the external world, all these are manifestations of the Eternal Energy (*Shakti*). They also say that when these are properly analyzed, they appear as dreams, that the Absolute *Brahman* alone is the Reality, and all else is unreal. Even Eternal Energy (*Shakti*) is like a dream, unreal; but you may analyze and discriminate thousands of times, you cannot transcend the realm of Divine Energy (*Shakti*) unless you have reached the highest state of *samādhi*, or superconsciousness.

"The very thoughts like: 'I am meditating,' 'I am thinking on the Absolute,' are within the realm of *Shakti*. They are the manifested powers of that Eternal Energy. Therefore the Absolute *Brahman* and the Eternal Energy are inseparable and one. The existence of one implies that of the other, as fire and its burning power. If you admit the existence of fire, how can you deny its burning power? No one can think of fire without thinking of its burning power. In the same manner, we cannot think of the rays of the sun, without thinking of the sun himself. Again, we cannot think of the sun without thinking of his rays. Therefore, no one can think of *Brahman* as apart from *Shakti*, or *Shakti* as separate from *Brahman*. Likewise, no one can conceive of the phenomenal as independent of the Absolute, or of the Absolute as apart from the phenomenal. The same Eternal Energy, the Mother of all phenomena, is creating, preserving, and destroying everything. She is called Kālī, the Divine Mother. Kālī is *Brahman*, *Brahman* is Kālī, one and the same Being. I call Him *Brahman* when He is absolutely inactive; that is, when He neither creates, nor preserves, nor destroys phenomena; but when He performs all such actions, I call Him Kālī, the Eternal

Energy, the Divine Mother. They are one and the same Being, the difference is in name and form, just as the same substance water is called by different names in different languages, such as *jal*, water, *pāni*, etc. A tank may have four *ghāts*. The Hindus drink at one *ghāt* and call it *jal*; the Mohammedans drink at another and call it *pani*; while the English who drink at the third call it water. Similarly, God is one, only His names are different. Some call Him by the name of Allah, some God, some *Brahman*, others Kālī, others again Rāma, Harī, Jesus, Buddha."

Keshab (smiling): "Please tell us once more, revered sir, in what different ways Kālī, the Mother of the universe, is making Herself manifest in this world of Her sports (*līlā*)."

The Mother of the Universe and Her Sports

Shrī Rāmakrishna (smiling): "Oh, the Mother sports with the world, Her toy, under various aspects and names. Now She is the God unconditioned, absolute, formless (Mahā-Kālī): now the Everlasting as distinguished from Her works (Nitya-Kālī). Under another aspect She is the Goddess of burning *ghāts* or crematories, the dreaded Being who presides over death (Shmashāna-Kālī); now again does She stand before us ready to bless, to preserve Her children (Rakshā-Kālī); under another aspect She appears to be pleasing to the eye of Her devotees as the Mother with the dark blue color, consort of the God of Eternity and Infinity. Mahā-Kālī and Nitya-Kālī are described in the sacred books, the *Tantras*: 'When nothing was—neither sun, nor moon, nor planets, nothing but Darkness Deep, there was alone my Divine Mother, formless, the eternal consort of the Infinite.' As Mother with the dark blue color (Shyāmā), She is tender and loving. She is the bestower of all blessings and makes Her children fearless; She is worshipped in the Hindu household. As preserver, She appears in times of plague, famine, earthquake, drought, or flood. At cemeteries, burning *ghāts*, or crematories She appears in the form of the Destroyer. The dead body, the jackal, the spirits of destruction are Her terrible companions. She lives in the midst of those horrible scenes, of those fearful environments. Streams of blood, a garland of skulls thrown round Her neck, a girdle made of the hands of those that are dead, are the symbols that mark Her as the dread Mother, as the All-Destroyer."

Creation of the World

"Now look at Her mode of creation. At the end of a cycle, upon the destruction of the world, my Mother, good Matron that She is, puts together the seeds of creation. The mistress of a house has a hodgepodge pot of her own in which she keeps sundry things for household use. (Rāmakrishna, smiling) Yes, my friends, that is indeed so. The mistress of a house has such a pot in her possession. In it are kept the 'sea-foam' in a solid state, small parcels containing seeds of the cucumber, gourd, and so on. She brings them out when wanted. In much the same way my Mother keeps the seeds of creation after the destruction of the world at the end of a cycle."

Divine Mother Omnipresent

"My Mother, the primal Divine Energy, is both within and without this phenomenal world. Having given birth to the world, She lives within it. In the *Vedas*, we find the illustration of a spider and its web. She is the spider and the world is the web that She has woven. The spider brings the web out of itself and then lives in it. My Mother is both the container and the contained."

Kālī, Why Black?

"Is Kālī, the Divine Mother, black? She looks black from a distance, but when realized, She is not black. The sky looks blue from a distance, but look at it near you, it has no color. The water of the ocean is blue from a distance. Take a little up in the hand, and it has no color."

Saying this, the Bhagavān became intoxicated with divine love, and began to sing:

> Is my Divine Mother black?
>   O mind! What dost thou say?
> Though black, She with Her flowing hair
>   Illumines the lotus of the heart.

Divine Mother's Will

"Bondage and freedom, of both She is the maker. Through Her inscrutable power of *māyā*, a man of the world becomes bound by woman and gold. Again, through Her grace, he becomes free. She breaks all fetters and takes Her children across the ocean of the world.

"My Divine Mother is playful. The world indeed is Her sport. She does what She will and is blissful. It is Her pleasure to give freedom to one among a hundred thousand of Her children."

A Brāhmo: "Sir, She can, if She pleases, set everybody free. Why is it then that She has bound us hand and foot with the chains of the world?"

Shrī Rāmakrishna: "Well, I suppose it is Her will. Her will is to play with all these things. In the game of hide-and-seek, whoever touches the grand-dame is out. He no longer runs about. If all the players touch the grand-dame at the same time, how can there be any game? The grand-dame would not like it; for she is pleased to have the play go on."

Power of the Mind

"Everything is in the mind. Bondage and freedom are in the mind. You can dye the mind with any color you wish. It is like a piece of clean white linen; dip it in red and it will be red, in blue it will be blue, in green it will be green, or any other color. Do you not see that if you study English, English words will come readily to you? Again, if a *pandit* studies Sanskrit he will readily quote verses from sacred books. If you keep your mind in evil company, your thoughts, ideas, and words will be colored with evil; but keep in the company of *bhaktas*, then your thoughts, ideas, and words will be of God."

Sense of Sin

"Someone gave me a book of the Christians. I asked him to read it to me. In it there was only one theme—sin and sin, from the beginning to the end. (To Keshab) In your Brāhmo Samāj the main topic is also sin. The fool who repeats again and again, 'I am bound, I am bound,' remains in bondage. He who repeats day and night, 'I am a sinner, I am a sinner,' becomes a sinner indeed."

Saving Power of God's Name

"It is necessary to have absolute faith in the name of the Lord. 'What! I have uttered his holy name, can there still be sin in me?

Can I still be in bondage?' Krista Kishore was a pious Hindu, a *brāhmin* of *brāhmins*, who worshipped the Lord with single-minded devotion. He went to Brindāvan. One day, while visiting the shrines, he felt very thirsty. He went to a well, and finding a man standing there, he asked him: 'My man, can you draw some water for me?' The man replied: 'O holy sir, I belong to a low caste, that of a cobbler.' Krista Kishore thereupon said to him: 'It matters not. You say "Shiva" (the holy name of the Lord) and draw the water for me.'

"By repeating the blessed name of God, man's body, mind, and soul become absolutely pure. Why talk of sin and hell-fire? Repeat but once, 'I shall never again do the evil deeds that I have committed in the past,' and by thy faith in His hallowed name thou shalt be freed from all sins."

Prayer to the Divine Mother

"I used to pray to my Divine Mother for true devotion (*bhakti*) alone. With flowers in my clasped hands, I prayed: 'Do Thou, O Mother, grant that I may have pure and unalloyed devotion. Here is sin, here again is virtue; I lay them at Thy feet; oh take them both. Here is knowledge (of many things), here again is ignorance; oh take them both and grant that I may have devotion alone. Here is purity and here again is impurity; I desire neither of them. Here are good works, here are bad; both I lay at Thy feet; oh grant that I may have devotion alone and love for Thee.'"

Example of Janaka

"One living in the world may also see God. It was the case with Rājā Janaka, the great royal devotee, who realized while on the throne that the world was a structure of dreams. For a lover of God, however, such is not the feeling." And the Bhagavān sang:

He who has attained to *bhakti* or true devotion to the Lord says:

This world is the abode of happiness;
    I eat, drink, and enjoy its pleasures.
Janaka Rājā was a great potentate;
    In what was he lacking?

He harmonized God and the world
And tasted the joys of both.

Value of Solitude

"No one can suddenly become like Janaka. Rājā Janaka performed great penances and austerities in solitude for many long years. Even when living in the world one should occasionally go into solitude. It will bring great good to one who can sincerely and earnestly cry for God three days and three nights in solitude, alone. Indeed, one day passed in that way would be a great gain. People will shed a jarful of tears for wives and children, but who weeps one tear for the Lord? It is necessary to practice every now and then devotional exercises in solitude. A worldly-minded aspirant absorbed in various works and duties finds in the first stage of his spiritual life a great number of obstacles in the path of self-control and devotion. As a young tree planted on the footpath needs a fence around it that it may not be eaten up by sheep and cattle, so in the first stage of a spiritual aspirant, a fence is necessary; but when the tree grows large and the trunk and roots are thicker and stronger, no fence is required. Then it is not injured even if an elephant be tied to it."

Intense Devotion Necessary

"Along with this another thing is needed and that is intense devotion to God. The *gopīs* of Brindāvan had such devotion.[5] They had an intense love for Shrī Krishna, God-Incarnate."

The Bhagavān then said to Keshab and other devotees with great feeling: "You are Brāhmos; you believe that God is formless and you do not believe in God-Incarnate. Well, it matters not. You need not accept Rādhā and Shrī Krishna as Incarnations of the Supreme Being; but the intense love and yearning which the *gopīs* felt for Shrī Krishna is a thing which you may well make your own, for yearning is the next step leading to God-vision."

5 Brindāvan is the sacred forest near Mathurā in India. The milkmaids (*gopīs*) of Brindāvan loved the Lord Shrī Krishna, then living among them as a shepherd-boy.

It was ebb-tide. The steamer was going fast downstream towards Calcutta. It had got to the other side of the Howrah Bridge within sight of the Botanical Gardens. The captain had orders to go a little farther down. How far the steamer had actually proceeded was not known to those who were listening to Shrī Rāmakrishna and watching his movements. They listened with such rapt attention that they had no idea either of time or of distance.

Keshab now offered the Bhagavān puffed rice with the kernel of the coconut. All present were invited to partake of these. They took them in the folds of their cloth, ate and were very happy. It seemed as if a festival were being held on board the steamer. The Bhagavān noticed that Bijoy and Keshab were not quite at home in each other's presence. He said to Keshab: "Look, my dear sir, here is Bijoy. As to your quarrels, well, do not worry yourselves on their account. There was fighting even between Shiva and Rāma. Shiva was Rāma's spiritual *guru*. After a little fighting, they made it up and became once more as good friends as ever. But the fighting went on among their followers. The gibbering of the ghosts and the chattering of the monkeys could not so easily be quieted down. You too will be very good friends, once again. But your followers, I dare say, will follow your example. These differences, you know, are things that cannot be avoided. There was the tug of war even between father and son. Take the case of Rāma and his sons Lava and Kusha. Take another case: The mother fasts on Tuesday for the welfare of her daughter, but the daughter, quarrelling with the mother, fasts on Tuesday for her own welfare, as if her welfare were different from that gained by her mother's fasting. In the same way, you, Keshab, have a religious society (*samāj*) of your own, and Bijoy, too, must have a separate society of his own. Well, there is room for all kinds of things under Providence—even for quarrels and differences. Opposition adds zest to a thing. Rāmānuja[6] held the doctrine of *Vishishtādvaita* (Qualified Non-Dualism). His

6 Rāmānuja was the founder of the *Vishishtādvaita*, or Qualified Non-Dualistic School of *Vedānta*. He was born about 1017 A.D. at Sri Parambattur, a town near Madras in Southern India. His doctrines were distinct from the absolute non-dualistic philosophy of Shankarāchārya. He is said to have lived for one hundred and twenty years and died in 1137 A.D. He has now millions of followers among all classes of Hindus in India.

guru, however, was an Advaitist (Non-Dualist, without any qualification). They had their differences. Master and disciple disputed and refuted each other's opinions. This is natural. Be it so; still to the master the disciple is always his own."

The Nature of Disciples Must be Examined

They all rejoiced. Shrī Rāmakrishna said to Keshab: "You do not study and examine the nature of your disciples. For that reason they drop away. All men look alike, but they differ in their nature. In some the *sattva* quality is predominant, in others *rajas*, and in the rest *tamas*. *Pooli* (cakes) all look alike on the outside, but the contents vary; some may contain sweet thickened cream, others coconut sweetened with sugar, while others may have boiled *kalai* (pulse) with no sweetening."

Earnestness of a True Seeker

"It is a difficult task to teach others. One can become a true spiritual teacher only when one has realized God and received a divine commission (*ādesha*) from Him. So commissioned were Nārada, Shukadeva, and Shankarāchārya. If you are not commissioned, who will listen to you? You know Calcutta and her fondness for the latest sensation. They say they want water and they begin to dig a well at one place; but they give it up as soon as they find that the earth is hard and stony. They then set to work to dig at another place. Suppose the soil is sandy there; they will as readily give up digging at that spot. They will look about for another locality. That is the way with these people. Their good opinion is by no means worth having."

Divine Commission

"Divine commission cannot be obtained by mere imagination. Verily I say, the Lord can be realized and He will speak to thee. Then thou mayest receive His commission. What great power lies in such Divine command! By it mountains may be shaken to their foundation. What can a mere ordinary lecture do? People may listen to it for a time, but they will soon forget it. It will not produce a lasting impression and they will not live according to it."

Ordinary Spiritual Teachers are Blind

"For the teaching of divine truths a badge of authority is indispensable. A man who tries to teach others without it will be laughed at. He cannot get realization himself and he tries to show the way to others. It is like the blind leading the blind. In this way more harm is done than good. When God is realized the inner spiritual sight opens and it is then that the true teacher can perceive the sickness of the soul and can prescribe the proper remedy. Without God's command a man easily becomes egotistic and thinks: 'I have the power to teach others.' Such egotism is the result of ignorance. In ignorance one feels, 'I am the doer'; but when one realizes that 'God is the Lord and doer of all, I cannot do anything,' then one becomes absolutely free even in this life. All misery and restlessness proceed from the sense of 'I' and 'me,' 'I am the doer,' 'I am the actor.'"

First See God, Then Help the World

"You talk glibly of doing good to the world. Is the world contained in a nutshell? Besides, who are you to do good to the world? First practice devotional exercises and realize God. Attain to Him. If He graciously gives you His powers (*shakti*), then you can help others, and not till then."

A Brāhmo devotee: "Revered sir, are we to give up all works until we have seen God?"

Shrī Rāmakrishna: "No, why will you give up all works? Meditation upon God, chanting His holy name, and other devotional exercises are daily works which you should have to perform."

The devotee: "But what about household works and business affairs?"

Pray that Worldly Work May Grow Less

Shrī Rāmakrishna: "Oh! you will also perform those, but only so far as is absolutely necessary for living in the world; and you should at the same time pray in solitude unto the Lord with tears in your eyes for His grace, and for strength to do your duties without seeking any reward. Say when you pray: 'Lord, grant that my work in the world and for the world may grow less and less day by day, for I see that my work growing manifold only makes me lose sight of Thee. Sometimes I think that I do my duties unattached to the world, but I know not how I deceive myself and do them through attachment instead. I give alms to the poor, and behold, I seek for fame, oh I know not how!'"

God-Vision and Philanthropic Works

"Shambhu[7] talked of founding hospitals and dispensaries, schools and colleges, of building roads, sinking wells, and digging tanks for the good of all. I said to him: 'Yes, whatever comes in your way and is absolutely necessary you will do; even that, without seeking any reward. Do not seek more work than you can well perform. If you do you will forget the Lord. A man desired to see the shrine of the Divine Mother. On his way he stopped and spent all the day in distributing alms to the poor. When he went to the shrine, the door was closed and he could not see the holy of holies. The wise ones should first see the Holy Mother, by pushing their way through the crowd assembled at the gate of the temple, and after seeing Her, they may then turn their attention to almsgiving and other good works, if they so desire.'

"All good works are for the realization of God. Works are the means and God-vision is the end. Therefore I said to Shambhu: 'Suppose you see God, or that God manifests Himself to you, will you say to Him: "Lord, do Thou grant that I may have lots of dispensaries and hospitals, schools and colleges!" A true devotee shall rather pray in this wise: "Grant, O good Lord, that I may have a niche in the lotus of Thy feet, that it may be my privilege to live always in Thy holy presence and that I may have deep and unalloyed devotion unto Thee."'"

Path of Bhakti Yoga Best for This Age

"*Karma yoga* is very difficult. It is difficult in this materialistic age (*Kali yuga*) to get through all the works, all the duties laid upon us by the sacred books. Verily in this age, earthly life depends entirely upon material food. Work and duties, there is scarcely time enough

7 Bābu Shambhu Charan Mullick was a Hindu multi-millionaire of Calcutta. He had a large garden-house near the temple of Dakshineshwar where many a time he entertained Bhagavān Rāmakrishna.

for them. Yes, in this age the one means of realizing God is *bhakti* or sincere devotion and love for Him, and earnest prayer and the chanting of His holy name and divine attributes. (To Keshab and other devotees) Your path, too, lies through devotion and self-surrender to the Lord (*bhakti yoga*). Blessed are ye who sing the name of Harī and chant the praises of my Divine Mother. Your path is right. (To Keshab) You talk against child marriage and the caste system, about female emancipation and female education. I say one thing is needful—the realization of God and devotion to Him. First realize God and all other things shall be added unto you."

Parable of the Deserted Temple

"There was a young man named Podo in a certain village. In that village was an old dilapidated temple. The holy image of God once worshipped there had disappeared and it was now the home of small bats. One day at nightfall the villagers were surprised to hear the sound of bells, gongs, and conch-shells issuing from the deserted temple. Men, women, and children all flocked to the place. They thought that some devotee must be worshipping some image of God newly set up within the temple by performing the *āratī*, the evening ceremony of waving the lights and offering flowers, fruits, and holy water. With folded hands they all stood listening to the sacred sounds before the temple. One of them, more curious than the rest, had the courage to go inside. To his surprise he saw that Podo was ringing the bell and blowing the shell; but the floor was as dirty as before with impurities of all kinds and there was no image of God on the altar! He then called out, saying: 'O Podo, thou hast no Mādhava (Shrī Krishna, God-Incarnate) in the temple; how is it, then, that thou hast raised all this clamor by blowing the conch-shell? And behold! thou hast not even taken the trouble to cleanse the temple by removing the impurities and dirt of years and washing the floor with the holy water of the Ganges!'"

First Cleanse the Heart

"First realize God in the temple of your heart. With that in view, you must cleanse it of all impurities, all sin and iniquity, all attachment to the world caused by the power of the senses. It is then that the time comes for blowing the shell, if need be. Talk of social reforms! You may well do so after realizing God. Remember, the *rishis* of old gave up the world in order to attain to God. This is the one thing needful. All other things shall be granted unto you."

The steamer had come back to Kolāghāt (Calcutta). All on board held themselves in readiness to land. As they came out of the cabin they saw that the full moon had bathed the bosom of the Holy Ganges and the adjoining banks with her mellow light. The Bhagavān with two or three disciples got into a cab which had been kept waiting for him on the bank. Nandalāl, Keshab's nephew, also got in. He wished to go with the Bhagavān for some distance. When all had seated themselves in the cab, Shrī Rāmakrishna asked: "Where is Keshab?" In a few moments Keshab came up smiling and inquired who were going with him. Being satisfied with the answer, he bowed down to the ground before the Bhagavān, who affectionately bade him adieu.

The cab set out. The Bhagavān was filled with supreme joy as the carriage drove along. Suddenly he said: "I am thirsty; what is to be done?" Nandalāl stopped the carriage before the gates of the India Club and went upstairs to bring water. It was brought in a glass tumbler. The Bhagavān, smiling, asked: "Is the glass well washed?" Nandalāl replied: "Yes." The Bhagavān drank the water. He was childlike in his simplicity. He leaned through the window to look at the various objects on both sides. His joy knew no bounds as he saw men, animals, carriages, houses, the moonlight, the lighted streets!

It was getting late. The Bhagavān asked to go back to the temple at Dakshineshwar. It was about half-past ten and he wished to leave for the garden.

Chapter 6

Sunday at the Temple

The nineteenth of August, 1883, fell on Sunday and was the first day after the full moon, so the devotees had leisure to come and see their beloved Master at Dakshineshwar. His visitors were from all classes of people—*sannyāsīs*[1] and *paramahamsas*,[2] Hindus, Christians, Brāhmos, Shāktas, Vaishnavas, and Shaivas—women as well as men. It was noon. Shrī Rāmakrishna was seated in his usual place in his room. A disciple (M.) came and saluted him, falling at his hallowed feet. The Bhagavān made him sit down and kindly inquired after the welfare of himself and of his family. A short while after the Bhagavān began to talk to him upon the *Vedānta*. He said:

Non-Dualistic Vedantins

"The *Ashtāvakra Samhitā*[3] deals with the knowledge of the *Ātman* (Self). The knowers of the Self declare: 'I am He, I am that supreme Self.' This is the view of all the *sannyāsīs* belonging to the non-dualistic (*Advaita*) school of *Vedānta*. But it is not meet that a man of the world should hold such a view. He is doing all kinds of work; how at the same time can he be that highest Self, the Absolute *Brahman*, who is beyond all actions? The non-dualistic Vedantins hold that the Self has no attachment to anything. Pleasure, pain, virtue, vice, can never affect the Self in any way; but they do affect men who think that their soul is the same as the body. Smoke can blacken only the wall, but not the space through which it moves. There was a certain devotee named Krishna Kishore who used to say that he was '*kha*,' or empty space. He meant that he

1 *Sannyāsīs* are those who have renounced the world and its pleasures for the sake of the Lord.

2 *Paramahamsas* are those who have attained to *nirvikalpa samādhi*, or *Brahma jnāna*.

3 *Ashtāvakra Samhitā* is a work containing the highest exposition of the *Advaita Vedānta*, written by the ancient sage Ashtāvakra, who was the preceptor of King Janaka.

was the same as the highest Self, *Brahman* the Absolute, who is sometimes likened to *ākāsha* (infinite space) because nothing can be predicated of it. A true philosopher has some right to say this. As for others, such a sentiment is altogether out of place."

Thought of Freedom Brings Freedom

"But it is good for everyone to cherish the idea that he is free. 'I am free,' 'I am free'; if a man constantly says this, he is sure to be free. On the other hand, he who always thinks that he is in bondage brings bondage on himself in the end. The weak-minded man who always says, 'I am a sinner,' 'I am a sinner,' is sure to have a fall. A man should rather say: 'I repeat the holy name of God; how can there be any sin in me, or bondage of the world?'"

Māyā and Dayā

Then turning towards the disciple, the Bhagavān said: "Today my mind is not at ease. I hear from Hridai[4] that he has been ailing much. Is this anxiety due to *māyā* (attachment) or *dayā* (compassion) towards him?"

The disciple did not know what to reply and remained silent.

Shrī Rāmakrishna: "Do you know what is *māyā*? Love towards one's own father, brother, sister, wife, child, nephew, niece, is called *māyā*, and compassion means loving all beings equally. Now what is this, my anxiety, due to—*māyā* or compassion? But Hridai did a great deal for me. He served me much. He never hesitated to do all sorts of menial services for me. My mind will be set at rest if he can get the money he needs. Now whom am I to ask for money? And how can I ask, being a *sannyāsī*?"

At two or three o'clock in the afternoon two great devotees, Adhar[5] and Balarām, came and prostrated themselves before him and

4 Hridāya Mukherji was an old servant of Shrī Rāmakrishna and served him for nearly twenty-five years in the temple of Dakshineshwar—till 1881. He was a remote nephew of Shrī Rāmakrishna. "Hridai" was a pet abbreviation of his name used by Shrī Rāmakrishna.

5 Adhar, whose full name was Bābu Adharlāl Sen, was a rich Hindu Deputy Magistrate of Calcutta. He was a devoted householder disciple of Shrī Rāmakrishna, who often sanctified his home by his holy visits.

took their seats. They asked him how he was doing. The Bhagavān replied: "Well, my body is all right, but not so is the mind." He did not mention anything about Hridāya's illness.

A short while after Narendra (Swāmī Vivekānanda) and Vishvanātha Upadhyāya,[6] the Nepalese Resident in Calcutta, entered. Bowing down to Shrī Rāmakrishna, they took their seats. Shrī Rāmakrishna asked Narendra to sing. There was hanging on the western wall of the room a *tānpurā* (a stringed musical instrument). Narendra took it down and began to tune it. He began to sing:

> 1. In the temple of the heart dwelleth the eternal Truth.
> Ever beholding His glorious and lovely form, when shall we dive in the sea of His beauty?
>
> 2. In the form of infinite wisdom the Lord will enter my soul.
> The restless mind filled with wonder will take refuge at His blessed feet.
> Immortal bliss, like embodied nectar, will rise in the firmament of the soul.
>
> 3. At Thy sight we shall be mad with joy even as the *chakora*[7] is maddened at the sight of the moon.
>
> 4. O King of kings, there is none like Thee, all good and peaceful.
> At Thy feet, O Beloved, I shall offer myself and thus fulfill the aim of my life.
>
> 5. Even here shall I enjoy heavenly bliss, so great a privilege where could I find?

6 Vishvanātha Upadhyāya was a *brāhmin* scholar and a devotee of Shrī Rāmakrishna. He was like a consul of the Nepal Government to the British.

7 *Chakora* is the name of a kind of aquatic bird.

6. O Lord, beholding Thy pure and perfect form, all sins will take flight, even as darkness vanishes before light.

7. O kindle in my heart the light of burning faith, fixed firm like the polar star, and thus, O Friend of the meek, fulfill my one desire. Day and night merged in the bliss of Thy love. O I shall forget myself having attained to Thee.
(O when will this come?)

Samādhi of Rāmakrishna

Shrī Rāmakrishna had lost himself in deep *samādhi* as soon as he had heard the words "Immortal bliss like embodied nectar." There he sat with clasped hands, turning his face toward the east. He was diving deep into the ocean of beauty of the All-Blissful One. Returning from *samādhi*, the Bhagavān murmured in an indistinct voice: "Thou art I, I am Thou. Thou eatest, Thou and I eat. What is this? Have I jaundiced eyes? I see Thee everywhere. Wherever I cast my eyes, I see Thy form." Then He repeated the holy name of Krishna: "O Friend of the meek and gentle! O Lord of my heart! O Divine Shepherd!" After repeating this a few times, he again went into *samādhi*.

Coming back to sense-consciousness, he opened his eyes and found that the room was full of people of every class. Narendra, seeing that the Bhagavān was in *samādhi*, had left the room and gone to the eastern veranda. In the meanwhile the Bhagavān looked for him in the room, but he was not there. The *tānpurā* (musical instrument) was lying on the ground. The devotees all had their eyes fixed upon the Bhagavān, who began thus, referring to Narendra: "He has lighted the fire. It matters not whether he remains in the room or leaves it!"

Bliss Comes in Meditation

Then turning towards Vishvanātha and his other numerous devotees, he said: "Meditate upon God, the sole Existence, Knowledge, and Bliss Eternal, and you also shall have bliss. That Being of Knowledge and Bliss is always here and everywhere, only It is covered and obscured by ignorance. The less is your attachment towards the senses, the more will be your love for God."

Vishvanātha: "The more we near our home at Calcutta, the farther we are from Benares, and the more we near Benares, the farther we are away from our home."

Lover of God

Bhagavān: "As Shrīmatī (Rādhā)[8] approached Shrī Krishna, she perceived more and more the charming fragrance of His sweet person. The more one approaches God, the more does one's love towards Him increase. The more the river nears the sea, the more it is subject to ebb and flow. The Ganges of knowledge flowing in the soul of a wise man runs only in one direction. To him the whole universe is a dream. He always lives in his own true Self (*Ātman*). But the Ganges of love in a devotee's heart does not run in one direction. It has its ebb and flow. A devotee laughs, weeps, dances, sings. He wants sometimes to enjoy his Beloved, to merge into his Beloved! He swims in Him, dives, rises up in his joy as merrily as a lump of ice floats upon the water."

God the Absolute and God the Creator One

"But in fact, God the Absolute and God the Creator are one and the same Being. The Absolute Existence-Intelligence-Bliss is the All-knowing, All-intelligent, and All-blissful Mother of the universe. The precious stone (*māni*) and its brightness cannot be separated in thought, for we cannot think of the stone without its brightness, nor can we think of the brightness apart from the stone. The Absolute Existence-Intelligence-Bliss, the Undifferentiated, appears as differentiated into many. He has various names applied to Him according to the various powers manifested. That is the reason of His having many forms. Hence a devotee has sung: 'O Mother Tārā;[9] Thou art even all that.' Wherever there is action, such as creation, preservation, and destruction, there is *Shakti* or Intelligent Energy. But water is water whether it is calm or disturbed. That one Absolute Existence-Intelligence-Bliss is also the eternally Intelligent Energy which creates, preserves, and destroys the universe. Thus it

8 Shrīmatī Rādhā was the beloved consort of Shrī Krishna, the greatest of the saviors among the Hindus.

9 Tārā is another name of the Divine Mother of the universe.

is the same Vishvanātha whether he does nothing or performs his worship or visits the Governor-General. In all cases it is the same Vishvanātha, only these are his different *upādhis* or states."

Vishvanātha: "Yes, sir, that is so."

Soon twilight began to fall. The devotees one after another took leave of the Bhagavān. The day was drawing to a close. The temple-servant was arranging the lights. The priests were busy saying their prayers as they stood waist-deep in the sacred waters of the Ganges, purifying themselves body and soul. They were shortly to go to their respective temples to perform the *āratī*, the evening ceremony. The young men of Dakshineshwar had come with their friends to take a walk in the garden. They were strolling about the rampart, enjoying the sweet evening breeze made fragrant by the flowers and watching the slightly undulating breast of the swiftly-flowing Ganges. Some of them, perhaps the more thoughtful, could be found going about by themselves in the solitude of the sacred trees called the *Panchavati*. Bhagavān Shrī Rāmakrishna also looked at the Ganges for some time from the western veranda.

It was evening. The lamp-lighter had lighted all the lamps of the big temple. The old maid-servant came and lit the lamp in the Bhagavān's room and burned incense there. In the meantime the *āratī* ceremony had begun in the twelve shrines dedicated to Shiva. It began soon after in the temples of Kālī, Mother of the universe, and of Shrī Vishnu. The united and solemn sound of gongs, bells, cymbals, grew more solemn and sweet as it was echoed back by the murmuring Ganges below.

It was the first lunar day after the full moon. A short while after nightfall the moon rose. Gradually the tops of the trees in the garden, as well as the big temple compound, were bathed in her balmy light. At the magic touch of her radiance the waters of the Ganges shone bright like silver and flowed on dancing with great joy.

When at nightfall Shrī Rāmakrishna bowed down to the Divine Mother, he repeated the holy names of God, keeping time all the while by clapping his hands. In his room there were pictures of various Incarnations of God. He bowed before each picture, repeating the holy name of each. He also repeated his favorite *mantrams*, each having some lofty, unifying principle running through it, such as:

(1) *Brahma-Ātmā-Bhagavān.* (The Absolute *Brahman* of the *Vedānta*, true Self, and the Personal God of the *bhakta* are three in one and one in three.)

(2) *Bhāgavat-bhakta-Bhagavān.* (The Word, the devotee, and the Personal God are three in one and one in three.)

(3) *Brahma-Shakti, Shakti-Brahma.* (God the Absolute and the Creative Energy are one and the same.)

(4) *Veda-Purāna-Tantra-Gītā-Gāyatrī.* (God of the scriptures and the holy texts.)

(5) *Sharanāgata, sharanāgata.* (I take refuge in Thee. I am Thine, I am Thine.)

(6) *Nāham-nāham, Tuhū-Tuhū.* (Not I, not I, but Thou, but Thou.)

(7) *Āmi Yantra, Tumi Yantrī.* (I am the machine; Thou art the One who runs the machine.)

After all these repetitions were ended, he meditated upon the Divine Mother with clasped hands.

A few of the devotees had been walking about in the garden during the evening. When the *āratī* ceremonies were over in the temples, one after another they came together in Shrī Rāmakrishna's room. He was sitting on his seat with devotees before him on the floor. He said: "Narendra, Rākhāl, and Bhavanātha—these are *nitya-siddhas* (perfect even from their birth). They need no training. What training they go through is more than they need. You see that Narendra never cares for anyone. He was with me in Vishvanātha's carriage the other day. When he was requested to sit upon the better seat, he paid no heed at all. Moreover, he never shows to me that he knows anything, lest I praise him before men. He has no *māyā*, no attachment. He looks as if he were free from all bondage. For a single individual he has many gifts and many noble qualities. He is also very courteous in his manners. He knows how to control his senses; he has said that he will not marry, but will live a pure life. That is good. I always go into *samādhi* when I see him."

Character and Associations

"We mold our character according to the company we keep; and we keep such company as is in harmony with our character. For this reason the *paramahamsas* (perfected souls) like to keep the company of innocent children because their minds are pure, simple, and unstained by worldliness."

As Shrī Rāmakrishna was speaking these words, a worthy *brāhmin* entered the room and bowed down at his feet. The Bhagavān had known him before and loved him because he was sincere and simple. He had studied *Vedānta* in Benares, the seat of great learning. Rāmakrishna said to him: "Well, you have not been here for a long time. How are you?"

The *brāhmin*, smiling, replied: "Revered sir, the duties of the world, as thou knowest, take most of my time."

He then took his seat and Rāmakrishna continued: "You remained in Benares for a long time. Tell us what you saw there. Let us hear something about Dayānanda.[10]"

Brāhmin: "Yes, I met Dayānanda. Thou hast also seen him."

Rāmakrishna: "Yes, I went to see him once. He was staying in a garden-house not very far from here. That day he had an appointment with Keshab Sen. He was a great scholar; he also believed in the deities (*devas*), but Keshab did not, whereupon he said: 'If God created all these phenomena, could He not create deities?' He believed in one God, but without form."

Brāhmin: "In Benares, Dayānanda had long theological discussions with the other *pandits*. In the end all the *pandits* unanimously stood on one side, while he stood alone on the other; and then the *pandits* drove him from the city by raising the outcry:

10 Dayānanda Saraswati was a *sannyāsī* of the *Advaita Vedānta* school. He was a great Vedic scholar, speaker, and a Hindu reformer of the nineteenth century. He wrote Sanskrit commentaries on the *Vedas* and was the founder of a reformed Hindu sect known as the Ārya Samāj. He died in 1883 A.D.

'Dayānanda's position is false and must not be accepted!' I also saw Colonel Olcott, the Theosophist. The Theosophists believe in the existence of the *mahātmās*, the realm of the moon, the realm of the sun, and the astral realms. They believe that the astral bodies go to these places and so on. Revered sir, what dost thou think of Theosophy?"

Devotion to the Supreme

Rāmakrishna: "*Bhakti*, devotion to the Supreme, is the only thing worth having. Do they seek *bhakti*? Then it is good. If their aim be the realization of God, then they are all right; but by simply dwelling upon these realms and *mahātmās* one cannot search after God. One should practice *sādhana* (devotional exercises) to attain true *bhakti*. One should have extreme longing for realization. Realization of God does not come so easily; it requires a great deal of *sādhana*. One should gather up all the mental activities and concentrate them upon Him. A man asked: 'Why can I not see God?' I replied: 'If you wish to catch a big fish, which lives in deep water, you will have to make many preparations to attract him. You must get the line, rod, hook, and float; you must put on savory bait; then when you see bubbles in the water, you may know that he has come near. Similarly, if you wish to see God, devote yourself to the practice of true *bhakti*.'"

Divine Love and Its Various Aspects

"In divine love the sense of 'I' and 'mine' exists, as was shown by the mother of the Divine Incarnation, Krishna. For her, Krishna was only a son and not the Lord of the universe. She loved to nurse Him and take care of Him, always calling Him 'my Krishna,' and feeling the same anxiety about Him that an earthly mother would feel about her son. When a certain saint spoke to her, saying: 'Your Krishna is the absolute Master of the world; He is not human,' Yashodā, the mother of Krishna, replied: 'Oh no, he is not the Lord of the universe; he is my child. I cannot think of him as other than my child.' Divine love is manifested by various relations; the closer the relation, the stronger the tie of love. The relation of a servant to his master was manifested by Hanumān; the relation of a friend to his friend was shown by Arjuna to Krishna; while the *gopīs* were devoted to the Lord as their divine husband."

Parable of the Tiger

"Some people think that they are bound (*baddha*), that they will never attain to divine wisdom, or to divine love. But all this fear vanishes from the heart of a true disciple if his *guru*, or spiritual guide, be gracious to him. There was a flock of sheep in the woods; suddenly a tigress jumped into their midst. At that moment she gave birth to a cub and died on the spot. The kind-hearted sheep took care of the cub, and brought it up among them. They ate grass, the cub followed their example; they bleated, the cub also learned to bleat. In this manner the cub grew up not as a young tiger but like a sheep. One day a full-grown tiger came that way and watched with wonder the grass-eating tiger. The real tiger drew nearer, but the cub began to bleat. Then the real tiger dragged him to the edge of a lake and said: 'Look here! Compare your face with mine. Is there any difference? You are a tiger like me; grass is not your food; your food is animal flesh.' But the grass-eating tiger could not believe it. After a long time the real tiger convinced him that he was of the same species. Then he gave him a piece of flesh to eat, but he would not touch it; he began once more to bleat and to seek for grass. At last, however, the real tiger forced him to eat animal flesh; at once he liked the taste of the blood, gave up his grass-eating and bleating, and realized that he was not a sheep but a tiger. He then followed the real tiger and became like him."

Human Soul, the Child of God

"The human soul is the child of God, but it does not know it, and therefore it lives like an ordinary mortal (sheep); but when, by the grace of the *guru*, he realizes his true nature, he becomes free from all fear and attains to perfection. Therefore I say, when the grace of the *guru* comes, all fear vanishes. He will make you know who you are and what you are in reality. You will have to do very little for yourself after you have received that grace. You will then be able to distinguish between the Real and the unreal and to realize that God is Truth and the world is unreal."

Parable of the False Sādhu

"A fisherman came to a garden at night and threw his net in the pond to catch some fish. Hearing the noise, the owner sent his men to capture him. The men came with torches in their hands to discover the thief. In the meantime the fisherman dropped his net, covered his face with ashes, and sat under a tree, pretending to be a holy man absorbed in meditation. The men could not find the thief; they simply noticed that a holy man was meditating under a tree, so they returned to the owner and told him what they had seen. Everybody then brought flowers, fruits, and sweets to the holy man and paid him great honor and respect. Next morning crowds of people came to see the *sādhu* (anchorite) and offered him money and various other things. The fisherman thought: 'How strange it is! I am not a holy man, still people have so much respect for me and I have received so many gifts. If I become a genuine *sādhu*, how much more I shall get! Undoubtedly I shall see God.' If merely feigning to be a holy man could so far awaken him, what can be said of him who has practiced all virtues in order to become a true holy man! He will realize what is Real and what is unreal, that God is Truth and the world is unreal."

A devotee: "Where shall I meditate on God?"

Rāmakrishna: "The heart is the best place. Meditate on Him in your heart."

Chapter 7

Some Incidents in the Life of Shrī Rāmakrishna (As Told by Himself)

Days of Struggle

"I practiced austerities for a long time. I cared very little for the body. My longing for the Divine Mother was so great that I would not eat or sleep. I would lie on the bare ground, placing my head on a lump of earth, and cry out loudly: 'Mother, Mother, why dost Thou not come to me?' I did not know how the days and nights passed away. I used to have ecstasy all the time. I saw my disciples as my own people, like children and relations, long before they came to me. I used to cry before my Mother, saying: 'O Mother! I am dying for my beloved ones (*bhaktas*); do Thou bring them to me as quickly as possible.'"

All Desires Fulfilled

"At that time whatever I desired came to pass. Once I desired to build a small hut in the *Panchavati* for meditation and to put a fence around it. Immediately after I saw a huge bundle of bamboo sticks, rope, strings, and even a knife, all brought by the tide in front of the *Panchavati*. A servant of the temple, seeing these things, ran to me with great delight and told me of them. There was the exact quantity of material necessary for the hut and the fence. When they were built, nothing remained over. Everyone was amazed to see this wonderful sight.

"When I reached the state of continuous ecstasy, I gave up all external forms of worship; I could no longer perform them. Then I prayed to my Divine Mother: 'Mother, who will now take care of me? I have no power to take care of myself. I like to hear Thy name and feed Thy *bhaktas* and help the poor. Who will make it possible for me to do these things? Send me someone who will be able to do these for me.' As the answer to this prayer came Mathur Bābu,[1]

1 Mathur Bābu was the son-in-law of Rānī Rāshmani, the founder of the temple garden at Dakshineshwar. He recognized the divine powers and superhuman

who served me so long and with such intense devotion and faith! Again at another time I said to the Mother: 'I shall have no child of my own, but I wish to have as my child a pure *bhakta*, who will stay with me all the time. Send me such a one.' Then came Rākhāl (Brahmānanda).

"Those who are my own are parts of my very Self."

Visit to Zoological Garden

In referring to the time of joyous illumination which immediately followed his enlightenment, he exclaimed: "What a state it was! The slightest cause aroused in me the thought of the Divine Ideal. One day I went to the Zoological Garden in Calcutta. I desired especially to see the lion, but when I beheld him, I lost all sense-consciousness and went into *samādhi*. Those who were with me wished to show me the other animals, but I replied: 'I saw everything when I saw the king of beasts. Take me home.' The strength of the lion had aroused in me the consciousness of the omnipotence of God and had lifted me above the world of phenomena."

Divinity Everywhere

"Another day I went to the parade-ground to see the ascension of a balloon. Suddenly my eyes fell upon a young English boy leaning against a tree. The very posture of his body brought before me the vision of the form of Krishna and I went into *samādhi*.

"Again I saw a woman wearing a blue garment under a tree. She was a harlot. As I looked at her, instantly the ideal of Sītā[2] appeared before me! I forgot the existence of the harlot, but saw before me pure and spotless Sītā, approaching Rāma, the Incarnation of Divinity, and for a long time I remained motionless. I worshipped all women as representatives of the Divine Mother. I realized the Mother of the universe in every woman's form.

"Mathur Bābu, the son-in-law of Rāshmani, invited me to stay

character of Shrī Rāmakrishna and became his devoted disciple.

2 Sītā was the consort of Rāma, the Divine Incarnation and the hero of the *Rāmāyana*. She was the perfect type of womanhood according to the Hindus.

Shrī Rāmakrishna
Calcutta, December 10, 1881

Rāmakrishna's birthplace of Kāmārpukur

Holy Mother (Sāradā Devī)
Calcutta, November 1898

Mahendranāth Gupta, or M
Dakshineshwar, February 23, 1927

Swāmī Abhedānanda (Kālī)

Swāmī Vivekānanda (Narendra)
Belagaum (Western India), 1892

Group of Rāmakrishna's disciples, Calcutta, 1902: From left to right: Swāmīs Trigunātīta (Sāradā), Shivānanda (Tārak), Vivekānanda (Narendra), Turīyānanda (Harī), Brahmānanda (Rākhāl), and below, Sāradānanda (Sarat)

Kālī, the Divine Mother.
Rāmakrishna worshipped this image in the Dakshineshwar temple.

A group of devotees, standing by Rāmakrishna's body (obscured) after his passing away. 1. M.; 2. Sarat (Sāradānanda); 3. Kālī (Abhedānanda); 4. Tārak (Shivānanda); 5. Gangādhar (Akhandānanda); 6. Gopāl (Advaitānanda); 7. Bāburām (Premānanda); 8. Niranjan (Niranjānananda); 9. Narendra (Vivekānanda); 10. Balarām Bose; 11. Shashi (Rāmakrishnānanda); 12. Lātu (Adbhutānanda); 13. Rākhāl (Brahmānanda); 14. Jogin (Yogānanda)

Panchavati, the scene of Rāmakrishna's spiritual practices, early nineteenth century

Kālī Temple and gardens at Dakshineshwar, early nineteenth century

in his house for a few days. At that time I felt so strongly that I was the maid-servant of my Divine Mother that I thought of myself as a woman. The ladies of the house had the same feeling; they did not look upon me as a man. As women are free before a young girl, so were they before me. My mind was above the consciousness of sex.

"What a divine state it was! I could not eat here in the temple. I would walk from place to place and enter into the house of strangers after their meal hour. I would sit there quietly, without uttering a word. When questioned, I would say, 'I wish to eat here.' Immediately they would feed me with the best things they had."

Visit to Devendranāth Tāgore

"Once I wished to meet Devendranāth Tāgore.[3] He is a very rich man, but in spite of his enormous wealth he is devoted to God and repeats His holy name. For this reason I desired to know him. I spoke about him to Mathur Bābu. He replied: 'Very well, Bābā, I will take thee to him; he was my classmate.' So he took me and introduced me to him, saying: 'This holy man has come to see you. He is mad after God.' I saw in him a little pride and egotism. It is natural for a man who has so much wealth, culture, fame, and social position. I said to Mathur Bābu: 'Tell me, does pride spring from true wisdom or from ignorance? He who has attained to the highest knowledge of *Brahman* cannot possess pride or egotism, such as "I am learned," "I am wise," "I am rich," and so on.' While I was speaking with Devendranāth Tāgore, I went into a state from where I could see the true character of every individual. In this state the most learned *pandits* and scholars appear to me like blades of grass. When I see that scholars have neither true discrimination nor dispassion, then I feel that they are like straws; or they seem

3 Devendranāth Tāgore (1817-1905) was a Hindu multimillionaire of Calcutta. In 1841 he became a follower of Rājā Rāmmohan Roy, the founder of the Ādi Brāhmo Samāj, and in 1844 he became the *āchārya*, or the spiritual leader of this theistic Hindu church. During the latter part of his life he retired from the world and devoted his time entirely to spiritual studies. He was the father of the great poet Rabindranāth Tāgore.

like vultures who soar high in the heavens, but keep their minds on the charnel-pits below on the earth. In Devendra I found both spiritual knowledge and worldly desire. He has a number of children, some of whom are quite young. A doctor was present. I said: 'When you have so much spiritual knowledge, how can you live constantly in the midst of so much worldliness? You are like Rājā Janaka; you can keep your mind on God, remaining amid worldly pleasures and luxury. Therefore I have come to see you. Tell me something of the Divine Being.' Devendra then read some passages from the *Vedas* and said: 'This world is like a chandelier, and each *jīva* (individual soul) is like a light in it.' Long ago, when I spent nearly all my time meditating at the *Panchavati*, I saw the same thing. When Devendra's words harmonized with my experience, I knew that he must have attained to some true knowledge. I asked him to explain. He said: 'Who would have known this world? God has created man to manifest His glory. If there were no light in the chandelier, it would be all dark. The chandelier itself would not be visible.' After a long conversation Devendranāth Tāgore begged me to come to the anniversary of the Brāhmo Samāj. I answered: 'If it be the will of the Lord. I go wherever He takes me.'"

Distaste of Worldly Conversation

"Nothing but discourses on God appealed to me at this period. If I heard worldly conversation, I would sit in a corner and weep bitterly. When I went with Mathur Bābu to Benares, I was sitting with him in the drawing-room when some friends came in to see him and began to discuss worldly affairs. 'So much we have gained, so much we have lost.' Hearing this I was in tears and cried aloud: 'Mother, why hast Thou brought me here? I was much better off in the temple. I have come to the Holy City to hear only of lust and gold; but there in the temple I did not have to listen to such conversation.'"

Longing to Hear About the Supreme

"I was at this time like a young boy and so Mathur Bābu fulfilled all the desires that arose in my mind. My heart and soul, however, were constantly longing to hear about the Supreme Being. I searched for the places where the holy scriptures were expounded. There was a *brāhmin* in the neighborhood who was a great *pandit* and who had true faith. I used to go to hear him very often. A saint lived nearby on the bank of the Ganges and I wished to go with this *brāhmin* to see him; but a priest who looked upon the world as a dream discouraged me by saying: 'The body of a saint is an earthly cage; what good can one obtain by visiting such a cage?' I spoke of this to the *brāhmin* and he replied: 'He who thinks of God, he who repeats His holy name and has renounced everything for the sake of the Lord, must not be regarded as an earthly cage. The priest does not know that the form of a devotee is a spiritual form full of divine intelligence.'

"This *brāhmin* once asked me why I had thrown away my brāhminical thread. I replied: 'When the storm of divine ecstasy overtook my heart and soul, it blew away all signs of caste and creed. If you once become mad after God, then you will understand me.' But after some time this *brāhmin* himself caught the madness of divine ecstasy. He would utter nothing but '*Om*, *Om*,' and sit in silence in his own room. He would not mix with or speak to anyone. His friends and relatives called in physicians. He told one of them: 'You can cure my disease, but do not take my "*Om*" from me.'"

Absolute Frankness

"During this period I was absolutely outspoken. I observed no formality or etiquette; I was fearless. Once I met a rich *zamindār* and asked him: 'What is our highest duty? Is not the attainment of God our highest duty?' He replied: 'We are men of the world; salvation is not for us. When even Yudhishthira,[4] the purest and the most perfect of mortals, had to see purgatory in a vision because he had once wavered for half a second from absolute Truth, what can we expect for ourselves?' I could not bear his words and rebuked him

4 Yudhishthira was the hero of the *Mahābhārata* and a Hindu emperor of ancient India.

sharply, saying: 'What kind of man are you, that you think of the momentary vision of purgatory? You must not think of that, but think of Yudhishthira's truthfulness, forgiveness, patience, right discrimination, renunciation, devotion, and love for God.'

"At another time I went to see a *zamindār* who had the title of *rājā* (king), and I told him plainly that I could not call him *rājā* because he was not really one.

"One day I saw a pious *brāhmin* who was counting his beads on the bank of the Ganges. I stood near him and knew that his mind was not fixed on God but on earthly things. Immediately I roused him by striking him on the shoulder. At another time Rāshmani, the founder of the temple, was praying in the temple while I was singing the holy song of the Divine Mother. I perceived that her mind was on worldly objects and instantly I roused her in the same manner. In amazement she folded her hands and remained motionless before me."

Visit to Keshab Sen

Keshab Chandra Sen was suffering from a serious illness. Bhagavān Shrī Rāmakrishna was very anxious to see him, so he came one day with a few of his disciples to Keshab's home, where he was received by some of Keshab's disciples. They led him to the drawing-room and seated him on a couch. The room was fitted up with modern furniture. The Bhagavān looked at it for a moment; then his mind turned within and he went into *samādhi*. After recovering sense-consciousness, he spoke thus:

Body and Ātman

"There are two, the physical body and the *Ātman*; the body is born, so it must die, but *Ātman* is deathless. It is separate from the body, like a nut in the shell; but when the nut is unripe, it is difficult to separate the kernel from the shell; so it is with worldly people who have not realized God. Their *Ātman* remains attached to the body; but in true knowledge the *Ātman* appears as separate from the body."

At this moment Keshab entered the room. He was extremely thin and looked almost like a skeleton. He could hardly stand on his feet. With great difficulty he walked to the couch and sat at the feet of Bhagavān Shrī Rāmakrishna. The Bhagavān came down from the couch and sat on the floor. Keshab touched his forehead to the floor and remained prostrate before him for some time. Rāmakrishna held Keshab's hand and said:

Perfect Knowledge Brings Realization of Oneness

"So long as there is knowledge of variety, so long there is bondage. When perfect knowledge comes, man realizes one Spirit in all. In that state he also sees that the same One has become the individual soul, and the phenomenal world with its various states and elements. It is true that the universal Spirit dwells everywhere, but His manifestation varies. In some places there is greater manifestation and in others less. Wherever there is greater manifestation of the Spirit, there is also greater manifestation of divine powers."

Unity and Variety

"First you will have to realize unity by discrimination: 'Not this, not this.' Then after reaching this state of realization, when you come down to phenomena, you will discover that variety has come from unity and the same unity is the goal of variety. The difference in the manifestation of *shakti* or power makes the variety. When the flood of spiritual realization comes in the soul, like a sheet of water the universal Spirit covers everything. All distinctions vanish. Then a boat can pass over a field and the way from one place to another becomes straight across the water."

Keshab was listening with rapt attention. Although the room was crowded, absolute silence prevailed. The Bhagavān, looking at Keshab, then asked:

Meaning of Keshab's Illness

"How are you? How do you feel? You are suffering; but your illness has a deep meaning. In this body you have gone through various stages of spiritual development; the body is now suffering from the reaction. When the spiritual waves arise, the consciousness of the body vanishes; but it tells upon the body in the end. When a big steamer plies in the waters of the Ganges, I have seen the waves dash against the shore for some time after; the larger the boat, the stronger the waves; sometimes they break down the banks. If an elephant enters a small hut, it shakes it and breaks it into pieces; so when the elephant of the spiritual Ideal enters into the body, it shakes and sometimes shatters it. What happens, do you know? If there be a fire in the house, it burns up many things. Similarly, the fire of divine wisdom burns all passion, anger, and other enemies, and in the end destroys the sense of 'I, me, and mine.' The body is then wrenched and shattered. You may think that everything is finished, but so long as there is the least sign of illness, so long He will not make you free. If you enroll yourself as a patient in a hospital, you cannot come out before you are absolutely cured."

Keshab began to smile. The Bhagavān continued: "Hridai used to say, after seeing the condition of my body: 'I have never seen so much spirituality with such a state of body!' But although my body was weak, still I never stopped talking of God with others. At one time, I remember, I was thin like a skeleton, yet I would continue discussions on spiritual subjects for hours."

Everything the Will of God

Then shedding tears of sympathy for Keshab, the Bhagavān said: "It is His will. Everything happens by Thy will, O Lord! Thou doest Thy work; by mistake people say, 'I do.' The gardener sometimes uncovers the roots of rose-bushes that the dew may fall upon them. Sometimes he trims off some of the roots so that the flowers will become larger. Perhaps the Lord is preparing you to do greater work. But I feel very unhappy when you are ill. Last time when you were ill, I was so anxious about you that I would cry at night and pray to my Divine Mother for your recovery. Sometimes I said to my Mother: 'If Keshab passes away, with whom shall I talk about God?' But this time I do not feel the same way."

At this moment Keshab's aged mother came near the door and addressed the Bhagavān, saying: "May Keshab be cured of his illness?"

The Bhagavān replied: "Pray to my blissful Divine Mother. She will remove all pain and trouble. (To Keshab) Do not spend so much time with your family and children. Their company will drag you to worldliness. You will feel better if you think of God and talk about Him."

Keshab's mother: "Do thou bless my Keshab."

Rāmakrishna: "What power have I? God will bless him. Thou doest Thy work, O Divine Mother! People say by mistake, 'I do it.' Two are the occasions when the Lord smiles. First, when brothers remove the chains which partition off the family property, saying: 'This is mine and that is thine'; and secondly, when the physician of a dying patient declares: 'I shall make him live.'"

Keshab then began to cough and could not remain longer, so he bowed down before the Bhagavān, saluted him, and with great difficulty walked out of the room. A Brāhmo devotee said: "Bhagavan, lay thy hand on his head and bless him."

Rāmakrishna replied: "It is not for me to bless anyone."

He then gently touched him on his arm and said to the Brāhmo devotee: "I cannot say to anyone, 'Be thou cured.' I never asked my Divine Mother for that power. I simply ask for pure love and nothing else."

Shrī Rāmakrishna then rose to leave. Keshab's disciples accompanied him to the door with great reverence, and he passed from the house with his disciples.

Chapter 8

Feast at the Garden-House of Shurendra

Shrī Rāmakrishna was invited by one of his beloved disciples, Shurendra,[1] a householder, to a feast arranged in his garden-house at Kānkurgāchi near Calcutta.

These feasts were invariably occasions for the gathering of his disciples, devotees, and admirers. They were times of real festivity and rejoicing, during which the holy name of God was chanted to the accompaniment of *mridangas* and other musical instruments. All the while the Bhagavān could be seen at his best, singing, dancing with the joy of the Lord, and frequently lost in that blessed state of ecstasy or *samādhi*. When the singing of devotional hymns and the spiritual excitement which came with it were over, the company present would be treated by the Bhagavān to one of those celestial conversations, so laden with sermons for the spiritual welfare of humanity, which will never die in the memory of those who had the rare privilege of listening to him.

Rāmakrishna's Ecstasy

The first part of the day was given to *sankīrtan* (singing forth the name of the Lord). They were singing the songs telling of the separation of the *gopīs* from the Lord Shrī Krishna, who had gone to Mathurā. In the course of the songs, the Bhagavān was frequently in a state of *samādhi*. They were singing. Suddenly he rose to his feet, saying: "O my friend, do thou bring my beloved Krishna to me or take me over to the place where He is." The Bhagavān, it would appear, had merged his personality in that of Rādhā, the chief of the *gopīs*. He realized that he and Rādhā were one. With those words he stood speechless and motionless, with fixed half-closed eyes that moved not, evidently having lost all sense-consciousness. Coming to himself, he again, in a voice that drew tears

1 Bābu Shuresh Chandra Mitrā was a devoted householder disciple of Rāmakrishna. The Bhagavān used to call him Shurendra.

from the eyes of those who heard him, cried out: "O my friend, do me this favor and I shall be thy most devoted servant. Remember it was thou that taughtest me my love for the Beloved."

The chorus went on singing. Rādhā was made in the song to say: "Oh! I will not go to the bank of the Yamunā to draw water, for coming up to the *kadamba* tree I am put in mind of my own, my Beloved." Rāmakrishna, heaving a sigh, said: "Ah, me!" As the chorus chanted aloud the name of the Lord, the Bhagavān was again on his feet and in *samādhi*. Recovering his sense-consciousness, he could only repeat inarticulately: "Kitma, Kitma," for "Krishna, Krishna."

The *sankīrtan* was brought to a close by the Bhagavān himself leading the chorus in the well-known piece: "Victory to Rādhā, victory to Govinda," and dancing with his disciples, who formed a ring around him.

The Madness of Love for the Lord

The dancing and singing had all taken place in the reception-hall. The Bhagavān then withdrew into one of the adjoining rooms to the west. To a disciple he said, talking of the *gopīs*: "How wonderful was their devotion! At the sight of the *tamāl* tree they were seized with the very madness of love."

Disciple: "This was also the case with Chaitanya. Looking at the forest he thought it was Brindāvan, the sacred birthplace of Shrī Krishna, that was before him!"

Bhagavān: "Oh! if any one is but favored with a single particle of this ecstatic love! What devotion! What intense love! Of this devotion they not only had the full measure, a hundred percent, but a great deal more than that. This is called the madness of divine love. The chief thing is to have intense love and sincere and earnest longing for God. On whatever path you may travel, whether you believe in the Divinity with or without form, whether you have faith in God-Incarnate in a human form or not—if you have intense love and sincere longing for Him, you are sure to attain to Him. He alone knows what He is like. He Himself will make you realize His divine nature. Why should you be mad after the things of the world? If you must be mad, be mad for God.

"There is a madness of divine love, a madness of *bhakti*, or ecstasy, and a madness of *jnāna*. Rādhā had the madness of divine love. Hanumān showed the madness of true devotion. When Sītā was forced by Rāma to prove her chastity by going through the ordeal of fire, Hanumān, although a devotee of Rāma, was so maddened that he wished to kill his Lord, the Divine Incarnation. I saw a true *jnāni*, who wandered like a madman. He came to the temple garden. He had so realized the oneness of the Spirit in every living creature that when he saw a dog eating the remains of a dish, he held him by the ears and said: 'Brother, wilt thou eat all?' He then took a portion and ate with the dog. He said to Hridai: 'When the holy waters of the Ganges and the water of the gutter appear the same, then will come the realization of divine oneness.'

"At one time I had this madness. I used to walk like a madman, seeing the same Spirit everywhere and recognizing neither high nor low in caste or creed. I could eat even with a *pariah*. I had the constant realization that *Brahman* is Truth and the world is unreal like a dream. Once Mathur Bābu took me in a boat. The Mohammedan crew were cooking and I was about to eat with them, but Mathur Bābu would not let me. In that state I used to bow down before everybody and would ask them to repeat the holy name of the Lord. As in a violent storm a screen of dust rises, hiding the trees of different kinds and making all trees appear alike, so in that storm of spiritual vision I could not distinguish one man from another as high or low."

A devotee: "Bhagavan, how can a man live in the world and experience any of these kinds of madness?"

Shrī Rāmakrishna: "These states are not for those who are living in the world and performing the duties of the world, but for those who have absolutely renounced internally and externally. External renunciation is not for those who live in the world. They should practice internal renunciation or mental non-attachment."

(To a disciple) "A man brought a bottle of wine; I went to touch it but could not."

Disciple: "Why, Bhagavan?"

Divine Intoxication

Rāmakrishna: "When divine bliss is attained, one becomes intoxicated with it, he does not need to drink wine. When I see the feet of my Divine Mother, I feel as intoxicated as if I had drunk five bottles of wine. In this state one cannot eat anything and everything."

Disciple: "As regards eating, one should eat what one gets."

Food for a Bhakta

Rāmakrishna: "That depends upon the spiritual state. In the path of *jnāna* that produces no harm; when a *jnāni* eats, he pours the food as an offering in the fire of Kundalinī. But for a *bhakta* it is different. A *bhakta* should eat only pure food, such food as he can freely offer to his beloved Lord. Animal food is not for a *bhakta*. But at the same time, I must say, if a man loves God after eating the flesh of a pig, he is blessed, and wretched is the man who lives on milk and rice, but whose mind is absorbed in lust and gold. Once I took as *mantram* the name of Allah from a Mohammedan teacher and repeated the name for several days and ate their food."

The Bhagavān then came back into the hall followed by his disciples and seated himself. A pillow was placed for him to recline upon. Before touching it, he said, "*Om tat sat*" (*Brahman* is the only Reality). The pillow was, of course, one which had been used by the unholy men of the world, and the Bhagavān was purity itself. It was getting late, but no dinner was being served and the Bhagavān became a little impatient like a child. Shurendra, the host, was a beloved disciple of the Lord. The Bhagavān said: "Shurendra's disposition has grown admirable. He is very generous; those who go to him for help never come away disappointed. Then he is very outspoken. He is bold enough to speak the truth."

Truthfulness

"In this age truthfulness is the best of all ascetic practices. He who is firm in truthfulness attains to God. Lack of truthfulness destroys all virtue. For this reason, when I say anything even inadvertently, such as, 'I shall go there. I shall do that,' I must go, because I have said it. I may lose my firmness in truthfulness if I do not keep my word to the very letter. Openness as opposed to dissimulation is the fruit of the practice of many religious austerities in one's previous incarnations. In a well-known song by Tulsī Dās[2] it is said: 'Give up dissimulation and cunning.' Do you not see that whenever God has taken a human form, this great virtue of guilelessness has never failed to come to view? Look at Dasharatha, the father of Rāma, and Nanda Ghosh, the father of Shrī Krishna. They were both free from guile. (To a young disciple) Like men of the world, you have accepted a position in an office, but you are working for your mother. Otherwise I should have said: 'For shame! For shame! You must serve only the Lord.' (To Māni Mullick) This young man is open and guileless to a degree; only nowadays he occasionally tells untruths, that is all. The other day he said that he would come to see me, but he did not. (To Mahendra) You went to see Bhagavān Dās; how did you like him?"

Mahendra: "Yes, revered sir, I went to see him. The great Vaishnava sage has become very old. He was lying down when I saw him; a disciple put some food into his mouth. He can hear only when addressed in loud tones. After hearing thy name, he said to me: 'You need not fear anything, Rāmakrishna is a divine manifestation. To worship his name is to worship God.'"

Here Mahima came in and the Bhagavān exclaimed: "This is a visit quite unexpected! We expect at most a shallop in this poor river of ours, yet here comes a ship! But then it is the rainy season!"

The conversation next turned on the spiritual aspect of feasts and the Bhagavān said to Mahima: "Why is it that people are fed at a feast? Do you not think that it is the same as offering a sacrifice to God who is the living fire in all creatures? But bad men not God-fearing, guilty of adultery and fornication, should on no account be entertained at a feast. Their sins are so great that several cubits of earth beneath the place where they eat become polluted."

2 Tulsī Dās was a great Hindu poet who lived between 1544 and 1624 A.D. He was a devoted worshipper of Rāma. His Hindī poem, *Rāmāyana*, or the history of Rāma, as well as proverbs and other verses, are to this day household words in every town and rural district where the Hindī language is spoken. He is regarded by the people as a Hindu saint of the Vaishnava sect.

Protāp Chandra Mozoomdār, a member of the Brāhmo Samāj, entered and saluted Shrī Rāmakrishna. The Bhagavān, as usual, returned his salutation with his well-known modesty, bowing very low. Mozoomdār said: "Revered sir, I have recently been to Darjeeling."

Shrī Rāmakrishna: "But you do not appear to be much the better for the change. What is the matter with you?"

Mozoomdār: "The same complaint to which Keshab Chandra Sen succumbed."

Egotism Rises from Ignorance

A certain Marāthā lady was then spoken of. Mozoomdār said that she had been to England and had embraced Christianity. He asked the Bhagavān whether he had ever heard of the woman. The Bhagavān replied: "No, but from what I hear from you, I should think she must be a person who wishes to make a name for herself. Egotism of this kind is not good. Those who seek for fame are under a delusion. 'I do this or that,' this sense arises from ignorance. But 'O Lord, Thou art doing everything' is true knowledge. God is the real Actor, others are actors in name only."

The Ego of a Calf

"The calf says: '*hāmmā*' or '*aham*' (I). Now look at the troubles caused by the self which says 'I, I.' In the first place, the calf is sometimes taken into the field where it is yoked to the plough. It is there made to work on from morning till evening, alike in the sun and in the rain. Its troubles are not yet over. It is very often killed by the butcher. Its flesh is eaten as meat. Its skin is tanned into hides which are then made into shoes. The sufferings of the calf in this state know no bounds. But that is not all. Drums are made with the skin which is thus mercilessly beaten, sometimes with the hand and sometimes with the drumstick. It is only when out of its entrails are made strings for the bows used for carding cotton that the troubles of the poor creature are over. And that is because it no longer says, '*hāmmā, hāmmā*' (I, I), but '*Tuhū, Tuhū*' (It is Thou, O Lord! It is Thou!). Similarly, when *jīva* (ego) says, 'O Lord! Not I but Thou art the doer and actor, I am merely an instrument in Thy hands,' it becomes free from all the world's troubles and attains to absolute freedom from birth and rebirth in this world of sorrow and suffering."

A devotee: "How can *jīva* become free from egoism (*ahamkāra*)?"

Bhagavān: "Egoism does not leave until one has realized God. If anyone has become absolutely free from egoism (*ahamkāra*) you must know that that person has seen and realized Divinity."

Devotee: "Revered sir, what are the signs of one who has seen and realized God?"

Signs of One Who Has Realized God

Bhagavān: "The signs of one who has seen God are thus described in the *Bhāgavatam*. There are four kinds. First, his conduct is like that of a child. A truly wise man who has seen the Lord becomes like a child. A child has no real egoism. He is not bound by any custom. The self of the child is nothing at all like the self of the grown-up man. The second sign is that one who has seen God does not care for his body or his dress. Purity and impurity seem to him the same. Third, such a one sometimes acts like a madman, now laughing, now weeping, and the next moment talking to himself; now dressed like a *bābu* (gentleman) and now taking his one garment under his arm and going quite naked like a child. Lastly, he may remain inert and motionless for a long time in the state of *samādhi*."

Devotee: "After God-vision does egoism (*ahamkāra*) disappear entirely?"

Bhagavān: "Sometimes the Lord wipes out the last stain of egoism, as in the state of *samādhi*. Again, sometimes He leaves a faint trace of egoism, but that is harmless. It is like that of an innocent child, who knows not the doing of injury to anyone. The steel sword is turned into gold by the touch of the Philosopher's Stone. It still retains its shape but it does not injure anyone."

Bhagavān to Mozoomdār: "You have been to England and America. Tell me all about what you saw there."

Mozoomdār: "Sir, people in England mostly worship what thou callest *kānchan* (gold), but there are some good men and women who are not so attached to worldliness. Generally speaking, one sees nothing but worldly activity (*rajas*) everywhere from beginning to end."

Attachment to Work

Bhagavān: "I have seen the same thing here too. Why in England and America alone? Attachment to work is to be found in every country. That worldly activity is the first chapter of life. So long as the *rajas* quality predominates, attachment to work increases. One cares more for one's own worldly good—riches, honor, fame. It gradually leads to ignorance which makes one forget God, the Reality of the universe. God cannot be realized until the *sattva* qualities, such as devotion, right discrimination, dispassion, and compassion for all, prevail. All attachment to lust and gold proceeds from *rajas* and *tamas* qualities, but work cannot be renounced entirely. Propelled by nature (*prakriti*) you plunge into work even against your wish. Therefore I say you should work with non-attachment; in other words, you should work without seeking the fruit.

"In a great religious ceremony we give alms to the poor and do various other charitable works and may think that we are absolutely unattached to the results of such works, but in the end we find that the desire for name and fame has crept up in the heart, we do not know how. But he alone who has seen and realized God can become absolutely unattached to work and its result."

A devotee: "What is the path for those who have not realized God? Is it necessary for them to give up all work and worldly activity?"

Path of Devotion

Rāmakrishna: "In this age (*Kali yuga*) the path of devotion and love (*bhakti yoga*) is easy for all. The practice of Nārada's *bhakti* is better adapted to this *yuga*. One should repeat the holy name of the Lord and chant His praises and with earnest and sincere heart, pray to Him, saying: 'O Lord, grant me Thy divine wisdom, Thy divine love. Do Thou open my eyes and make me realize Thee.'

"When *karma yoga* is so difficult to practice, one should pray to the Lord in this manner: 'O Lord! Do Thou reduce our *karma* to a minimum, and the little work that we daily perform, may we do it with non-attachment by Thy grace. O Lord! Do not let our desire for work increase in number and bind us to the ties to worldliness.'"

Attainment of God-Vision

"No one, however, can avoid work (*karma*). Every mental action is a *karma*. 'I am thinking,' 'I meditate,' 'I feel,' each of these is a *karma*. The more one attains to true devotion the less becomes one's worldly work. The pleasures of the world do not satisfy such a soul. They lose their charm. How can one who has tasted the sherbet made with pure crystallized sugar be pleased with the taste of a drink made with molasses or treacle? On one occasion a *karma yogī* (Shambhu) said to me: 'May thy blessings be upon me so that my wealth be spent in building hospitals and dispensaries, in making roads, in sinking wells for travelers, in establishing schools, colleges, and in other good works.' Whereupon I replied: 'Shambhu, all these works are good when they are performed with non-attachment. But that is very difficult. In any case you should always keep in mind that the end and aim of your human existence is the attainment of God and not hospitals and dispensaries. Suppose the Lord appears before you and graciously offers to fulfill your desires. Will you then pray for dispensaries and hospitals, tanks and wells, roads and serais, or will you say: 'O Lord! Grant that I may have pure and unalloyed love for Thee and unswerving devotion to Thy feet, that I may always feel Thy presence and realize Thee under all conditions?'

"Hospitals, dispensaries, and all these things are transitory; God alone is the Reality, all else is unreal. Once placed face to face with the Vision Divine we see them as no better than dreams and then we pray for more light, more wisdom, more divine love, the love which lifts a man to God, the love which makes us realize that we are really sons of the Supreme Being, of whom all that can be said is that He exists, that He is knowledge itself in the highest sense, and that He is the eternal fountain of love and bliss. Again, when one attains to God-vision, one feels that God alone is the real actor in the universe, the doer of all things, and that we can do nothing. If God does everything, then why, instead of realizing Him, shall we get entangled in the meshes of worldly works? First realize God; then, if it be His will, many hospitals and dispensaries may be established. Therefore, I say, never lose sight of this goal of life that I have pointed out for you, but move onward through the practices of devotion and love. When you have advanced far enough you will know that God alone is the Reality, that all the things of the world are unreal and that the highest end and aim of life is the attainment of God."

Parable of a Wood-Cutter

"There was a wood-cutter who led a very miserable life with the small means he could procure by daily selling a load of wood brought from a neighboring forest. Once a *sannyāsī*, who was passing by that way, saw him at work and advised him to go further into the forest, saying: 'Move onward, my child, move onward.' The wood-cutter obeyed the injunction and proceeded onward until he came to a sandalwood-forest, and being much pleased he took away with him as many sandal logs as he could carry, sold them in the market and derived much profit. Then he began to wonder within himself why the good *sannyāsī* had not told him anything about the wood of the sandal-tree, but had simply advised him to move onward. So the next day he went on beyond the place of the sandalwood until he came upon a copper-mine, and he took with him all the copper that he could carry, and selling it in the market, got more money by it. Next day, without stopping at the copper-mine, he proceeded further still, as the *sādhu* had advised him to do, and he came upon a silver-mine and took with him as much of it as he could carry, sold it and got even more money, and so daily proceeding further and further, he found gold-mines and diamond-mines and at last became exceedingly rich. Such is also the case with the man who aspires after true knowledge. If he does not stop in his progress after attaining a few extraordinary and supernatural powers, he at last becomes really rich in the eternal knowledge of Truth.

"So go on, my children and never lose sight of your ideal! Go onward and never stop until you have reached the goal. Arriving at a particular stage, do not get the idea that you have reached your journey's end. Work is only the first stage of the journey. Bear in mind that doing works *unattached* is exceedingly difficult, that therefore *bhakti yoga*, the path of love, is better suited to this age, and that work, even if unattached, is not the end of your life, but only a means to an end. So march on and never halt till you have come up to the great Ideal of your life—the realization of God."

Then turning to Mozoomdār the Bhagavān said: "You are an educated and intelligent man, you are a deep thinker. Keshab and yourself were like the brothers Gaur (Chaitanya) and Nitāi.[3] You have had enough of this world—enough of lectures, controversies, schisms, and the rest. Do you still care for them? Now, it is high time for you to collect your scattered mind and turn it towards God. Plunge into the ocean of Divinity."

Mozoomdār: "Yes, revered sir, that I ought to do. There is no doubt about it. But all this I do simply to preserve Keshab's name and reputation."

Story of a Man and His Cottage

Rāmakrishna (smiling): "You believe that you are doing all this, as you say, for Keshab, but after a while this idea will change and you will think differently. Let me tell you a story. A man built a cottage on a mountain-top. It cost him hard labor and much money. After a few days there arose a cyclone and the cottage began to rock to and fro. He was very anxious to save it, so he prayed to the Wind-god, saying: 'Lord, I beseech Thee, do not destroy this cottage'; but the Wind-god did not listen. He prayed again, but the cottage kept on rocking. Then he thought out a plan to save it. He remembered that in the mythology Hanumān was the son of the Wind-god. Instantly he cried out: 'Lord, I beg of Thee, spare this cottage for it belongs to Hanumān, Thy son.' But the Wind-god did not listen. Then he said: 'Lord, I pray Thee, spare this cottage, for it belongs to Hanumān's lord, Rāma.' Still the Wind-god did not listen. Then, as the cottage was about to topple over, the man, to save his life, ran out of it and began to swear, saying: 'Let it go to destruction! What is that to me?' You may now be anxious to preserve Keshab's name, but console yourself with the thought that it was after all owing to God's will that the religious movement connected with his name was set on foot, and that if the movement has had its day, it is also owing to that same divine will. Therefore dive deep into the sea." And the Bhagavān sang:

3 Gaur is the abbreviated form of Gaurānga, another name of Chaitanya. Nitāi is the abbreviated form of Nityānanda, the most powerful preacher among the followers of Chaitanya. He is regarded by the Vaishnavas of this sect as the spiritual brother of Gaurānga.

1. Dive deep, dive deep, dive deep, O my mind! into the sea of beauty.
Make a search in the regions lower, still lower below the bottom of the sea:
Thou wilt surely find the jewel of *prema* (intense love of God).

2. Within thy heart Brindavān (the abode of the God of love).
Search, search, search; searching Thou wilt find it.
Then in the heart shall burn, burn, burn the lamp of wisdom without ceasing.

3. Who is it that steers the boat on land, on land, on land?
Says Kubir: Listen, listen, listen; meditate on the lotus feet of *guru.*

"Do you hear the song? You have finished your lectures, quarrels, and fights. Now dive in this ocean. There is no fear of death in this sea. It is the sea of Immortality. Do not fear that one becomes unbalanced by meditating on God. I once said to Narendra (Vivekānanda)—"

Mozoomdār (interrupting): "Who is this Narendra?"

God, the Sea of Immortality

Bhagavān: "Oh, there is a young man of that name, Well, I said to Narendra: 'God is like a sea of immortal syrup. Would you not dive deep into this sea? Suppose, my boy, there is a basin containing the syrup of sugar and that you are a fly anxious to drink the sweet liquid. Where would you sit and drink?' Narendra said in reply: 'Why! from the edge of the basin. If I go far from the edge I may be drowned and lose my life.' Thereupon I said to him: 'My boy, in the sea of Divinity there is no fear of the kind. Do you not know that it is the sea of Immortality? Whosoever dives into this sea does not die but obtains everlasting life.' He who is mad after God can never become unbalanced or insane."

Ideal of a Wet-Nurse

Mozoomdār made inquiries about the disciples. He asked whether those who came to the Bhagavān were getting better in the spirit day by day. The Bhagavān said: "I place before them the ideal of a wet-nurse as teaching them how to live in this world. The maid-servant referring to her master's house says, 'This is our house.' All the while she knows that her home is far away in a distant village, to which her thoughts are always fixed. Again, referring to the master's child in her arms, she will say: 'My Harī has grown very wicked,' or 'My Harī likes to eat this or that,' and so on. But all the while she knows that Harī is not her own. I tell those who come to me to live a life unattached like this maid-servant. I tell them to live unattached in this world, to be in the world but not of the world, and at the same time to have their mind directed to God, the heavenly home from whence all come. I tell them to pray for love of God (*bhakti*), which will help them so to live."

As Mozoomdār rose to take leave, the Bhagavān said to him: "What shall I say? It is better that you cease to have anything to do with all those things—schisms, controversies, etc. All quarrels and disputes spring from egotism and attachment to the world. These keep men away from God. Therefore abandon all earthly attachment and fix your mind on the Almighty."

Compassion and Attachment

Mozoomdār then saluted the Bhagavān and withdrew. After he had gone, a devotee asked: "Revered sir, thou didst go to see Vidyāsāgara, what dost thou think of him?"

Rāmakrishna: "Vidyāsāgara is a very learned scholar. He is kind and charitable, but he has no spiritual consciousness. There is gold inside; if he had been aware of it, he could not have devoted so much of his time to external work. Eventually his work would have been finished. If he knew that God was dwelling within his heart, his mind would have been fixed in thinking and meditating on Him. Some people have to perform work without attachment for a long time before true dispassion for the world comes; then the mind runs towards God and becomes absorbed in Him. Whatever work Vidyāsāgara has done for others has been very good and helpful. To be kind and compassionate is also good; but there is a difference between compassion and attachment. Compassion is good, but attachment is not. Attachment is love for wife, children, brother, sister, father, mother, and other relatives, while true compassion is equal love for all living creatures."

Mahendra: "Is compassion also a bondage?"

Sattva, Rajas, and Tamas

Rāmakrishna: "This question is not for ordinary mortals. Compassion is the result of the *sattva* quality. The *sattva* quality is protective, the *rajas* quality is creative, and *tamas* is destructive; but *Brahman* the Absolute, is beyond these three qualities, *sattva, rajas*, and *tamas*. It is also beyond *prakriti* or nature. Where there is Absolute Reality, no quality of nature can reach. As a thief cannot go to the exact spot where the treasure is, because he is afraid of being caught, so *sattva, rajas*, and *tamas*, like thieves, cannot go to the realm where is the treasure of the Absolute."

Parable of the Three Robbers

"A man was going through the woods. On his way he was caught by a band of three robbers. They took away everything he had. Then the first robber asked: 'What is the use of keeping this man alive?' And drawing his sword, he was about to kill him, when the second robber stopped him saying: 'What good will be done by killing him? Tie his hands and feet and throw him to one side.' So they bound his hands and feet and went away leaving him by the roadside. After they had gone for a while, the third robber returned and said to him: 'Ah! are you hurt? Come, let me untie the cords and release you.' Then when he had removed the cords, he said: 'Now come with me. I will show you the road.' After walking for a long distance, they found the road, and then the robber said: 'Look, there is your home. Follow the road and you will soon reach it.' The man, thanking him, replied: 'Sir, you have done me a great service. I am greatly obliged to you. Will you not come with me to my house?' The robber answered: 'No, I cannot go there; the guard would find me out.'

This world is the wilderness. The three robbers are the three *gunas* (qualities) of nature—*sattva, rajas*, and *tamas*. *Jīva* or the individual soul is the traveler; self-knowledge is the treasure. The *tamas* quality tries to destroy the *jīva*, the *rajas* quality binds him with the fetters of the world, but the *sattva* quality protects him from the actions of *rajas* and *tamas*. By taking refuge with the *sattva* quality, *jīva* becomes free from lust and anger, which are effects of *tamas*; the *sattva* quality also emancipates the *jīva* or the individual soul from the bondage of the world. But *sattva* quality itself is also a robber. It cannot give divine wisdom, or the knowledge of the Absolute. It leads one, however, up to the path of the Supreme Abode and then it says: 'Behold, there is thy home!' Then it disappears. Even the *sattva* quality cannot go near the abode of the Absolute."

Parable of the Four Travelers

"What the Absolute is, no one can tell. He who has attained the Absolute cannot give any information about it. Four travelers discovered a place enclosed by a high wall, with no opening anywhere. They were very anxious to see what was inside. So one of them climbed to the top of the wall and as he looked in, he shouted with amazement and joy: 'Ha! ha! ha!' and without giving any information to his fellow-travelers, he jumped inside. The others did likewise. Whoever climbs to the top of the wall jumps inside with extreme joy and never comes back to give the news of what he has found. Such is the realm of the Absolute. The great souls who have realized the Absolute have not come back, because after attaining the highest knowledge of *Brahman*, one absolutely loses the sense of 'I.' The mind ceases to be active, and all sense-consciousness vanishes. This state is called the *Brahma jnāna* or divine wisdom."

A devotee: "Revered sir, did not the perfected soul Shukadeva attain to *Brahma jnāna*, the knowledge of the Absolute?"

Rāmakrishna: "Some say that Shukadeva saw the ocean of the Absolute *Brahman* and touched its water, but he did not go into the water; therefore he was able to come back and teach mankind. Others believe that he attained to the Absolute *Brahman* and then returned to help humanity."

Devotee: "Does sectarianism exist after the knowledge of the Absolute (*Brahma jnāna*) has been attained?"

Sectarianism and Brahma Jnāna

Rāmakrishna: "I was talking with Keshab Sen of this *Brahma jnāna*. Keshab asked me to say more about the Absolute. I replied: 'If I say more, your sect and creed will vanish.' Keshab answered: 'Revered sir, then I do not wish to hear more.' Still, I said to Keshab: '"I, me, mine," this is ignorance; "I am the doer," "I am the actor," "This is my wife, these are my children, my property, wealth, fame," all these arise from ignorance.' Keshab replied: 'Revered sir, nothing will be left, if the sense of "I" be abandoned.' I answered: 'Keshab, I do not ask you to abandon the whole of the sense of "I"; but leave out the unripe "I"—"I am the doer," "my wife, my children, I am the teacher," abandoning this sense of "I," retain the ripe "I"—"I am His servant, I am His devotee," "I am not the doer, but He is the Actor."'"

Devotee: "Can the ripe 'I' make a sect?"

Keshab and His Disciples

Rāmakrishna: "I said to Keshab: '"I am the leader of a sect, I have founded a sect, I am teaching others," all these proceed from the sense of the unripe "I."' Therefore I asked Keshab to abandon this 'I.' I also said to him: 'You talk of your sect, many members of your sect have resigned.' Keshab replied: 'Revered sir, after remaining for three years under my instructions, they have now joined another sect, and at the time of leaving, they criticized and slandered me.' I said to him: 'You do not understand the inner nature of your disciples. You must study their predominant traits and must not make disciples indiscriminately.'"

Rām Bābu:[4] "Bhagavan, I do not see what good has been done by the New Dispensation of Keshab Sen. If Keshab himself had realized God, the condition of his disciples and followers would have been different. In my opinion he has had no realization."

4 Rām Bābu was a devoted householder disciple of Shrī Rāmakrishna. He was a scientist and a teacher of chemistry in the Medical College of Calcutta. He was a good speaker and writer.

A Spiritual Leader Must Renounce the World

Shrī Rāmakrishna: "Oh yes, he must have some realization; otherwise why should so many people honor and respect him? Why do they not honor and respect the leaders of other branches of the Brāhmo Samāj in the same way? Without divine will no one can command such respect from the masses. A man cannot become a true spiritual leader unless he practices absolute renunciation. Without this people will have no faith in him. They will say: 'This man is worldly. He himself enjoys the pleasures of flesh and wealth, yet he tells that God is Truth while the world is unreal like a dream.' The world will not receive his teachings unless he has renounced everything. A few people may listen to him and follow him. Keshab Sen was in the world and had his mind on worldly things. He tried to support his family by giving lectures and by marrying his daughter to a prince, thus protecting his worldly relations and social position. Once Keshab asked me: 'Why can I not see God?' I answered: 'Because you have absorbed yourself in seeking of the honor and respect of people, in education and so on. So long as the child is absorbed in playing with its dolls, the mother does not come. But when the child throws away the doll and cries for the mother, the mother cannot stay away. You think that you are a leader, but the Divine Mother thinks: "My child believes that he has become a leader and is happy; let him enjoy his belief."'"

The Absolute and the Divine Mother

"I also told him to believe the Divine Mother, that the Absolute and the Divine Mother are one. The Divine Mother is the Eternal Energy. They are inseparable. They appear as separate so long as we are conscious of the body and as we try to describe them by words. Eventually Keshab believed in the Divine Mother. Once he came with his disciples to see me. I asked him to deliver a lecture, so he did and after it I had a long talk with him. I said: 'He who is the Personal God manifests in one form as His devotee and in another form as His Word.' Then I went on to say to him: 'You are living in the realm of *māyā* (worldliness). This *māyā* does not let anyone know God. It keeps all in ignorance.'"

Delusive Power of Māyā

"How wonderful is its power! It entangles even a Divine Incarnation and makes him suffer from hunger, thirst, sorrow, misery, like an ordinary mortal. Do you not see how Rāma, the Divine Incarnation, suffered for Sītā? How with great sorrow, He wept bitterly when Sītā was stolen away from him? In the Hindu mythology there is a story that Vishnu incarnated in the form of a boar to destroy the demons; but after destroying the demons, He did not care to return to His heaven, He wanted to live as a boar. He had some little ones and he was happy with them. The *devas* of the heaven thought: 'How is it that our Lord does not come back? What has happened?' Then they went to Shiva and asked Him to persuade Vishnu to return to His heaven. Shiva came and entreated Him, but He was taking care of His young ones and paid no heed. Then Shiva tore open His body with His trident and freed Him from His self-delusion. Vishnu then laughed and returned to His heavenly abode. Such is the power of *māyā*! To go beyond its realm and rise above the *gunas* (qualities) is extremely difficult. He who has attained to God has transcended *māyā* with its qualities."

CHAPTER 9

Visit to a Hindu *Pandit* and Preacher

It was the day of the great car festival of Jagannāth. The streets of Calcutta were crowded with people. Boys and girls were playing along the way and amusing themselves by blowing horns and pipes made of palm-leaves. A light rain was falling and the roads were wet and muddy. About four o'clock in the afternoon the Bhagavān came out of Ishān's[1] house and entered a carriage which was waiting for him at the door. Immediately after taking his seat he lost sense-consciousness and went into that state of pure God-consciousness which he had often called his *ādesha* (divine commission). The disciples followed their divine Master on foot, for they were eager to be present at this memorable meeting with Pandit Shashadhar,[2] the great preacher of the *Vedānta* philosophy and religion.

The *pandit* was visiting a friend in Calcutta. As Shrī Rāmakrishna's carriage drew up at the entrance-door, he was warmly welcomed by the host and his people. Coming upstairs the Bhagavān met Shashadhar advancing towards him. He appeared to be a middle-aged man with a fair complexion and around his neck was thrown a rosary of *rudrāksha* beads. He came forward with a reverential air, saluted the Bhagavān, and led him to the parlor which was intended for his reception. The disciples and others went in after him and seated themselves as near him as they could. Among the disciples present was Narendra. The Bhagavān, smiling in his semiconscious state, said: "Very good, very good! Well, what kind of lectures do you give?"

Shashadhar: "Revered sir, I try to explain the truth taught by the holy scriptures."

1 Ishān Chandra Mookerjee was a pious *brāhmin* householder. He regarded Shrī Rāmakrishna as the incarnation of divine wisdom.

2 Pandit Shashadhar Tarkachurāmani was a Sanskrit scholar of great renown and an eloquent preacher of the philosophy and religion of *Vedānta*. By his powerful speeches he succeeded in checking the materialistic tendency of the Hindu students of Bengāl. He also gave rational explanations of the rituals and ceremonies described in the Hindu scriptures.

Bhagavān: "For this age *bhakti yoga*, communion with God by love, devotion, and self-surrender, as practiced by the Rishi Nārada, is enjoined. There is hardly time for *karma yoga*, for doing the works laid upon man by the scriptures. Do you not see that the well-known decoction of the ten medicinal roots (*dasamul pāchan*) is not the medicine for fevers of the present day? The patient runs the risk of being carried off before the medicine has had time to take effect. 'Fever-mixture' is therefore the order of the day. Teach them *karma* if you like, but leave aside the head and tail of the fish. I tell people not to bother with the long ritual of *sandhyā*, but to repeat only the short *Gāyatrī*.[3] You are welcome to talk of work to such people if you must."

Effect of Lectures on Worldly Men

"Give thousand of lectures, you cannot do anything with the worldly men. Can you drive a nail into a stone wall? The head will be broken without making any impression on the wall. Strike the back of an alligator with a sword, it will receive no impression. The mendicant's bowl (of gourd-shell) may have been to the four great holy places of India but still be as bitter as ever. But you will learn this truth gradually. A calf cannot stand on its legs all at once. It falls down, gets up, falls again, and then it learns to stand and run. You do not know who is a *bhakta* (godly) and who is worldly; but that is not your fault. When a heavy storm blows, one cannot distinguish tamarind from mango tree.

"It is true, however, that no one can absolutely renounce all works without realizing God. The question is, how long should *sandhyā* (rituals) and other ceremonial works be practiced? So long as the holy name of the Lord does not bring tears of love to the eyes and produce horripilation in the body. When you are uttering '*Om Rāma*,' if tears of love come to your eyes, you will know for certain that the term of your *karma* (works and duties) is over. You are no longer obliged to perform *sandhyā* and other works.

3 *Gāyatrī* is the most sacred and the most universally used of all Vedic prayers among the Hindus. It is a Sanskrit *mantram* or formula which means: "Let us meditate on that glorious self-effulgent light of the Divine Sun; may He enlighten our *buddhi* or understanding." This is still the daily prayer of all the Hindus of the upper three castes.

You have risen above *karma*. When the fruit appears, the blossom drops off. The true *bhakti* is the fruit, while work is the blossom.

"When the daughter-in-law of the house is with child, she cannot do much work; so the mother-in-law daily reduces the number of her duties. As the time of her delivery draws near, the mother-in-law seldom allows her to do anything; and when the child is born, she fondles and caresses it and ceases altogether to work."

All Rituals and Samādhi

"*Sandhyā* merges into *Gāyatrī*; *Gāyatrī* into *Om*, and *Om* ultimately loses itself in *samādhi*. As the sound of a bell—ding, dong—gradually fades away into the infinite, so the soul of a *yogī* gradually rises with the *nāda* (the sound of *Om*) and becomes merged in the Absolute *Brahman* in *samādhi*. Into this *samādhi* eventually enter all *karma*—*sandhyā*, *Gāyatrī*, and other works. In this manner the *jnānis* are freed from all rituals and religious exercises."

As the Bhagavān was talking of *samādhi*, a strange heavenly expression came over his sweet, radiant face. He lost all outward consciousness. After remaining speechless in this state for some time, he came down and like a child said, "Give me a little water." This call for water was the usual sign of his return to the plane of sense-consciousness. Then he murmured: "O Mother! The other day Thou didst show me Vidyāsāgara. Then I desired to see another *pandit* and Thou hast brought me here."

The Necessity of Practice

Then turning to Shashadhar, the Bhagavān said: "My son, add to your spiritual strength, go through devotional exercises a little longer. You have hardly got up into the tree, how can you expect to lay your hand upon its fruits? But you are doing all this for the good of others." Saying this the Bhagavān bowed to Shashadhar and continued: "When I first heard your name, I inquired whether this *pandit* was merely an ordinary *pandit* or one who had attained right discrimination (*viveka*) and dispassion (*vairāgya*). He is not a true *pandit* who does not possess right discrimination."

The Divinely-Commissioned Teacher

"If there has been a commission (*ādesha*) from the Supreme, then there is no harm in teaching others. Such a divinely-commissioned teacher is invincible. No one can defeat him. If one single ray from the Goddess of Wisdom falls upon a man, it brings him such power that before him the greatest *pandits* become like worms of the earth. When a lamp is lighted, swarms of moths rush towards it without waiting to be called. So he who has received a divine commission, for him there is no need to seek followers or make known the time of his lectures. His own power of attraction is so great that people of their own accord crowd around him. Then kings and nobles flock to him saying: 'We have brought mangoes, sweets, money, jewels, and shawls; of these what will you accept?' To such people I say: 'Take them away, I do not want any of them.'

"Does a magnet ever say to the iron, 'come to me?' No; drawn by the magnet, it goes of itself. Such a man may not be a *pandit*, still do not think for a moment that he lacks in knowledge. Is true wisdom acquired by reading books? There is no end to the wisdom of one who has received a divine commission. That wisdom comes from God, and it is endless. Therefore I ask whether you have received any commission (*ādesha*) from the Lord?"

Hāzrā (to the *pandit*): "Oh! I dare say he must have received something of that kind. Is it not so?"

Shashadhar's host: "He has not obtained *ādesha*, but he is lecturing only from a sense of duty."

Bhagavān: "If a man has received no divine commission, what good will his lectures do? A true teacher of mankind must possess great spiritual power (*Shakti*). In Calcutta there are many veteran wrestlers. One must try one's strength on such men and not on novices in wrestling. Chaitanya Deva was an *Avatāra*. Tell me how much of that which even he did is now preserved? What good will be done by the lectures of one who does not hold the badge of divine authority? Therefore I say: 'You must be absorbed in the holy feet of the Almighty.'"

Different Paths to God

"There are infinite ways which lead to the sea of immortality. The main thing is to fall into that sea; it matters not how one gets there.

Suppose there is a reservoir of nectar, a single drop of which falling into the mouth will make one immortal. You may drink of it either by jumping into the reservoir or by slowly walking down along its slope. The result will be the same even if you are pushed or thrown into it by another. Taste of that nectar and become immortal.

"Innumerable are the paths. *Jnāna*, *karma*, *bhakti* are all paths which lead to the same goal. If you have intense longing you will surely reach God. *Yoga* (communion with God) is of four kinds: *jnāna yoga*, *karma yoga*, *rājā yoga*, and *bhakti yoga*."

Jnāna Yoga

"*Jnāna yoga* is communion with God by means of right discrimination and knowledge in its highest sense. The object of a *jnāni* is to know and realize the Absolute. He discriminates between the Absolute Reality and the unreal phenomena by saying: 'Not this,' 'Not this,' until he comes to a point where all discrimination between the Real and the unreal ceases and the Absolute *Brahman* is realized in *samādhi*."

Karma Yoga

"*Karma yoga* is communion with God by means of work. It is what you are teaching. The performance of duties by householders, not for the sake of obtaining their result but for glorifying the Supreme, is that which is meant by this method of *yoga*. Again, worship, repetition of the name of the Lord, and other devotional exercises are also included in it, if they are done without attachment to their fruits but for the glorification of God. The end of *karma yoga* is the same as the realization of the Impersonal Absolute or the Personal God or both."

Rājā Yoga

"*Rājā yoga* leads to this communion through concentration and meditation. It has eight steps. The first is *yama*, which consists in non-injuring, truthfulness, non-covetousness, chastity, and the non-receiving of gifts. The second is *niyama*, which includes austerities, forbearance, contentment, faith in the Supreme Being, charity, study, and self-surrender to the Supreme Will. The practice of various physical postures is comprised in *āsana*, the third; while *prānāyāma* or breathing exercises constitutes the fourth step. The fifth is *pratyāhāra* and consists in making the mind introspective and one-pointed. Concentration or *dhāranā* is the next; *dhyāna* or meditation is the seventh; and *samādhi* or the state of superconsciousness the eighth."

Bhakti Yoga

"*Bhakti yoga* is communion by means of love, devotion, and self-surrender (*bhakti*). It is especially adapted to this age. The path of absolute knowledge is exceedingly difficult. The term of human life at the present day is short and entirely dependent on material food. Moreover, it is almost impossible to get rid of the idea that the soul is one with the body. Now, a *jnāni* or philosopher may declare: 'I am not this body, gross or subtle; I am one with *Brahman*, the Absolute. I am not subject to the necessities and conditions of the body—hunger, thirst, birth, death, disease, grief, pleasure, pain.' Such assertions, however, will not make him free from these bodily conditions so long as he is on the plane of relativity. He may be compared to a person who is suffering from the intense pain of a wound but who is trying to deny it by mere words of mouth.

"When the *kundalinī* is awakened, true *bhakti*, divine love and ecstasy are attained. Through *karma yoga* one can easily attain to various psychic powers. But when *karma yoga* leads to *bhakti yoga*, divine realization comes. Then all duties, rituals, ceremonials, drop off like the petals of a flower when the fruit has grown. When a child is born, the young mother does not discharge any other duties, but fondles the child the whole day. As she is free from all household duties, so a *bhakta* becomes free from the bondage of work after realizing God. The true *bhakta* says: 'O Mother, *karma* with attachment I fear, for it proceeds from selfish motives, and as a man soweth so shall he reap. I see again that work without attachment is exceedingly difficult. If I work through attachment I shall forget Thee; therefore I do not desire such *karma*. Grant that my work may become less and less so long as I do not attain to Thee. Till then may I have strength to do unattached the little work that is left for me, and may I be blessed with unselfish love and devotion to Thee! Mother, so long as I do not realize Thee may my mind be not attached to new works and new desires! But when

Thou wilt command me to work I shall do it not for myself but only for Thee.'"

A devotee: "Revered sir, what is *hatha yoga*?"

Hatha Yoga

Rāmakrishna: "*Hatha yoga* deals entirely with the physical body. It describes the methods by which the internal organs can be purified and perfect health can be acquired. It teaches how to conquer the various powers of *prāna* and the muscles, organs, and nerves of the body. But in *hatha yoga* the mind must always be concentrated on the physical body. A *hatha yogī* possesses many powers, such as the power of levitation; but all these powers are only the manifestations of physical *prāna*. So the practice of *hatha yoga* will bring one control over the body, but it will carry one only so far. *Rājā yoga*, on the contrary, deals with the mind and leads to spiritual results through discrimination, concentration, and meditation."

Concentration

"Perfect concentration of the mind is necessary in the path of *rājā yoga*. The mind is like the flame of a lamp. When the wind of desire blows, it is restless; when there is no wind, it is steady. The latter is the state of the mind in *yoga*. Ordinarily the mind is scattered, one portion here, another portion there. It is necessary to collect the scattered mind and direct it towards one point. If you want a whole piece of cloth, you will have to pay the full price for it. *Yoga* is not possible if there be the least obstacle in the way. If there be a small break in the telegraphic wire, the message will not reach its destination. A *yogī* controls his mind, the mind does not control him. When the mind is absolutely concentrated, the breath stops, and the soul enters into *samādhi*."

Meditation

"At the time of true meditation the body and senses become absolutely still like a piece of wood. When I first saw Keshab Sen in the Ādi (original) Brāhmo Samāj, I saw him sitting in meditation with other members; his mind was entirely withdrawn from the external world and his body was perfectly motionless like a wooden stump; then I said to Mathur Bābu: 'This man has hooked the fish.'

Meditation is possible even with eyes wide open, even when one is conversing with another. Suppose you have a toothache. You may perform all works, but your mind will remain concentrated on the spot where the pain is. Similarly, if you have true concentration on God, your mind will remain fixed even when your body is moving or your mouth is speaking. I used to close my eyes at the time of meditation. Then I thought: 'If God exists after closing the eyes, why should He not exist while the eyes are open?' I opened my eyes and saw the Divine Being everywhere. Man, animals, insects, trees, creepers, moon, sun, water, earth, in and through all these the Infinite Being is manifesting Himself. He who thinks upon God for a long time possesses divine substance within him. Through him flow divine powers. A great singer, or one who is perfect in instrumental music or in any other art or science, also possesses a portion of divine power. This is the doctrine of the *Bhagavad Gītā*—'Wherever there are signs of greatness, there is the manifestation of divine power.'"

A devotee: "Revered sir, what happens after death?"

What Happens After Death

Rāmakrishna: "Keshab Sen asked me the same question. So long as a man remains in ignorance, in other words, so long as he has not realized God, he will be subject to rebirth; but after divine realization one does not come back to this earth, nor is he born in any other world. Potters after making earthen pots dry them in the sun. Have you not seen that there are pots which are baked in fire and others that are unbaked? When a pot of unbaked clay is broken, the potter uses the same clay to make a new pot; but if a baked pot is broken, the pieces are of no further use and he throws them away. Similarly, when the ego is not baked in the fire of wisdom, after death it will appear in another form and be born again and again. If a fried grain is planted, it will not germinate; in the same manner, he whose inner nature is fried in the fire of wisdom is no longer subject to evolution, but attains to absolute freedom from rebirth."

Dualistic and Monistic Vedānta

"In the *Purānas* the doctrine of dualistic *Vedānta* prevails, which teaches that the *jīva* is one thing and God is another: 'I am distinct and separate from you.' This body is like a bowl; mind, intellect, and egoism are like water within it, while the Personal God is the sun which is reflected in the water; and this reflection or image of the Divine Being can be perceived by the *jīva* in ecstasy. In monistic *Vedānta*, however, *Brahman*, the Absolute, is the Reality and all else is unreal like a dream. Egoism is like a stick which lies upon the waters of the infinite ocean of Existence-Intelligence-Bliss Absolute, and makes it appear as divided; but when the stick is removed, the apparent division ceases and the waters of the ocean remain undivided. The knowledge of this indivisible oneness brings the highest state of *samādhi*, where this egoism is entirely obliterated. But the great spiritual teachers like Shankarāchārya kept a little egoism of knowledge to teach mankind."

The Signs of a True Jnāni

"A true *jnāni*, or knower of the Absolute, may be recognized by certain signs. A real *jnāni* does harm to no one. His nature becomes like that of an innocent child. As a burnt rope retains its shape and appears from a distance like a real rope, but in truth a breath can blow it away, so the egoism of a *jnāni* is merely apparent. A child has no attachment for anything. It may build a toy house; if anyone touches it, it cries; but the next moment the child will itself break it to pieces. So a true *jnāni* lives in the world, but unattached. He may possess things of great value, but he has no attachment for them. In monistic *Vedānta* the waking state is no more real than the dream state. A woodcutter was dreaming a happy dream, but being suddenly awakened by someone, he explained with annoyance: 'Why did you awaken me? I was a king and the father of seven children. My children were all receiving education in the various sciences. I was seated on the throne and ruling over my country. Why did you destroy so happy and delightful a state?' The man replied: 'Oh! It was only a dream. What does it matter?' The woodcutter said: 'Get away, you fool! You do not understand that my being a king was as real as my woodcutting. If it be true that I am a woodcutter, then it is equally true that I was a king.'"

Jnāna and Vijnāna

"*Jnāna* is to know the *Ātman* through the path of discrimination: 'Not this, not this.' When this discrimination leads to *samādhi*, then the *Ātman* can be apprehended. But *vijnāna* is complete knowledge or realization. Some have heard of milk, some have seen it, but others have tasted it. So with God. Those who have heard of Him are still in ignorance; those who have seen Him are *jnānis*; but those who have tasted or realized Him are *vijnānis*. After seeing God, when one makes acquaintance with Him and realizes Him as the nearest and dearest of all, that is *vijnāna*. At first it is necessary to discriminate 'Not this, not this,' that is, God is not the elements of nature, He is not the senses or sense-powers, He is not this mind, not this intellect, not this egoism; He is beyond all the categories of nature. To go to the roof, one must climb step by step, leaving one step after another. The staircase is not the same as the roof. After coming out on the roof, however, one can easily see that both roof and staircase are of the same material. The same Infinite *Brahman* appears as the Personal God, *jīva*, and the twenty-four categories of nature. You may ask why this earth is so hard and solid, if it has come out of *Brahman*? His omnipotence can make everything possible."

Rāmakrishna (to old Gopāl, Swāmī Advaitānanda): "What! Do you still wish to visit holy places?"

Gopāl: "Yes Bhagavan, I would like to travel a little more."

Parable of the Bird on the Mast

Rām Bābu (to Gopāl): "The Bhagavān says, after traveling to many places one should settle down in one spot. This he explains by the parable of the bird on a ship's mast. A bird was sitting on the mast of a vessel as it sailed out to sea. After a long time the bird realized that there were no trees around or land in sight. He flew towards the north to find land, but being disappointed, he returned to the mast, rested a while and flew towards the south. Still finding no shore, he came back again, tired and exhausted. In the same manner he went in all directions, but finding nothing but water and water everywhere, he at last rested on the mast and became content."

Parable of a Man Seeking a Light

Rāmakrishna: "So long as God seems to be outside, in different places, so long there is ignorance. But when God is realized within, that is true knowledge. A man woke up at midnight and desired to smoke. He wanted a light, so he went to a neighbor's house and knocked at the door. Someone opened the door and asked him what he wanted. The man said: 'I wish to smoke. Can you give me a light?' The neighbor replied: 'What is the matter with you? You have taken so much trouble and awakened us at this hour, when in your hand you have a lighted lantern.' What a man wants is already with him; but he still wanders here and there in search of it."

Rām Bābu: "Bhagavan, now I have understood why a *guru* asks his disciple to visit holy places—to give him experience and to increase his faith in his teachings."

Pandit: "Revered sir, how far did your holiness go on pilgrimages?"

Pilgrimages

Rāmakrishna (smiling): "Well, I went to some places. Hāzrā went farther and higher up, to Hrishīkesha[4] in the Himālayas. I did not go so far or so high up. The vulture and the kite soar very high, but their eyes are all the while directed to the charnel-pits below. Do you not know what the charnel-pits are? Lust and gold. If in going on a pilgrimage a man does not acquire *bhakti*, then his pilgrimage is fruitless; for *bhakti* is the end of all; it is the one thing needful.

"Do you know what the vulture and the kite are? They are those who talk on lofty subjects and say: 'We have performed most of the works enjoined in the holy scriptures,' but whose minds are immersed in worldliness and strongly attached to wealth, name, fame, and sense-pleasures."

Pandit: "Yes, revered sir, that is true. Going on a pilgrimage is like casting aside the precious stone worn on the breast of Vishnu and wandering about in search of other jewels."

4 Hrishīkesha is a sacred place of pilgrimage on the banks of the holy river Ganges at the foot of the Himālayas.

Rāmakrishna: "Again, you should know that although you may give thousands of instructions, still they will not produce results until the time is ripe. A child before going to sleep says to its mother: 'Mamma dear, awaken me when I shall feel hungry.' The mother replies: 'Do not worry about that, my child; thy hunger will awaken thee.' In the same manner one yearns after God when the proper time comes for it."

Grace of God

The conversation then passed to another subject—the grace of God. The Bhagavān said: "Once a number of Sikh soldiers came to the temple. I met them before the temple of the Divine Mother. One of them said: 'God is all-merciful.' I asked: 'Indeed, is it so? How did you come to know this?' 'Why, sir, is not the Lord feeding and taking care of us?' I said: 'Is that so extraordinary? God is the father of us all. If the father does not look after his own children, who will? Shall outsiders from another neighborhood come and take care of them?'"

Narendra: "Then we should not call Him merciful?"

Bhagavān: "Am I forbidding you to call Him all-merciful? What I mean is that the Lord is our nearest and dearest and not like a stranger."

Pandit: "Priceless are these words!"

The Bhagavān here asked for a fresh glass of water. He would not take the one already offered and it was therefore carried away. It appeared that he looked upon it as unfit to be offered to the God in him, being made impure by the "feverish" touch of some wicked men.

Pandit (to Hāzrā): "You who live with the Bhagavān day and night must enjoy the highest Bliss."

Bhagavān (smiling): "This day I have had the rare pleasure of looking at the moon of the second lunar day. Do you know why I say the moon of the second lunar day? Sītā said to Rāvana:[5] 'Thou art the full moon, and my Rāmachandra is the moon of the second

5 Sītā is the faithful and devoted wife of Lord Rāmachandra, who is regarded as an Incarnation of God. She was stolen by Rāvana, King of Ceylon, who brought her to his capital, Lankā. Hence the war described in the epic *Rāmāyana*, which ended with the destruction of Rāvana and many of his people.

lunar day.' Rāvana was highly pleased, for he did not understand the meaning. Sītā meant to say that the fortune of Rāvana had reached its climax like the full moon and that now it must be on the wane; but the fortune of Rāmachandra is like the moon of the second lunar day, which will increase day by day."

Here the Bhagavān rose to take leave. The *pandit* and his friends bowed down before him with great reverence and devotion. He then departed, followed by his disciples.

Chapter 10

Gathering of Disciples at the Temple

Shrī Rāmakrishna was seated on his seat as usual with his face to the north. The western and northern doors of the apartment in which he latterly passed his days looked out on the sacred waters of the Ganges. Balarām, Rākhāl, and other devotees and visitors were seated on a mat spread out on the floor of the room. They were singing hymns to the accompaniment of musical instruments. One of the songs had particular reference to the six lotuses marking different stages of the *yogī*'s progress towards union with the Universal Spirit. At the close of this song the Bhagavān said:

Seven Mental Planes

"The six lotuses, mentioned in the science of *yoga*, correspond to the seven mental planes mentioned in the *Vedānta*. When the mind is immersed in worldliness, it makes its abode in the lowest lotus at the end of the spine. Sexual desires rise when the mind is in the second lotus, the sexual organ. When it is in the third, the navel, the man is taken up with the things of the world—eating, drinking, begetting children. In the fourth mental plane the heart of the man is blessed with the vision of divine glory and he cries out: 'What is all this! What is all this!' In the fifth plane the mind rests in the throat. The devotee talks only on subjects related to God and grows impatient if any other subject comes up in the course of conversation. In the sixth plane the mind is localized between the eyebrows. The devotee comes face to face with God; only a thin glass-like partition, so to speak, keeps him separate from the Divine Person. To him God is like a light within a lantern, or like a photograph behind a glass frame. He tries to touch the object of his vision, but he cannot. His perception falls short of complete realization, for there is the element of self-consciousness, the sense of 'I,' kept to a certain extent. In the last or seventh plane it is in perfect *samādhi*. Then all sense-consciousness ceases and absolute God-consciousness takes its place."

Sages Who Have Reached the Seventh Plane

The Bhagavān continued: "Some sages, who have reached the seventh or highest plane and have thus attained to God-consciousness, are pleased to come down from that spiritual height for the good of mankind. They keep the ego of *vidyā*, or, in other words, the higher Self. But this ego is a mere appearance. It is like a line drawn across a sheet of water. Hanumān was blessed with the vision of God both with form and without form; but he retained the ego of a servant of God. Such was also the case with the wise men Nārada, Sanaka, Sananda, and Sanat Kumāra[1] of ancient times."

Here the question was asked whether Nārada and others were *bhaktas* only and not *jnānis*. The Bhagavān replied: "Nārada and others had attained the highest knowledge (*Brahma jnāna*), but still they went on like the murmuring water of the rivulet, talking and singing. This shows that they too kept this ego of knowledge. They were *jnānis* (knowers), but they talked and sang the praises of the Personal God for the good of others. A steamboat not only reaches its destination itself but also carries numbers of people on board to the same place. Preceptors such as Nārada are like steamboats."

Avatāras

"The *Avatāras* or Incarnations of God are born with divine powers and divine qualities. They can go anywhere and can stay in any state of existence from the highest to the lowest. They can stand on the top of the house and come down by the stairs to the ground floor and can go back to the roof again. They possess the power both to come down and to return. In a seven-story palace a stranger can go only to the outer quarters, but the king's own child, the prince of the house, is free to go to every corner."

Avatāras and Ordinary Jīvas

"As in fireworks there is a kind of flower-pot which sends off one kind of flower for a while, then another kind and still another, possessing, as it were, an innumerable variety of flowers, so are the

1 For Nārada, see note 3, p. 15. Sanaka, Sananda, and Sanat Kumāra were the three *rishis* or seers of Truth in ancient India.

Avatāras. Then there is another kind of flower-pot which when lighted, burns a little and then goes off all at once. Similarly ordinary *jīvas*, after long practice and devotional exercises, go up at once in *samādhi* and do not return."

Souls Eternally Free

"There is another class who may be called eternally free. From their birth they seek after God and do not care for anything of the world. We are told of a fabled species of bird called '*homā*,' which live so high up in the heavens, and so dearly love those regions, that they never condescend to come down to the earth. Even their eggs, which when laid in the sky begin to fall to the earth by the force of gravity, are said to be hatched during their downward course, and the fledglings, finding that they are falling down, at once change their course and begin to fly upwards towards their home, drawn thither by instinct. Men such as Shukadeva, Nārada, Jesus, Shankarāchārya and others are like those birds, who even in their boyhood give up all attachment to the things of this world and betake themselves to the highest regions of true knowledge and divine light. Those who come with the *Avatāras* are either souls who are eternally free or who are born for the last time."

Two Classes of Paramahamsas

"The holy men (*paramahamsas*) may be divided into two classes. First, those who declare the Supreme Being to be the Formless One. Generally speaking, holy men of this class are comparatively selfish, because they care only for the liberation of their own souls. Those of the second class say that God is with form as well as formless, and that He manifests Himself to His devotees as a Being with form. Have you ever seen a canal running over into the water of the river with which it is connected? The canal has sometimes no trace left, being entirely one with the river-water. But very often there may be noticed a slight movement in the water which proves its separateness from the river. Almost the same is the case with the *paramahamsa* belonging to the second class. His soul becomes one with the Universal Spirit. Still the ego of knowledge (*vidyā*) or a slight trace of individuality is kept to mark his separate existence from the Deity."

Ego of Knowledge

"Again, such a holy man may be compared to a jar or pitcher of water. A pitcher filled with water to the brim gives sound only when a portion of the water is poured out into another vessel. Similarly the *paramahamsa* keeps silent except when his water of wisdom is poured out into the soul of the disciple. Thus he retains the ego of knowledge for the purpose of teaching others.

"Again, suppose a person digs a well. He is thirsty and drinks the water of that well. Yet when his thirst is quenched it is not unusual for such a person to keep the digging implements—the hack, the shovel, the spade—for the sake of others who may want them for the same purpose. In the same way a *paramahamsa* of the second class, who may have drunk the waters of everlasting life and have thus quenched his spiritual thirst, is often anxious to do good to mankind. With this in view he retains the ego of knowledge, the ego of love, and the ego of the preceptor."

Divine Communion

"Communion with God may be compared to the process of involution. When one communes with the Supreme Being one's personality becomes absolutely united with the Divine Personality. This is the state of *samādhi*. Then, again, when one returns to the human plane and comes back to the starting-point one sees that the world and the ego or self are evolved from the same Supreme Being; and that God, man, and nature are interrelated, so that if you hold on to one of them you realize the others."

Fire of Bhakti Destroys Sins

"Call with *bhakti* (love) upon His hallowed name and the mountain of your sins shall disappear as a mountain of cotton-wool will vanish if it catches one spark of fire. Worship through fear of hell-fire is intended for beginners."

Then turning to some of the company present who were singing, the Bhagavān said: "Will you sing songs which describe the enjoyment that is realized by the human soul after God-vision? Rākhāl (Swāmī Brahmānanda, one of his young disciples), do you remember the song the other day at Nabin Neogi's house, 'Be intoxicated with the joy of the Lord'?"

One of the company then said: "Revered sir, may we be favored with a song from thee?"

Bhagavān: "What shall I sing? I sing pretty much like yourselves. Very well; when the time comes, I will sing." So saying, he remained silent for a while. The first song that he then sang was about Shrī Chaitanya Deva and Shrī Krishna, that is, from the point of view of the Vaishnavas (dualistic *bhaktas*). The last was regarding the Divine Mother.

The Devotee and Her Ecstatic Love

1. The waves of the divine love come dashing against my body. The swell of the sea of love causes the fall of the unrighteous; nay, it drowns the whole universe.

2. I think of diving deep near the bottom of the sea, but the alligator of ecstasy has swallowed me up. Who is there to feel for me and, holding me by the hand, drag me out of the water?

The Mother of the Universe, and the Machine of the Human Body

1. What a fine machine of the human body hath the Divine Mother made!
How wonderful are the sports She is playing through the machine only six feet long!

2. Dwelling within the machine, She holds in Her hand the string that sets it in motion; but the machine thinks: "I move by my own will," not knowing who causes it to move.

3. The "machine" that has realized Her will not have to be born again. She Herself is tied in some machines by the string of *bhakti* (love).

At the end of the song the Bhagavān was in *samādhi*. His eyes were fixed and half-closed. His pulse and the heart-beat were suspended. Sense-consciousness had left him, giving place to pure God-consciousness. Returning a little to the semi-conscious state he talked to the Holy Mother, saying: "Do not trouble, O Mother! Come down to this plane. Be still, O Mother! What Thou wishest, O Mother, for everybody shall come to pass. What shall I say to these people?"

Discrimination and Renunciation

"Nothing can be achieved in the path of spirituality without discrimination (between the Real and the unreal) and renunciation (non-attachment to riches, honor, sensual pleasures). Renunciation is of many kinds. One kind springs from the acute pain due to worldly misery. But the better kind of renunciation arises from the realization that all worldly blessings are unreal even when they are within reach. Thus, having all, the man renounces everything for the sake of God."

Time Necessary for Religious Awakening

"Everything rests upon time. For all religious awakening we must wait. But in the meanwhile the precepts of a *guru*, the spiritual teacher, should be carefully followed, for the impression of these precepts in the mind of a worldly man may be of great help in time of need. Another reason is that constant hearing of those precepts may gradually remove the evil effects of worldly attachment. As the effects of drunkenness can be removed by making the drunkard drink rice-water, so the intoxication of the worldly-minded people can be cured by the constant hearing of the precepts of a holy *guru*. The number of those who attain divine wisdom is very limited. So the *Gītā* says: 'Among thousands a few only strive for the realization of God, and among thousands of such seekers after Truth a few succeed in reaching the goal.'"

Three States of Consciousness in Ecstasy

"Chaitanya Deva was the incarnation of divine love or *bhakti*. He came to teach mankind true *bhakti*. He used to have three states of consciousness in ecstasy. First, consciousness of the gross and subtle body. At this time he would repeat the name of the Lord and sing His praises in *sankīrtan*. Second, consciousness of the causal body alone. In this state he would become intoxicated with ecstatic joy, and retaining partial consciousness of the external, he would dance in company with other *bhaktas*. Third, consciousness of the Absolute. In this state he would enter into the highest realm of *samādhi*, and rising above all sense-consciousness, his body would remain apparently lifeless. These states correspond to the five sheaths of the soul in *Vedānta*. According to *Vedānta*, the gross body includes the material form which is the outermost sheath and the sheath of *prāna* or the sense-organs and sense-powers. The subtle body includes two sheaths, mental and intellectual. The causal body is the sheath of joyfulness. Beyond these five is the true Self, the Absolute. When the mind reaches this state, the highest *samādhi* or God-consciousness is the result."

How to Pray

"How to pray is the next question. Let us not pray for things of this world, but pray like Nārada. Nārada said to Rāmachandra: 'O Rāma, grant that I may be favored with *bhakti*, love, devotion, and self-surrender to Thy lotus feet.' 'Be it so,' said Rāma. 'But wilt thou not ask for anything else?' Nārada replied: 'Lord, may it please Thee to grant that I may not be attracted by Thy *māyā*, which fascinates the creatures of this world.' Rāmachandra said once more: 'Be it so, Nārada; but wilt thou not ask for something else?' Nārada replied: 'No, Lord, that is all I pray for.'"

Degrees of Knowledge

"*Jnāna* (knowledge) varies in degrees and kind. There is first the knowledge belonging to men of the world—ordinary mortals. This knowledge is not sufficiently powerful. It may be compared to the light of a lamp which illuminates only the inside of a room. The knowledge of a *bhakta* (devotee) is a stronger light and may be compared to the light of the moon which causes to be visible things outside the room as well as those inside of it. But the *jnāna* of an Incarnation of God is still more powerful and it may be likened to a yet stronger light—the resplendent glory of the sun. Such light is the illuminator of the moon as well as of the whole world. Nothing is problematic to the Divine Incarnation (*Avatāra*). He solves the most difficult problems of life and soul as the simplest things in the world. His exposition of the most intricate questions in which humanity is interested is such as a child can follow. He is the sun of divine knowledge whose light dispels the accumulated ignorance of ages."

Spiritual Knowledge and the Worldly People

"So long as a man is immersed in worldliness he cannot attain to knowledge divine and cannot see God. Does muddy water ever reflect the sun or any surrounding object? Spiritual knowledge is occasionally visible in worldly people, but very seldom. It does not last long. It is like the light of a lamp. No, no, it is like a ray of the sun—as if a ray were coming through a very small hole in the wall. Worldly people repeat the holy name of the Lord, but there is no longing in the heart. They have no persistence. Whether they attain God or not, they do not care. They are bound by *karma* and must reap the results of their works. Is there no remedy for this state, or no hope for the worldly man? Yes, there is. Drop a purifying agent, say a piece of alum, into muddy water; the water is purified and the impurities settle down at the bottom of the vessel. Discrimination of the Real from the unreal phenomenal universe and non-attachment to the world are the two purifying agents. Thus it is that the worldly man ceases to be worldly and becomes pure.

"Worldly people have the knowledge of diversity, which is the same as ignorance. But true knowledge makes one realize the unity of existence. 'This is gold, that is brass' is ignorance, while 'all is gold' is true knowledge. All differentiation ceases, when true knowledge comes."

Shankara and the Pariah

"Shankara[2] was a great *jnāni*. He had true Self-knowledge; he realized one *Brahman* everywhere and in all beings. He recognized no distinction in caste or creed. At one time, however, he had the consciousness of difference; he would differentiate a *pariah* from a high-caste *brāhmin* or a sage. He would not touch a *pariah* after bathing in the sacred river Ganges. One day a *pariah* was carrying animal flesh along the river bank as Shankara was coming from his bath and the *pariah* ran against him. Shankara exclaimed: 'Sirrah, how darest thou touch me?' The *pariah* replied: 'Neither hast thou

2 Shankara, same as Shankarāchārya.

touched me nor have I touched thee. The *Ātman* is pure. It is neither body nor the elements of the body. It is far above the twenty-four categories of the universe. Thou art the real *Ātman*: so am I. How can I touch thee?' Shankara bowed down before the *pariah* and lo! the *pariah* transfigured himself into Shiva, the Lord of Wisdom. At that moment Shankara's spiritual eyes were open and he realized the absolute oneness of the *Ātman*. 'I am pure and spotless *Ātman*, eternally free': this is the nature of true Self-knowledge."

Spiritual Practices

"Spiritual practices (*sādhana*) are absolutely necessary for Self-knowledge; but if there be perfect faith, then a little practice will be enough. One must have faith in the words of the *guru* or spiritual master. Vyāsa[3] was about to cross the river Yamunā when the *gopīs* (shepherdesses) arrived. They also wished to go across, but there was no ferry-boat. They asked Vyāsa, 'Lord, what shall we do?' Vyāsa replied: 'Do not worry, I will get you across the river; but I am very hungry. Can you give me something to eat?' The *gopīs* had with them a quantity of milk, cream, and fresh butter. He consumed them all. The *gopīs* then asked: 'What about crossing the river?' Vyāsa stood near the edge of the water and prayed: 'O Yamunā! as I have not eaten anything today, by that virtue I ask thee to divide the water, so that we can walk across thy bed and reach the other side.' No sooner did he utter these words than the water parted and the dry bed was laid bare. The *gopīs* were amazed. They thought: 'How could he say, "as I have not eaten anything today," when just now he has eaten so much?' They did not see that this was a proof of firm faith; that Vyāsa had the faith that he did not eat anything, but that the Lord who dwelt within him was the real Eater."

Stages of Spiritual Practice

"The first stage of spiritual practice is association with spiritual people, the company of holy men. The second stage is faith in things relating to the Spirit. The third stage is single-minded devotion to one's ideal. The ideal may be one's *guru*, the spiritual teach-

3 The author of the *Vedānta Sutras* and many of the *Purānas*.

er, the Impersonal *Brahman*, the Personal God or any of His manifestations. The fourth stage is the state of being struck speechless at the thought of God. The fifth stage, when the feeling of devotion to God reaches the highest point; it is called *mahābhāva*. The devotee sometimes laughs, sometimes weeps like a madman. He loses all control over his body. This state is not attained by ordinary human beings who are not capable of conquering the flesh. It is reached by Incarnations of God who appear in this world for the salvation of mankind. In the sixth stage, *prema* or ecstatic love, goes hand in hand with *mahābhāva*. It is the most intense love of God and is strictly the highest state of spirituality. The two marks of this stage are the forgetfulness of this world and the forgetfulness of self, which includes one's own body."

After delivering this sermon, the Bhagavān said to his audience that he would be glad to answer any question. But none asked any, so the Bhagavān continued:

Attainment of Knowledge Gradual

"Knowledge (*jnāna*) cannot be communicated all at once. Its attainment must be gradual. Suppose a fever is of a severe type. The doctor would not give quinine under such circumstances. He knows that such a remedy would do no good. The fever must first leave the patient, which requires time, and then the quinine will take effect. Sometimes the fever will go off without the help of quinine or any other medicine. Precisely the same is the case with the man who seeks for knowledge. To him religious precepts often prove useless so long he is immersed in worldliness. Allow him a certain time for enjoyment of the things of the world, then his attachment to the world will gradually wear off. This is exactly the moment for the success of any religious instructions that may be given to him. Till then all such instructions will be entirely thrown away like pearls before swine. Many come to me and I have observed how some of them are anxious to listen to my words. But others of the company appear to be restless and impatient in my presence. They say to their friends in whispers: 'Let us go, let us go. Well, if you wish to stay, we will go to the boat and wait for you there.' Spiritual awakening is very much a question of time. The teacher is a mere help."

The meeting then broke up.

The Bhagavān left his seat and went out into the veranda next to the western door of his room and for a time looked on the sun which was sinking rapidly towards the horizon. Then he gazed down upon the holy waters of the sacred stream before him. A disciple was walking alone in front of the temple on the embankment of the Ganges. He was watching Balarām and others getting into a boat to return to Calcutta. It being midsummer, the sacred waters of the river were broken into waves. The day was drawing to its close; it was past five, the sky was cloudy, and the clouds presented a most wonderful sight, especially towards the north. In the foreground was the *Panchavati*, backed by a line of tall willow trees, with the silver stream flowing past on their right. In the background were the beautiful dark blue clouds and the dark stream beneath.

The disciple was looking on this charming scene. Suddenly his attention was arrested by the Bhagavān coming from the south in the direction of the *Panchavati* and the willow trees. As Shrī Rāmakrishna, smiling like a child of five, came up, the beautiful picture seemed to be more than complete. There was the universe on one hand, and on the other the One Soul who reflected the universe and saw it in its real nature. Yes, the disciple felt that in that presence he was as near the solution of the problems of life as he could be. It was this presence that made everything—the images of gods and goddesses, men, women, and children, trees, flowers, leaves, every inch of ground in that temple instinct with spirituality and full of the joy of the Lord. Yes, he felt truly that it was the God-man before him that had thrown an irresistible charm over everything in that wonderful place—over every object, divine or human, animate or inanimate. He felt like one spellbound in that presence!

It was evening. After the usual prayers and other religious exercises enjoined on the pious Hindu were over, there was yet another meeting between the Master and the same disciple. The disciple then asked, referring to the apparently contradictory systems of religious faith among the Hindus: "Bhagavan, is this a contradiction: some among the Hindus hold that Shrī Krishna is identical with Kālī, the Divine Mother, while others hold that Shrī Krishna is the *Ātman*, the Absolute, and that Rādha is *Chitshakti*, the Self-Conscious Power that rules the universe, the Creator, Preserver, and Destroyer, the Personal God?"

God is Infinite

Bhagavān: "The former view is that of the *Devī Purāna*. Be it so, but there need be no contradiction. God is infinite. Infinite are the forms in which He manifests Himself. Infinite also are the ways leading to Him."

Disciple: "Oh, I see! The end in view is to get on the roof of the house. The means may be various, as thou hast often said—a single rope, a bamboo, a wooden ladder, or a staircase?"

Bhagavān: "Quite so. That you can understand this so quickly is due to the grace of God. Without His grace doubt is never cleared up. Our attitude towards God should be like that of Hanumān, who said to Rāmachandra: 'Lord, I care not for a special time or place for meditation. What alone I am concerned with is to meditate upon Thee.'"

Love of God the One Thing Needful

"Suppose you go into a garden to eat mangoes. Is it necessary for you first to count the number of trees in the garden, which may be many thousands, then the number of branches, which may be hundreds of thousands? Certainly not; you should at once, on the contrary, proceed to eat. In the same way, it is useless to enter into all sorts of discussions and controversies regarding God, which would only cause a waste of time and energy. One's present and most important duty is to love God, to cultivate *bhakti* or devotion."

Disciple: "Bhagavan, I greatly desire that my work in the world should become a little less than now. The pressure of work stands in the way of giving one's whole mind to God, does it not?"

Bhagavān: "Oh yes, no doubt that is so; but a wise man may work *unattached* and then work will not do any harm to him."

Disciple: "But that depends upon the possession of an extraordinary power of will derived from the realization of God. First realization of God, then work without attachment. Is it not so Bhagavan?"

Power of Desire

Shrī Rāmakrishna: "I must say you are right. But the probability is, you must have desired these things in your previous incarnations. This reminds me of the story narrated in one of the sacred books. It is said that Shrī Krishna had made His abode in the heart of Rādhā: so long there was no *līlā* (the life of sport that He lived in Brindāvan). But He felt the desire to take the form of a human being; the consequence of this desire was that He came to Brindāvan. Such is the power of desire. Your duty now is to pray without ceasing for love of God, so that the bondage of work shall gradually fall off."

Disciple: "Is Pandit Shashadhar making any progress in this direction—in the culture of *bhakti* or devotion?"

Renunciation

Bhagavān: "Yes; but his tendency is in the direction of the path of knowledge. These men belong to a class of their own. They do not see that this way is exceedingly difficult. It is sufficient if one can give up the world in the mind. Outward renunciation is not absolutely necessary."

Disciple: "Yes, Bhagavan, I understand by renunciation not only the absence of attachment to things of this world. It is non-attachment to things of this world *plus* something. That something is the love of God."

State of God-Vision

Bhagavān: "You are right. I am glad that you see this. God-vision cannot be made clear to others. The state of things that comes about may, however, be described to a certain extent. You have no doubt been to the theater to witness a dramatic performance. Before the performance commences, you must have noticed that the people are very busy talking to one another on a variety of subjects—politics, household affairs, official business. But no sooner does the curtain go up and men, mountains, cottages, rivers are presented to view than all noise ceases, all conversation ends, and each individual spectator is all attention to the novel scene that is being enacted before him. Pretty much the same is the state of him who is blessed with God-vision."

Chapter 11

Shrī Rāmakrishna at the Sinthi[1] Brāhmo Samāj

Bhagavān Shrī Rāmakrishna had been asked to attend the anniversary meeting of the Brāhmo Samāj, which that year was held in the beautiful garden-house of a gentleman named Beni Bābu.[2] The morning service was over when the Bhagavān arrived in a carriage with certain of his disciples and took his place on a raised seat set apart for him on the veranda overlooking a large quadrangle. Crowds of devotees, followers, and members of the Brāhmo Samāj gathered round him in a circle. The prayers, music, and other exercises of a devotional nature then continued. On hearing the music, Shrī Rāmakrishna went into *samādhi* and remained motionless for some time. Then regarding his sense-consciousness, he opened his mouth and in rapt tones began to speak thus:

Psychic Powers

"The realization of God is not the same as psychic power. There are many *yoga* powers, but do you remember what Krishna said to Arjuna about them? When you see one who exercises any of these powers, you may know that such a one has not realized God, because the exercise of these powers requires egotism (*ahamkāra*), which is an obstacle in the path of supreme realization."

Danger of Psychic Powers

"There is, indeed, great danger in possessing psychic powers. Nangtā (Totāpurī)[3] thus taught me this truth: A *siddha* (a man

1 Sinthi, a village about four miles north of Calcutta.

2 Beni Bābu was a follower of the Brāhmo Samāj. He regarded Rāmakrishna as the most divine man of the age.

3 Nangtā was the name by which Shrī Rāmakrishna called his spiritual teacher in the *Advaita Vedānta*. The word literally means, "One who does not cover his body with any clothes." Totāpurī was his real name. He was a *sannyāsī* monk of

who had absolute control over psychic phenomena) was sitting on the sea-shore. Suddenly there arose a violent storm, which caused him great distress. Desiring to stop it, he exclaimed: 'Let this storm cease!' His command was instantly fulfilled. A vessel was passing at a distance with all sails set. As the wind suddenly died away, the vessel capsized and all on board were drowned. The *siddha* was the cause of the disaster and therefore he had to take the sin of killing so many innocent people. As the result of this terrible sin, he lost his power and after death he had to suffer in purgatory."

The Siddha and the Elephant

"There was another *siddha*, who was very proud of his psychic powers. He was a good man and an ascetic. One day the Lord came to him in the form of a saint and said: 'Revered sir, I have heard that thou possessest wonderful powers.' The good man received him kindly and gave him a seat. At this moment an elephant passed by. The saint asked him: 'Sir, if thou desirest, canst thou kill this elephant?' The *siddha* replied: 'Yes, it is possible'; and taking a handful of dust he repeated some *mantram* over it and threw it on the elephant. Immediately the animal roared, fell on the ground in agony and died. Seeing this, the saint exclaimed: 'What wonderful power thou possessest! Thou hast killed such a huge creature in a moment!' The saint then entreated him, saying: 'Thou must also possess the power to bring him back to life.' The *siddha* replied: 'Yes, that is also possible.' Again he took a handful of dust, chanted a *mantram*, threw it on the elephant, and lo! the elephant revived and came back to life. The saint was amazed at the sight and again exclaimed: 'How wonderful indeed are thy powers! But let me ask thee one question. Thou hast killed the elephant and brought him back to life; what hast thou gained? Hast thou realized God?' Thus saying, the saint disappeared."

Desire for Powers Prevents Realization

"Most subtle is the path of spirituality. God cannot be realized so long as there is the least desire for powers in the heart. You cannot thread a needle so long as there are fibers at the point of the thread.

Shankara's school and was a great *Vedānta* scholar.

Krishna said to Arjuna: 'Brother, if thou wishest to realize me (God), thou must not desire any psychic powers. The possession of psychic powers brings pride and egotism, then one easily forgets God. So long as there is egotism, divine realization does not come.'"

Four Stages of Realization

"There are four different stages in the path of realization. First, that of a beginner, a *pravartaka*, or one who has just begun to worship God. Those who belong to this class begin to wear the sign of their creed, such as the rosary or the mark on the forehead; and they are very particular about the external forms of their sect. The second stage is that of a neophyte or a *sādhaka*. Those of this class are farther advanced. They do not parade their beliefs and do not attach so much importance to external signs. Their worship is internal. They repeat the Lord's name silently, pray without ostentation and feel some longing for God. The third stage is that of a *siddha*. What is a *siddha*? One who is firmly convinced in his heart and soul that God exists, that He does everything, that He is the Omnipotent Being, and who has obtained a first glimpse of Him. The fourth stage is that of a *siddha* of *siddhas*. One who has reached this stage has not only seen God but has made acquaintance with Him and has established a definite relation with Him—either that of a son to his father or that of a mother to her child, or that of a friend to a friend or of a brother to a brother, or the relation of husband and wife."

Faith and Realization

"To believe that fire is in the wood is faith. This is one thing, but it is another thing to bring that fire out of the wood, to cook something with it, to eat this and to attain peace and happiness afterwards. So to believe that God is in the world and to catch a distant glimpse of Him is one thing; but to come into direct communion with Him, to enjoy His company and taste divine bliss is another. No one can set a limit to the various aspects of God which a *bhakta* can realize. They rise ever higher and higher."

A devotee: "Bhagavan, why can some attain realization more quickly than others?"

Sudden Conversion

Rāmakrishna: "It depends upon the *samskāras* or impressions of previous lives. Nothing happens suddenly or by accident. A certain man drank an ounce of wine in the morning and began to act like a drunkard. People, seeing him, wondered why he should be drunk after taking one small glass of wine. Hearing them, however, another man replied: 'Because he has been drinking all night.' There have been many instances of sudden conversion. People living in the midst of wealth and luxury have suddenly renounced the world. Such sudden changes are the results of spiritual impressions acquired in the previous life. In the final incarnation of a *jīva*, *sattva* qualities prevail: his heart and soul long for realization, the mind becomes unattached to worldly pleasures and constantly remains fixed upon the supreme Being."

Firmness of Faith Necessary for Realization

"These people here believe in and worship God without form; that is right. (Addressing the Brāhmo devotees) Be firm only in devotion to one aspect, either in God with form or in God without form. Firmness in faith is the first thing necessary for realization. Nothing can be achieved without firmness. If you have firm faith in God with form you will attain to Him; similarly if you firmly believe in an impersonal and formless Deity, you will reach Him. Candy will taste sweet whether you bite it straight or crooked. But you will have to be firm and you will have to call upon Him with extreme longing. When a worldly man speaks of God, do you know what it seems like to me? It is just like children quarrelling in their play and taking the name of God in vain; or like a fop walking in the garden, stick in hand, who picks a flower and idly exclaims: 'What a beautiful flower God has made!' And even this mindfulness of God exists only for a moment, like drops of water on a red-hot iron. Firmness in devotion to one aspect is absolutely necessary. Dive deep. Without diving into the ocean no one can get the treasure. If you float on the surface, you cannot reach it. Learn to love God. Be absorbed in His love.

"I have heard your prayers and devotional exercises; but why do you speak so much of the phenomena which God has made? 'O Lord, Thou hast made the sky, the mighty ocean, the moon, the sun, the stars, and planets. O Lord, Thou hast made all these, and so on.' Why do you dwell upon these things? Seeing the beautiful garden of a rich man, everyone will exclaim: 'What a beautiful tree! What a handsome flower! What a large pond and what fine fish in it! What an artistic building! With what rich paintings is the drawing-room decorated!' At the sight of all this everyone is struck with wonder, but how many seek to know the master of the garden? A few only. Those who seek God with intense longing see Him, make acquaintance with Him, speak with Him, just in the same manner as I am speaking to you. I am telling you the truth when I say that God can be seen. Who will listen to me and who will believe me?"

God and the Scriptures

"Can God be found in the scriptures? After reading the scriptures, the highest knowledge that one can get is about the existence of a God; but God does not appear to him who does not dive below the surface. Until then doubts are not removed and divine knowledge does not come. You may read thousands of volumes, you may repeat verses and hymns by hundreds, but if you cannot dive into the ocean of Divinity with extreme longing of the soul, you cannot reach God. A scholar may delude the people by his knowledge of the scriptures and by his book-learning, but through these he will not attain to God. Scriptures, books, sciences, what good will they do? Nothing can be acquired without the grace of the Lord. Yearn after His grace, devote your energy to obtaining it and by His grace you will see Him and He will be glad to speak to you."

Sub-Judge: "Revered sir, is He more gracious to some than to others? In that case He would be partial and unjust."

Differences in Powers

Rāmakrishna: "How is that? Is a horse the same thing as an earthen pot? Vidyāsāgara asked me the same question. He said to me: 'Has God given greater powers to some than to others?' I replied: 'God pervades all living creatures equally. He dwells in me in the same way as He dwells in the smallest ant, but there is a difference in powers. If all human beings were equal in powers, then why have we come to see you, after hearing of you? Is it because you have two horns on your head? No, it is because you are kind, charitable, learned, and have many other qualities greater than in others. It is for this reason that your fame is so great. Do you not know men who alone can defeat a hundred men, and again a man who will run away from a single person?' If there be no difference in powers, why should people respect Keshab Chandra Sen so much? It is said in the *Gītā*, he whom many people respect and honor either for his knowledge or for his musical gifts or for his oratorial powers or for any other reason, in him, be assured, there is a special manifestation of divine power."

A Brāhmo devotee (to sub-judge): "Why do you not accept what he says?"

Rāmakrishna (to the Brāhmo devotee): "What kind of man are you? Do you not know that it is hypocrisy to accept an opinion outwardly without believing in it?"

Sub-Judge: "Revered sir, shall we have to renounce the world?"

Worship God in Solitude

Rāmakrishna: "No. Why should you renounce? You can attain to God while living in the world; but at first for a few days you will have to live in solitude and worship Him alone. It is necessary to have a quiet place near your house where you can occasionally be alone for hours at a time and yet go home for your meals. Keshab Sen, Mozoomdār, and others have told me that they are like Rājā Janaka, who lived in the world and yet attained to the highest realization. I replied: 'It is not an easy thing to be like Rājā Janaka. Rājā Janaka was at first a great ascetic and practiced extreme asceticism for many years. A man who writes English very fluently has not acquired that facility all at once; he has had to practice for a long time.' I also said to Keshab Sen: 'Without going into solitude, how can one cure so acute a disease as worldliness? It is like the worst form of typhoid fever. If you keep bottles of chutney and jars of water where a patient is suffering from this fever, he will surely be tempted to eat the one and drink the other and then it will be impossible for the best physicians to cure him. Objects of lust are like the bottles of chutney, and desire to enjoy is like the thirst after water. Worldly thirst has no end. And so long as the object of thirst is kept within the reach of the patient, how can he be cured?

Therefore I say, withdraw from the place where those objects are and remain in solitude for a time. Then when the disease is cured, you may live in the world without being tempted by it. It is then that you will live like Rājā Janaka.'

"But in the first stage you must be very watchful. In solitude steadily practice devotional exercises. When a fig-tree is young, it must be protected by hedge, otherwise it may be eaten up by sheep and cattle; but when the trunk has grown thick, the hedge is no longer necessary. You may tie an elephant to it without damaging it. If after practicing in solitude you have acquired true *bhakti* (devotion to God) and have gained spiritual strength, then you can go home and live in the world; nothing can corrupt you."

Sub-Judge (with great delight): "Revered sir, these are the most beautiful teachings. We need to practice in solitude, but we always forget it and think that we have at once become Rājā Janaka. It has given me great peace and joy to hear that it is not absolutely necessary to leave the world and that God can be realized even at home."

Renunciation and Worldly Men

Rāmakrishna: "Renunciation, why should you practice it? When you have to fight, it is better to do so from within the fort. You will have to fight against the senses, against hunger, thirst, and other desires. This fight is easier from within the fort of the world. In this age our life depends upon material food; if you cannot get anything to eat for a day, your mind will be turned away from God. A man once said to his wife: 'I am going to leave the world.' The wife was very practical and replied: 'Why wilt thou wander from house to house for food? When thou art in need of food, is it not better to go to one house than to ten or more?' Why should you renounce? It is so much more convenient to live at home. You do not have to worry about food; then you have your wife with you. Whenever your body needs anything, you will have it right at hand; when you are ill, you will have many hands to nurse you. Janaka, Vyāsa, Vasishtha, and others first attained God-consciousness and then lived in the world. They had two swords in their hands—one of wisdom and the other of work."

Sub-Judge: "Revered sir, how can we know that true wisdom?"

Rāmakrishna: "When true wisdom comes, God does not appear to be very far. He is no longer there, but here in the heart. He is no longer that but this. He dwells within all. Whoever seeks Him finds Him."

Sub-Judge: "I am a sinner; how can I say that God dwells in me?"

Rāmakrishna: "You always talk of sin and sinners; this is the Christian doctrine. Have faith in the holy name of the Lord. By the power of faith all sins will be washed away."

Sub-Judge: "Revered sir, how can I have such a faith?"

Rāmakrishna: "First be devoted to God. You have in one of your songs: 'O Lord, canst Thou be known without devotion, simply by good works and sacrifice?' That which brings true devotion and unselfish love for God you must pray for with earnest longing in silence. Shed tears of repentance until you have acquired these."

A Brāhmo devotee: "Revered sir, when will they get time? They have to work in their offices."

Resign All to God

Rāmakrishna (to sub-judge): "Well, resign yourself to the will of the Lord and draw up a power of attorney in His favor. If anyone depends entirely upon some good man, does he do any evil to him? Internally lay upon Him your whole burden and sit calmly, without anxiety. Whatever He has given you to do, do that. A kitten has no self-reliance. It mews and mews and stays where the mother cat places it. She may put it on a soft bed or on the hard floor of the kitchen; the kitten is always content and depends entirely on the will of the mother."

Sub-Judge: "We are householders with certain duties; how long shall we have to perform these?"

Householder's Duties

Rāmakrishna: "Of course you have your duties. You will have to bring up your children, sustain your wife, save enough to maintain your family after your death. If you did not do this you would be heartless and cruel. Even great sages like Shukadeva practiced loving-kindness. He is not a man who has neither heart nor kindness."

Sub-Judge: "How long shall we maintain our children?"

Rāmakrishna: "Until they have passed the age of minority. When the young bird is able to take care of itself, it pecks at the parent bird, if she tries to come near it."

Sub-Judge: "What is the duty towards the wife?"

God Provides for Those Who Have Realized Him

Rāmakrishna: "As long as you live you should give her spiritual advice and sustain and care for her. If she is faithful, save enough to make her comfortable after your death. But when God-consciousness comes, no worldly duties can bind you. Then if you do not think of the morrow, God will think for you. If you attain to God-consciousness, He will provide for the support of your family. When a *zamindār* dies, leaving a son under age, a guardian manages the estate for the child. These are legal affairs; you understand them all."

Sub-Judge: "Yes, revered sir."

Brāhmo devotee: "What is the sign of one who has attained true wisdom living in the world?"

Signs of True Wisdom

Rāmakrishna: "When the repetition of the name of the Lord will bring tears to the eyes, send a thrill through the whole body, and make the hair stand on end. The spiritual eye must be opened. It is open when the mind is purified. Then the presence of the Divinity will be realized everywhere and every woman will appear as Divine Mother. Everything is in the mind. The impure mind brings attachment to the world, and the purified mind brings the realization of God. The impure mind of a man becomes attached to a woman. Woman naturally loves man and man naturally loves woman, and from this spring attachment and worldliness."

Divine Mother in All Women

"Every woman represents divine motherhood. The same Divine Mother appears in all women under various forms. It is said in the scriptures that Nārada in prayer thus addressed Rāma: 'O Rāma, Thou art *Purusha*, Thou appearest in the form of all men, and Sītā, Thy *Prakriti*, appears in the form of all women. Thou art man and Sītā is woman. Wherever there is masculine form, it is thy manifestation; and wherever there is feminine form, it is the manifestation of Sītā, the Divine Mother."

Attachment to the Body

"So long as there is attachment to worldliness, and thirst for objects of lust, so long there is attachment to the body. As attachment to the world grows less, the mind goes towards the *Ātman* or the true Self and the attachment to the physical body becomes less. When the attachment to the world has entirely vanished, Self-knowledge comes and the *Ātman* is separated from the physical body. When an ordinary coconut is cut into halves, it is very difficult to separate the kernel from the shell; but when it is dried, the kernel becomes separate from the shell by itself. You can feel it by shaking it. A man who has realized God becomes like the dry coconut, his soul becomes separate from his body and all attachment to the body leaves him. He is not affected by the pleasure and pain of the body; he does not seek the comforts of the body; he moves from place to place like an emancipated soul. When you notice that tears flow and the thrill comes at the repetition of the name of the Lord, then you may know that attachment to sense-objects has become less and the devotee is on the path of realization. For instance, if the match is dry it will ignite the moment it is struck; but if it be wet, you can strike it fifty times and yet you cannot get a light. Similarly when the mind is soaked in the water of lust and thirst for worldly objects, divine enlightenment does not come in it, however hard you may try; it is merely waste of time and labor. But when that water dries up, spiritual illumination comes instantly."

Brāhmo devotee: "By what method can that water be dried up?"

The Divine Mother Will Cure Worldly Attachment

Rāmakrishna: "Pray to the Divine Mother with an earnest and sincere heart; when you see Her, the water of worldly attachment will dry up. Attachment to lust and wealth will drop away from you. If you can feel Her as your own mother, it will come to you at that very moment. Go to Her and importunately ask for what you want. An importunate child hangs on its mother's gown and begs a penny to buy a paper kite. The mother may be engaged in talking to other girls and at first she may not wish to give it, saying: 'No, your father has forbidden it. I'll speak to him when he comes home. You will spoil everything if you get a paper kite.' But when the child begins to cry and does not give in, then the mother says to her companions: 'Just wait a minute, let me quiet the child'; she then gets the key to her drawer, opens the money-box, and gives him what he is crying for. Similarly if you cry to your Mother and pray to Her, She will surely come to you."

Pride and Egotism

Then turning to the sub-judge, the Bhagavān said: "What is the cause of pride and egotism? Do they arise from knowledge or ignorance? Egotism is the quality of *tamas* arising from ignorance. It is a barrier which prevents the soul from seeing God. When it dies, all troubles cease. Of what avail is it to be egotistic? This body with all its comforts and luxuries will not last long. A drunkard, after seeing an image at the Durgā festival beautifully decorated with jewels and costly ornaments, exclaimed: 'Mother, you may decorate yourself with all these valuable things, but after three days they will take you out and throw you in the Ganges.' So I say to you all, whether you be a judge or any great personage, it is only for a few days. Therefore you must not be proud or egotistic about anything."

Three Classes of Character

"People's character can be divided into three classes—*tamas*, *rajas*, and *sattva*. Those who belong to the first class are egotistic; they sleep too much, eat too much, and passion and anger prevail in them. Those who belong to the second class are too much attached to work. They love nice, well-fitting clothes and are very neat; they care for a luxurious, richly furnished house; when they sit and worship God, they love to wear costly garments; when they give anything to charity they parade it. Those who belong to the third class are very quiet, peaceful, and unostentatious; they are not particular about their dress; they lead a simple life and earn a modest living, because their needs are small; they do not flatter for selfish ends; their dwelling is modest; they do not worry about their children's dress; they are not anxious for name, nor do they care for the admiration or adulation of others; they worship God, give charity, and meditate silently and in secret. This *sattva* quality is the last step of the ladder which leads to the roof of the Divinity. A person reaching this state does not have to wait long for God-consciousness. (To sub-judge) You said a little while ago that all men were equal, but now you see how characters vary."

Music for a time interrupted the teachings and Bhagavān Shrī Rāmakrishna, on hearing it, again went into *samādhi*. The Brāhmo devotees sang the *sankīrtan*, and when they finished, all those present resumed their seats, Bijoy taking his place just before Shrī Rāmakrishna. It was the hour for another Brāhmo service at which Bijoy, who was the leader of the Brāhmo Samāj, was to read from the *Vedas* and give an address. Before going to the platform, he asked Shrī Rāmakrishna's permission, saying: "Bhagavan, grant me thy blessing, then I shall begin the service."

Egotism and Knowledge

Rāmakrishna: "When egotism is gone, everything is accomplished. 'I am lecturing and you are listening,' this sense of egotism you must not have. Egotism proceeds from ignorance and not from knowledge. He who is free from egotism attains knowledge. The rain-water gathers in a low place, it runs off from a high place; similarly the water of wisdom gathers in the humble heart. It is very difficult to be a spiritual leader (*āchārya*). One easily loses a great deal by it. When many people show honor and respect, ordinary preachers become egotistic and are easily spoiled. They cannot go further. They merely gain a little fame. Perhaps people will say: 'Oh! Bijoy Bābu is a good speaker or he is very wise,' that is all. Never think, 'I am speaking.' I tell my Divine Mother: 'O Mother, I am merely an instrument in Thy hands. Thou dost everything. As Thou guidest me and makest me speak, so shall I speak.'"

Bijoy (very humbly): "Please give me thy permission. Without thy permission I cannot begin the service."

Rāmakrishna (smiling): "Who am I to permit you? Ask the permission of the Lord. When genuine humility comes, there is no fear."

Bijoy repeated his request and Shrī Rāmakrishna then said: "You can go and begin according to your custom, but keep your mind on God."

Bijoy began the service with a prayer to the Divine Mother. After the service was over, he came down from the platform and again sat near Shrī Rāmakrishna. The Bhagavān said to him: "You prayed to the Divine Mother; that was very good. They say that the mother's attraction towards her child is greater than the father's. You can urge your mother more strongly than you can your father. You have a stronger claim on anything that belongs to your mother than on anything of the father."

Bijoy: "If *Brahman* the Absolute be the Divine Mother, then is She with form or without form?"

Absolute Brahman and Divine Mother

Rāmakrishna: "The Absolute *Brahman* and the Mother of the universe are one and the same. Where there is no activity of any kind, that is the state of the Absolute *Brahman*, but where there is evolution and destruction, there is the manifestation of the Divine Mother. When the water of the ocean is calm, without a wave or ripple, that is like the state of the Absolute. When the water is in motion and with waves, it is the state of the Creative Energy or Divine Mother. Divine Mother is both with form and without form. You have faith in formless Divinity, therefore you can think of my Mother as formless. When your faith is firm, the Divine Mother will show you how She is. Then you will know that it is not that She is mere Absolute Existence; She will come to you and speak to you. Have faith and you will get everything. If you have faith in the formless Divinity, you must make that faith as firm as a rock. But do not be dogmatic; you must never dogmatize about God. You must not say that He is like this and not like anything else. You may say: 'I believe in a formless Divinity, but what else He is, is known to Him. I do not know, I cannot understand.' The small intellect of a man cannot grasp the whole nature of God. A vessel which can hold a pound only, how can it contain four pounds? If God reveals Himself to one by His grace and makes one understand His nature, then one realizes Him and not until then. The Absolute and the Divine Mother are one."

Bijoy: "How can we attain to the vision of the Divine Mother and the realization of the Absolute?"

Vision of the Divine Mother and the Absolute

Rāmakrishna: "With earnest longing and sincerity pray and cry. When the heart will be purified, then you will see the vision as in pure water you can see the reflection of the sun. Upon the mirror of the ego of the devotee is to be seen the reflection of the Absolute Mother of the universe with form. But the mirror should be thoroughly polished; if there be a speck of dirt the reflection will not be perfect. When the sun is to be seen on the water of the ego and when there is no other means of getting a view of the real sun, so long the reflected image of the sun should be considered as absolutely real. As long as the ego is real, so long the reflected image of the sun is real, not partially but absolutely. That reflected image of the sun is the Divine Mother. If you wish to reach the Absolute *Brahman*, which is impersonal and without attributes, then start from that reflected image and march towards the real sun. The Personal God or *Brahman* with attributes is the one who listens to prayers. Pray to Him and He will grant the highest wisdom, because the same Personal God has the impersonal aspect also, which is the Absolute *Brahman*. Divine Energy, which is the Mother of the universe, is another aspect of the same *Brahman*. All these merge into absolute oneness. The Mother can give *Brahma jnāna*, the knowledge of the Absolute, as also true devotion and absolute love. God is the internal ruler of all. Forsaking egotism, resign your will to His will; you will get everything you desire."

Become One with All

"When you mix with other people, you should love them all, become absolutely one with them. Do not hate anyone. Do not recognize caste or creed. Do not say that this man believes in a Personal God, that man believes in an Impersonal God; this man worships God with form, that man worships God without form; this man is a Hindu, that one is a Christian, or a Mohammedan. Saying this, do not condemn one another. These distinctions exist because God has made different people understand Him in different ways. The difference lies in the nature of the individuals.

Knowing this you will mix with all as closely as possible and love them as dearly as you can. Then when you go home, you will enjoy blissful happiness in your soul. Light the candle of wisdom in the secret chamber of your heart. By that light see the face of my Absolute Mother, and by that light you will also see the true nature of your real Self. When cowherds drive the cattle to a pasture from different quarters, the cows form themselves into one herd as if of the same family; but when they return at night, they separate, each going to its own home. So the *bhaktas* of different sects and creeds, when they meet, are like members of one family, but when they are by themselves, they show their peculiar beliefs and different creeds."

It was late in the evening, and Shrī Rāmakrishna, entering the carriage accompanied by a few devotees, returned to Dakshineshwar.

Chapter 12

At the House of Balarām, a Disciple

Shrī Rāmakrishna arrived from Dakshineshwar at the house of his disciple Balarām Bose about ten in the morning and had his dinner there. It was this house which the Bhagavān chose to make his chief "vineyard" on that day. Here he had bound devotee after devotee by the tie of divine love. It was here that he had so often sung the name of the Lord and danced at the head of his disciples. It seemed as if another Gaurānga (Chaitanya) had set up in the house of his disciple Shrivāsh a fair for the "buying and selling of divine love."

How great was the Master's love for his disciples! There in the temple of Kālī alone by himself he often cried like a child, he so longed to see them. Sleepless at night he would say to the Divine Mother: "O Mother! Deign to draw them into the fold! They are so devoted to Thee! Oh, how I long to see them! Mother, bring them to me or take me to them." Was this the secret of his coming to Balarām's house so frequently? He declared, indeed to everyone: "Balarām is a true *bhakta*, he daily worships the Lord of the universe. His offerings are therefore always acceptable." But whenever he came to his house, he would say: "Go and invite my Narendra and other disciples. Offering food to them is the same as offering it to God Himself. They, indeed, are not ordinary men. They are parts of Divinity manifest in the flesh." And many a time had the devotees met there "at the Durbar (court) of God's love."

Mahendra, who taught in a neighboring school, had heard that Shrī Rāmakrishna was visiting at Balarām's house, so having a little leisure he came about noon to see him. The midday dinner was over and the Bhagavān was in the drawing-room resting. His young disciples were seated round him. Mahendra, entering, bowed down and saluted his feet.

Shrī Rāmakrishna (affectionately): "Mahendra! You here! Is there no school today?"

Mahendra: "I have come directly from school. I had just now nothing of importance to attend to there."

A devotee: "No, revered sir, he is playing the truant."

Mahendra (to himself): "Ah me! It is as if some invisible force had drawn me to this place."

The Bhagavān then grew more serious and bade them take their seats. He said: "For some time past I have not been able to touch any metal. Can you tell me why it is? Once when I put my hand on a metal cup, it was hurt as if stung by a horned fish and the pain lasted for a long while. I had to use a metal pitcher and I thought that I should be able to carry it by covering it with a towel; but no sooner did I touch it than I had excruciating pain in my hand. Then I prayed to my Divine Mother: 'O Mother! I shall never touch metal again. Do Thou forgive me this time.'"

In the afternoon Shrī Rāmakrishna was still seated in Balarām's drawing-room. On his face was a sweet smile, the reflection of which was caught by the faces of the disciples. Girish Ghosh,[1] Shuresh Mitrā,[2] Balarām, Latu,[3] Chunilal[4] and many other disciples were present.

Rāmakrishna (to Girish): "You would better argue the point with Narendra (Vivekānanda) and see what he has to say."

Girish: "Narendra says: 'God is Infinite. We cannot even say that all that we hear or see—be it an object or a person—is a part of God. Infinity is one; how can it have parts? It cannot be divided.'"

Divine Incarnation

Rāmakrishna: "God may be Infinite or even greater than Infinite; but by His omnipotent will He can manifest His essence through

1 Girish Chandra Ghosh, the greatest Hindu poet, dramatist, and actor of modern India. He is the founder and manager of many theaters in Calcutta.

2 Bābu Shuresh Chandra Mitrā was a devoted householder disciple of Rāmakrishna.

3 Latu, the devoted servant of Rāmakrishna. Although he is illiterate he reached the height of spiritual ecstasy through his whole-hearted service and devotion for his divine Master. He is now one of the *sannyāsī* disciples of Rāmakrishna.

4 Bābu Chunilal Bose is a gentle householder disciple of Rāmakrishna.

human form and incarnate Himself among us. Indeed He does incarnate Himself as a human being. How He incarnates we cannot explain by words. One must feel it and realize it. By analogy we can get only a faint idea of it. For instance, if you have touched the horn, leg, or udder of a cow, have you not touched the whole cow? But for us human beings the milk is the most important thing and that you can get only from the udder, not from any other part of the body. The Incarnation of God is like the udder, through which flows the milk of divine love. In order to give mankind His essence of divine love and *bhakti* the Lord incarnates from time to time in a human form."

Girish: "Narendra says: 'Is it possible to fully comprehend God? He is the Infinite.'"

Rāmakrishna: "That is true. Who can fully comprehend God or even any of His attributes, great or small? Why is it necessary for us to know all His attributes? It is enough if we can see Him and realize Him. Moreover, he who has seen His Divine Incarnation has seen God. Suppose a man goes to the banks of the holy river Ganges and touches the water. He will say: 'I have seen and touched the holy river.' It will not be necessary for him to touch the whole river from its source to its mouth. If I touch your feet, then I have touched you. If you go to the ocean and touch the water, you have touched the whole ocean. As fire is all-pervading but is more manifest in burning wood, so God, although He is all-pervading, is more manifest in His incarnation."

Girish (smiling): "I, for my part, am searching after fire. I am eagerly looking for the place where I shall find it."

Seek God in Man

Rāmakrishna (smiling): "The element fire is more manifest in the wood. If you seek the divine element, you must seek it in man, for Divinity is more manifest in a human being than elsewhere. Again, if you see a man who is overflowing with divine love, who is mad after God, who is intoxicated by the wine of divine love, in that man you must know, I assure you, that the Lord has manifested Himself. It is true that God dwells everywhere, but His divine power (*Shakti*) is more manifest in some places than in others. In the *Avatāra* (God-Incarnate) the manifestation of *Shakti* is very great. Sometimes the manifestation of this divine power is complete and perfect. In fact *Avatāra* means the incarnation of *Shakti*, the divine power."

Girish: "Narendra says: 'He is beyond the reach of mind, words, and senses.'"

Rāmakrishna: "No, He is beyond the reach of impure mind only, but not of the purified mind (*manas*). He cannot be apprehended by ordinary intellect, but purified intellect (*buddhi*) can comprehend Him. Mind and intellect become purified when they are absolutely free from attachment to lust and wealth (*kāmini* and *kānchan*). Then purified mind and purified intellect become one. Indeed God can be realized by the purified mind. Is it not true that the sages and saints have realized Him? They realized the Supreme Spirit in the Self by their True Self."

Girish (smiling): "Narendra has been defeated by me in the discussion!"

Rāmakrishna: "Oh, no; on the contrary he says: 'Girish has such firm faith in the *Avatāra* in a human form that I feel that I should say nothing against it.'"

The Bhagavān then expressed a desire to listen to the chanting of hymns. Balarām's drawing-room was filled with visitors. Everyone watched the Bhagavān, eager to hear what fell from his lips and to mark what he would do next. Tārāpada was invited to sing, and sang a song describing the sports of the Shepherd of men, Shrī Krishna.

Shuresh Mitrā was seated at some distance from the Bhagavān. Shrī Rāmakrishna smiled on him affectionately and pointing to Girish, he said to him: "Do you talk of the wild life that you did live at one time? Here is one very much more than your match."

Shuresh (laughing): "That is indeed true, revered sir. He is my *dādā* (respected elder brother) in this regard."

Girish (to the Bhagavān): "I never paid attention to my studies in my boyhood. How is it, revered sir, that people insist on calling me learned?"

Scriptures and Realization

Rāmakrishna: "Do you know what I think about learning and the reading of the scriptures? Books and sacred scriptures all point the way to God. Once you know the way, what is the use of books? Now the time comes for devotional practices in solitude. A person had received a letter in which he was asked to send certain articles to his kinsmen. He was about to order the purchase of those things, when, looking for the letter, he found it was missing. He searched for a long time. His people also joined him in his search. At last the letter was found and his joy knew no bounds. With great eagerness he took it up and went through its contents. But after knowing what things were wanted, he threw the letter aside and set forth to collect the desired articles. How long does one care for such a letter? So long as one does not know its contents. The next step is to put forth one's effort to procure the things. Similarly the sacred books only tell us the means for the realization of God. Having once known them, you should struggle hard to acquire them and reach the goal. What is the use of mere book-learning? A *pandit* may know many sacred texts and sciences, but if his mind is attached to the world, if he enjoys the pleasures of the senses, he has not realized the spirit of the scriptures; he has studied them in vain."

Rāmakrishna then said to Girish: "Narendra is a young man of very high order. He is interested in everything—singing, playing on musical instruments, on the one hand, and in the study of various branches of knowledge on the other. He possesses the virtues of self-mastery, right discrimination, dispassion, and many other qualities. (Aside to a disciple) Just look at Girish's devotion to the Lord and his faith in Him."

Nārān,[5] to the Bhagavān: "Revered sir, shall we not have the pleasure of hearing thee sing?"

Upon this the Bhagavān chanted the name of the Divine Mother of the universe.

The Beloved Mother of the Universe

1. O my soul, do thou clasp to thy heart my beloved Mother,
Let thee and me alone have the pleasure of looking on Her;
Let Her be seen by none else, by none else!

5 Nārān was a young householder disciple of Rāmakrishna.

2. Desires—Oh, get out of their way, my soul; let us enjoy Her presence alone.
Only let us have the tongue for our sole companion to cry out to Her, saying, "Mother, Mother!"

3. There are evil desires, there are those which point to us the path leading to worldliness; Oh! Do not let them come near us.
Let the eye of wisdom that leads Godward keep watch and guard us from evil.

The Bhagavān then sang another song in which he placed himself in the position of the weary and heavy-laden men of the world, bending under the weight of their trials and sufferings:

The Mother and Her Weary Children

1. O Mother! Thou art made of bliss everlasting, why then is it denied unto me?

2. My soul, O good Mother, knows not anything but the lotus of Thy hallowed feet.
Why then does the Ruler of Death, the King of Justice, find fault with me? Tell me what answer to make to that dreaded King.

3. It was my heart's desire, O Mother, to repeat Thy sacred name and cross the ocean of death. Not even in my dream had I the least idea that I should be drowned by Thee in the shoreless ocean.

4. Day and night, O Mother, Thou the Consort of Eternity, have I been repeating Thy sacred name, which brings salvation unto Thy weary children. But alas! my endless troubles will never leave me. I only regret that if I am not saved, no one else will ever repeat Thy name.

The Bhagavān next sang about the joy of the Divine Mother:

The Great Mystery

With Shiva the Mother plays always, absorbed in blissful joy.
Deep drunk She is, but falls not.

She dances on the breast of Her consort,
The world quakes under the weight of Her feet.
Both have reached the climax of madness;
Both are fearless and free.

The disciples listened to the song in deep silence. What struck them was the change that had come over the Bhagavān. He was beside himself with the joy of the Lord—intoxicated with that unbounded bliss.

Twilight had fallen. The disciples would not leave their seats. With heads upraised and eager ears they listened to the sweet name of the Lord chanted by the Bhagavān, sweeter as repeated by him than by any whom they had ever heard before. Yes, they had never heard another child calling out so sweetly to its mother, saying, "Mother, Mother!" The Master had spoken today of the udder of the cow from which to draw the milk of divine love. Was it indeed given to those present to behold the vision of God-Incarnate in that very room? What else could have brought into the hearts of the disciples—of those who were weary and heavy-laden—the perfect peace and the joy that are of the Lord? Thus did some of the disciples think within themselves. They felt that they were truly blessed as they heard the Bhagavān chant the name of the Divine Mother and of Harī, the Lord God who taketh away all trouble, all sin, and iniquity.

The chanting of the names being over, the Bhagavān prayed to the Mother. It seemed as if the God of Love had taken a human form in order to teach man how to pray. He said:

Prayer to the Divine Mother

"Mother, I throw myself upon Thy mercy. May the lotus of Thy feet ever keep me from whatever leadeth Thy children away from Thee! I seek not, good Mother, the pleasures of the senses; I seek not fame. Nor do I long for those *siddhis* (*yoga* powers) which en-able one to perform miracles. What I pray for, O good Mother, is pure love for Thee, love untainted by desires, love without alloy, love which seeketh not the things of this world, love for Thee that welleth up unbidden from the depths of the immortal soul. Grant likewise, O Mother, that Thy child, bewitched by the fascinations of Thy enchanting powers (*māyā*) may not forget Thee; yes, forget Thee, entangled in the charming net of *samsāra* that Thou hast woven. O, grant that he may never be charmed into loving these! O good Mother, seest Thou not that Thy child hath none else in the world but Thee. I know not how to chant Thy name out of deep devotion. Devoid am I of knowledge that leadeth to Thee—devoid of genuine love (*bhakti*) for Thee! O, vouchsafe unto me that love out of Thine infinite mercy!"

This evening prayer—was it called for in the case of this God-Man, for him who chanted the name of the Lord day and night, for him out of whose hallowed mouth there flowed a never ceasing stream of prayers unto the Most High? Was it then that the Master observed these forms in order to teach mankind how to live and pray?

Girish had invited Shrī Rāmakrishna to his house. He must come that very night. The Bhagavān said to him: "Do you not think it will be too late?"

Girish: "No, revered sir; thou shalt come away as early as thou pleasest."

It was about nine in the evening. Balarām had made his offerings ready for Shrī Rāmakrishna's supper. The gracious Bhagavān would not wound his feelings. He said to Balarām: "Send over to Girish's house the food that you have prepared for me." Saying this, he set out, followed by his disciples. Going downstairs from the first floor, he became like another being; he looked as if he was lost in the thought of God—as if he had drunk deep! It seemed as if sense-consciousness was beginning to leave him. A disciple went forward to hold him by the hand, lest he should miss his footing. The Bhagavān said to him with great tenderness: "If you hold me by the hand, people will say, 'He is a drunkard.' Let me walk alone without any help." He crossed the next turning just a little way from Girish's house. What made him walk so fast? The disciples were left behind. No one knew what divine idea had found its way into his heart.

Rāmakrishna's Ecstasy

Here was Narendra coming! Many a day had the Bhagavān cried, calling "Narendra, Narendra," like one gone mad. But now Narendra was there before him and yet he exchanged no word with him. Shrī Rāmakrishna had come to the end of the lane leading to Girish's house. The disciples were all following. He now spoke to Narendra, saying: "Is it well with you, my child? I had not the power then to talk to you." Every word that fell from his lips was marked by tenderness. He had not as yet come to the door of the house, but all at once he stopped short. He looked at Narendra and said: "This is one of the two—the human soul, and the other is the cosmos." Was he indeed looking at the soul and the world? If so, in what light? He was gazing on the indescribable *Brahman*! One or two words had dropped from his hallowed lips, like some solemn texts from inspired scriptures. Or was it that he had gone to the edge of the infinite ocean and stood there speechless, looking on the boundless expanse, and had heard one or two echoes reverberating from the never-ceasing voice that comes up from the eternal deep?

Girish stood at the door of his house. He had come to receive the Bhagavān. Shrī Rāmakrishna came up with his disciples. At the blessed sight Girish fell at his feet prostrate and received on his head the dust of his hallowed feet and then rose at the Master's bidding. He led the way to the drawing-room, where the Bhagavān and his disciples took their seats. They longed to drink the nectar of his words which brought everlasting life.

He was about to take his seat when he found a newspaper lying by his side. As newspapers had to do with worldly-minded men, with worldly matters, with gossip and scandal, they were unholy objects in his eyes. He made a sign and the paper was put away. Thereupon he took his seat.

Among the disciples who sat at the feet of Rāmakrishna, Narendra did not believe in the Incarnation of God, while Girish had a burning faith that God incarnated Himself from age to age in this world of ours. The Bhagavān wished them to discuss the matter before him.

Shrī Rāmakrishna (to Girish): "I should like to hear you both talk over the matter in English."

The discussion was commenced. It was, however, carried on not in English but in Bengāli, with here and there an English word.

God Manifest

Narendra: "God is infinite; it is beyond our power to conceive Him by means of our poor intellect. God is in every human being, but He is not manifest in one particular individual."

The Bhagavān (affectionately): "I quite concur. He is in every object, in every human being; only there is a difference in the manifestation of divine energy in those objects. The divine energy manifest in some objects leads one away from God and is then called *avidyā* (ignorance). When it leads Godward it is called *vidyā* (knowledge). Again, the manifested energy is greater in some vessels and less in others. Thus it is that all men are not equal."

A disciple: "What is the use of all this idle talk?"

Bhagavān: "There is a great deal of use in it."

Girish (to Narendra): "How do you know that God does not take a human body, does not incarnate Himself?"

Narendra: "Oh! God is surely beyond the reach of words and the finite mind!"

God Realized by Purified Soul

Rāmakrishna: "Quite so; beyond the finite impure mind. But He can be realized by the purified intellect (*buddhi*). Purified intellect and purified soul are one. The holy sages (*rishis*) realized the pure universal Spirit by their purified intellect and purified soul."

Girish (to Narendra): "If God does not incarnate Himself in a human form, who will explain these difficult problems? He assumes human form to teach mankind divine wisdom and divine love. Who else has the power to teach in the same manner?"

Narendra: "Why, He will certainly teach me within the heart."

Bhagavān (affectionately): "That is indeed so. He will teach as internal ruler of the heart (*antaryāmin*)."

The discussion grew warm. It turned on matters too high for ordinary comprehension: Was infinity indivisible? What did Hamilton say as to the limit of human knowledge—and Herbert Spencer, Tyndall, and Huxley?

Rāmakrishna: "I for my part do not like these things. God is beyond the power of reasoning; He is something more. I see that whatever is, is God. What then is the necessity of reasoning about Him? I do actually see that whatever is, is God. It is He who has become all these things. This is a stage at which the mind and the intellect (*buddhi*) are lost in the Absolute and Indivisible Being. At the sight of Narendra my mind becomes merged in the Indivisible Absolute. What, pray, do you say to this?"

Girish (smiling): "Surely, revered sir, we do not pretend that we understand everything except this."

Rāmakrishna: "Thereupon at the end of *samādhi* I must come down two notes at least below the highest note in the scale before I can utter a word. *Vedānta* has been explained by Shankara. Another point of view is that of Rāmānuja, who has put forward the doctrine of *Visishtādvaita* (Qualified Non-dualism)."

Narendra (to the Bhagavān): "Sir, may I ask what is meant by *Visishtādvaita*?"

Qualified Non-Dualism

Rāmakrishna: "There is a doctrine called *Visishtādvaita*, the view of Rāmānuja; that the Absolute (*Brahman*) must not be considered apart from the world and the soul. The three form one: three in one and one in three. Let us take a Bel-fruit. Let the shell, the seeds, and the kernel be kept separate. Now suppose someone wished to know the weight of the fruit. Surely it would not do to weigh the kernel alone. The shell, the seeds, and the kernel are all weighed with a view to knowing the real weight of the fruit. No doubt we reason at the outset that the all-important thing is the kernel—not either the shell or the seeds. In the next place, we go on reasoning that the shell and the seeds belong to the same substance to which the kernel belongs. At the first stage of the reasoning we say, 'Not this, not this.' Thus the Absolute (*Brahman*) is not the individual soul. Again, it is not the phenomenal world. The Absolute (*Brahman*) is the only Reality, all else is unreal. At the next stage we go a little farther. We see that the kernel belongs to the same substance as that to which the shell and the seeds belong; hence the substance from which we derive our negative conception of the Absolute *Brahman* is the identical substance from which we derive our negative conceptions of the finite soul and the phenomenal world. Our relative phenomena (*līlā*) must be traced to that Eternal Being which is also called the Absolute. Hence, says Rāmānuja, the Absolute (*Brahman*) is qualified by the finite soul and the phenomenal world. This is the doctrine of the qualified non-dualistic *Vedānta*."

Intellectual Apprehension and Realization

After the discussion was over, the Bhagavan said: "I have observed that discrimination brings only intellectual apprehension of the Absolute, which is far from true realization. The latter can be acquired by meditation in solitude (*dhyāna*); but it is very different from realization through His grace. If He, out of His grace, makes us realize what is God-Incarnate and how He manifests through a human from, then it is no longer necessary to reason or to explain. Do you know how it is? As in a dark room someone rubs a match on the side of the box and all at once a light is struck. So, if the Lord is gracious enough to strike the light for us, the darkness of ignorance will be dispelled and all doubts will cease forever. Can He be realized by such discussions?"

The Bhagavān then invited Narendra to be seated by his side. He made many loving inquiries about him and caressed him.

Narendra: "Why, revered Sir, I have meditated in solitude on the Divine Mother for three and four days together, but nothing has come of it."

Bhagavān: "All in time; do not be impatient. Mother is no other than the *Brahman* the Absolute. Divine Mother is the Primeval Energy, but when She is without activity I call It the *Brahman*. But when It creates, preserves, and destroys the phenomenal world I call it *Shakti* (Energy), or Divine Mother. That which you call *Brahman* is the same as my Divine Mother. (To Girish) It is getting late."

Girish: "I am afraid I shall have to leave thee, revered sir, and go to my work, unfortunate that I am!"

Bhagavān: "No, you must serve both parties. Janaka served God unattached to the world and thus looked to the interests of this world and the next; he drank the cup of milk but did not forget the soul."

Girish: "I am thinking, revered sir, of giving up my profession."

Bhagavān: "No, no; you need not do any such thing. It is all right as it is. You are doing good to many."

Narendra (softly): "Just a moment ago he was addressing him as Lord, God-Incarnate, yet he still has such strong attachment to his professional work."

The Bhagavān had Narendra seated by his side. He fixed his eyes on him. He moved down to sit closer to him. Narendra did not believe that God incarnated Himself, but what did that signify? His love for him was still as great as ever. Touching his person the Bhagavān said to him: "Are your feelings wounded? Never mind; we, too, are of the same mind with you and feel for you."

Disputations Prevent Realization of God

Bhagavān continued: "So long as one reasons and argues about God, one has not realized Him. You both were engaged in discussion. I did not like it. How long does the noise continue at a feast to which many are bidden? So long as the guests have not begun to eat. As soon as the viands are served and they begin to partake of them, three-fourths of the noise is gone. Then the more the sweetmeats are passed around, the more the noise subsides. The nearer you come to God, the less you are disposed to argue. When you come up to Him, when you behold Him as the Reality, then all noise, all disputations are at an end. Then is the time for the enjoyment which comes in *samādhi*."

Saying this, the Bhagavān gently moved his hand over Narendra's sweet face and caressed him, repeating, "*Harī Om, Harī Om, Harī Om*."

Then what a miracle passed before the eyes of the disciples! Looking at the Bhagavān they saw his sense-consciousness beginning to leave him. Looking again, they saw that it had left him altogether. In this half-conscious state the hand of the Incarnation of divine love continued to rest on Narendra's body. Was he breathing into him the inspiration, the power that comes from above? Then yet other changes came over the Bhagavān. He said to Narendra, with folded hands: "A song do sing, then I shall get well; how else shall I be able to stand on my feet: 'My Nitāi! Oh! He is deep drunk, intoxicated with the wine of divine love, the love for Gaurānga.[6]'"

A short while and he was speechless again, speechless like a figure cut in marble. Drunk with the joy of the Lord, the Bhagavān went on, saying: "Take care, Rādhā, lest thou fall into the Yāmuna. O thou, mad with ecstatic love for Him who incarnated Himself at Brindāvan, the Lord Shrī Krishna!" Once more he was in deep *samādhi*! Coming back into sense-consciousness he repeated portions of a well-known song: "O my friend, how far is that blessed woodland, the land where is to be seen my own Beloved One? Look! Here comes the fragrance from the blessed person of my Beloved! I am unable to take a step forward, O my friend!"

Now the Bhagavān had lost all consciousness of the world. He was not mindful of anything or any person in this state. Narendra was seated before him, but apparently he did not see him. He had lost all sense of time and place. The mind, the heart, and the soul had all become absorbed in God. Suddenly he stood up, saying: "Deep drunk with the wine of divine love, with love, for Gaur.[7]" A few moments after he took his seat and said: "Yonder is a light coming this way, but I cannot even now say from which way the light comes." It was then that Narendra began to sing:

God-Vision

1. O Lord! Thou hast blessed me with Thy vision and Thou hast driven all my troubles away.
A charm Thou hast thrown over my soul.

2. Beholding Thee as the Reality, the seven worlds have forgotten their grief.

6 Nitāi, or Nityānanda, is the beloved disciple of Gaurānga, another name for Shrī Chaitanya. See note 3, p. 111.

7 Same as Gaurānga.

> Not to speak of my poor self, so worthy of Thy pity and Thy loving-kindness.

Listening to the song, the Bhagavān had once more lost all consciousness of the outer world. His eyes were closed. His body and limbs moved not. He was in deep *samādhi*. When the *samādhi* was over he asked: "Who will take me home to the temple?" A child looking for a companion! It was getting late and it was the night of the tenth day of the dark fortnight. Shrī Rāmakrishna wished to go back to the temple at Dakshineshwar. He seated himself in the carriage which was to take him there. The disciples stood on either side of the carriage to see him off. Even now was he deep drunk with the joy of the Lord! The carriage rolled away. The disciples looked after it for a few moments, then dispersed each to his own home.

Chapter 13

A Day at Shyampukur

Shrī Rāmakrishna was living at Shyampukur at the request of his householder disciples, who had hired a house for him there.

It was about half-past five in the afternoon of a day in October. Vivekānanda, Brahmānanda, Rāmakrishnānanda, Saradānanda, Abhedānanda and other disciples were with Shrī Rāmakrishna. The great national festival Durgā Pūjā had been celebrated only a few days ago but it was difficult for the disciples to take part in the festivities with their whole heart. How could they rejoice when their Master was suffering from a serious malady? Their one thought was to serve him, to nurse him, to attend to his smallest wants day and night. This devoted and unparalleled service of the Master led the way for the younger disciples (Vivekānanda and others) to the great renunciation of the world of which Bhagavān Shrī Rāmakrishna was the ideal example. Through their intense love for the Master they left their homes and sacrificed the duties and pleasures of life that they might give their whole soul to his service.

Notwithstanding his illness, hundreds of people came every day to pay reverential homage to him. They were eager to receive his blessing and to sit in his presence if only for a few minutes; for his presence brought peace and celestial happiness in the hearts and souls of all. Who had ever seen such unbounded compassion? He was anxious for the welfare of all those who came to him and was ever ready to help them by removing their doubts and opening their spiritual eyes. This was the time when Bhagavān Shrī Rāmakrishna showed to the world that he was not a man of this earth, but an embodiment of infinite divine love.

His charm and fascination were so great that everyone who came into his presence would lose the consciousness of time and place. Even men like Dr. Sircar, who was the busiest physician in Calcutta and who usually spent a few moments only with each patient, would remain with the Bhagavān hours together and sometimes the whole day. He had just now been paying Shrī Rāmakrishna a long visit. Rising to go, he said to the Bhagavān, who was then conversing with Shyām Bābu:[1] "Now that you have Shyām Bābu to talk to, I will bid you goodbye."

Shrī Rāmakrishna: "Would you not like to hear some songs?"

Doctor: "I should like it very much; but your feelings will be too much worked upon and you will go off into a state of ecstasy."

The doctor took his seat once more, and Vivekānanda sang to the accompaniment of instruments:

God and His Works

1. Wonderful, infinite, is the universe made by Thee! Behold, it is the repository of all beauty.

2. Thousands of stars do shine—a necklace of gold studded with gems. Innumerable are the moons and suns.

3. The earth is adorned with wealth and corn; full indeed is Thy storehouse. O Great Lord! Innumerable are the stars which sing, "Well done, Lord! well done!" They sing without ceasing.

Kālī, the Mother of the Universe

1. In the midst of the dense darkness, O Mother, breaketh forth the light of Thy formless beauty.
For this the *yogī* meditateth in the mountain cave.

2. In the lap of darkness infinite and borne on the sea of great *Nirvāna*,
The fragrance of peace everlasting floweth without ceasing.

3. O Mother! who art Thou, seated alone within the temple of *samādhi*, assuming the form of the Great Consort of the Lord of Eternity, and wearing the apparel of darkness?
The lotus of Thy feet keepeth us from fear; in them doth flash the lightning of Thy love for Thy children;
And loud laughter adorneth Thy spiritual face.

1 Shyām Bābu was a rich Hindu of Calcutta and an intimate friend of Dr. Sircar.

Doctor (to Vivekānanda): "It is dangerous for him—this singing. It will work upon his feelings with serious results."

Shrī Rāmakrishna (to Vivekānanda): "What does the doctor say?"

Vivekānanda: "Sir, the doctor is afraid lest this singing bring on ecstasy (*bhāva-samādhi*)."

Shrī Rāmakrishna (to the doctor, with folded hands): "No, oh no; why should my feelings be worked upon? I am very well."

But as soon as these words were uttered, the Bhagavān, who was already losing sense-consciousness, went into deep *samādhi*. His body became motionless. The eyes moved not. He sat speechless like a veritable figure of wood or stone. All sense-consciousness had ceased to be. The mind, the principle of personal identity, the heart, had all stepped out of their wonted course towards that one object, the Mother of the universe.

Again did Vivekānanda pour forth with his sweet, charming voice melody after melody.

In the midst of the songs, Shrī Rāmakrishna had come to himself again. The music was hushed. Then followed conversation with the Bhagavān, which was always charming alike to the learned and the illiterate, to the old and the young, to men and women, to the great and the lowly. The whole company sat mute and looked in silence on his divine face. Was there any trace now of that serious illness from which he was suffering? Joy alone was there, and radiance of celestial glory. Turning to the doctor, Shrī Rāmakrishna began:

Three Obstacles in the Way of Perfection

"Do give up shyness, doctor. One should not be shy in repeating before others the name of the Lord, or in dancing with joy while chanting His sweet name. Do not care what people may say. There is a proverb: 'Three obstacles lie in the way of perfection—shyness, contempt, and fear.' The shy man thinks: 'I, who am so unimportant, how can I dance in the name of the Lord? What will other great people say if they hear of it?' They may say: 'What a shame! The poor doctor has lost his head! He has danced while chanting the name of the Lord!' Give up all such foolish ideas."

Doctor: "That is not my line at all. I do not care what people say."

True Knowledge and Ignorance

Shrī Rāmakrishna (smiling): "On the contrary, you do care very much. Go beyond knowledge and ignorance, then you will realize God. Knowledge of diversity is ignorance. The egotism bred of erudition proceeds from ignorance. That knowledge by which we know that God exists everywhere is true knowledge. But to know Him intimately is realization (*vijnāna*)."

Realization

"Suppose your foot is pierced with a thorn, you require a second thorn to take it out. When the first thorn is taken out you throw both away. So in order to get rid of the thorn of ignorance you must bring the thorn of knowledge. Then you must throw away both ignorance and knowledge to attain to the complete realization of God, the Absolute, for the Absolute is above and beyond knowledge as well as ignorance. Lakshman once said to his divine brother: 'O Rāma, is it not strange that a God-knowing man like Vashishta Deva should have wept for the loss of his sons and would not be comforted?' Thereupon Rāma replied: 'He who has knowledge has also some ignorance. He who has knowledge of one object has also the knowledge of many objects. He who has the knowledge of light has also the knowledge of darkness, but *Brahman* the Absolute is beyond knowledge and ignorance and above virtue and vice, merit and demerit, purity and impurity.'"

Shyam Bābu: "Sir, may I ask what remains after both thorns are thrown away?"

The Absolute Brahman

Shrī Rāmakrishna: "What remains is the Absolute, called in the *Vedas Nitya-shuddha-bodha-rūpam* (the Unchangeable, the absolutely pure source of all knowledge). But how shall I explain it to you? Suppose someone asks you what is the taste of *ghee* (clarified butter) like? Is it possible to define it? The utmost that you can say is that it is precisely like the taste of *ghee*. A young girl once asked a friend: 'Your husband is come: tell me what short of joy you feel when you meet him?' Thereupon the married friend replied: 'My dear, you will know everything when you have got a husband of your own; how can I explain it to you?'

"In the *Purānas* we are told that the Mother of the universe incarnated Herself as the daughter of the presiding god of the Himālayas. Just after she was born, the king of the mountains was blessed with a vision of the various manifestations of the Omnipotent Mother. Then he said: 'O Mother! Let me see *Brahman* about whom there is so much in the *Vedas*.' The child Incarnate thereupon said: 'O father if thou wishest to see the Absolute *Brahman* thou must associate with the holy sages who have renounced everything. What the Absolute *Brahman* is cannot be expressed in words.' The *Tantra* has well said: 'All things with the sole exception of God the Absolute, have become defiled like leavings of food.' The idea is that the sacred scriptures of the world having been read and recited with the aid of the tongue have got defiled like food thrown out of the mouth. The Absolute *Brahman*, however, no one has ever been able to describe by word. Therefore it is said that the Absolute is not defiled by the mouth. Again, who can express in words the blissful joy that one experiences in the company of the Lord and in communion with the Absolute *Sat-Chit-Ānanda*? He alone knows who has been blessed with such realization."

Addressing the doctor, Shrī Rāmakrishna continued: "True knowledge does not come until egotism is entirely gone."

Prayer of a True Bhakta

"'When shall I be free?' When 'I' shall cease to be. The sense of 'I' and 'mine' is ignorance. The sense of 'Thou' and 'Thine' is knowledge. A true *bhakta* says: 'O Lord! Thou art the doer, Thou hast created everything, I am nothing but an instrument in Thy hands. I do only whatever Thou makest me do. All this is Thy wealth, Thy glory. Thine is the universe, Thine the family, Thine the relatives. Nothing belongs to me, I am Thy servant. Thine is to command and mine is to serve Thee with my whole heart and soul.'"

Egotism

"Egotism comes to all those who have studied a few books and have acquired a little learning. I had a talk with Tāgore[2] about the nature of God. He said to me: 'I know all about it.' I replied: 'He

2 Devendranāth Tāgore. See chap. 7, pp. 93-94.

who has been to Delhi does not go about telling others "I have been to Delhi" and so on. He who is a true gentleman does not boast of being a gentleman.'"

Shyam Bābu: "Sir, Tāgore has a great respect for you."

Vanity

Shrī Rāmakrishna: "My dear sir, shall I tell you of the vanity of the sweeper-woman in the temple at Dakshineshwar? She had a few ornaments on her person and she was so vain that whenever she walked along the road, if she found anyone near, she would shout: 'Get out of my way! Get out of my way!' What shall I say about the vanity of wealthy people of higher castes!"

A devotee: "If God is the one Actor in the universe, then whence come good and evil, virtue and vice? Do they exist by His will?"

The Lord Untouched by Good and Evil

Shrī Rāmakrishna: "In this world of relativity, good and evil, virtue and vice, exist, but they do not touch the Lord. God is unattached to them—like the wind which is unaffected by the good or bad odor which it carries. His creation is of dual nature, consisting of good and evil, real and unreal. As among trees there are some which bear good fruits, others poisonous, so among human beings there are good men and wicked, sinful men. Wicked people have their place in the world. Do you not see that wicked people are necessary to govern the law-breakers and evil-doers of a community?"

Shyam Bābu: "Sir, we are told on the one hand that man is punished for his sins, and on the other that God is the sole Actor, all creatures being humble instruments in His hands. How shall we reconcile these two things?"

Shrī Rāmakrishna: "You talk like a gold merchant weighing things with his delicate balance."

Calculating Intellect

Vivekānanda: "What the Bhagavān means to say is that you are talking like one who has a calculating intellect."

Shrī Rāmakrishna: "I say, O Podo (my foolish boy), eat these mangoes! What is the use of counting how many mango-trees there are in the garden, how many thousands of branches, how many millions of leaves, and so on? You are here to eat the mangoes. Eat them and go away. (To Shyam Bābu) You have come into this world to realize God by means of religious works. Your first effort should be to acquire love (*bhakti*) for the lotus feet of the Almighty. Why do you trouble yourself with other things? What will you gain by discussing philosophy? Do you not see that four ounces of wine are quite enough to intoxicate you? Why do you then inquire how many barrels of wine there are in the wine-shop? Of what use is such vain calculation?"

Doctor: "God's wine, again, is beyond all measure. The supply can never be exhausted."

Lay Cares on God

Shrī Rāmakrishna (to Shyam Bābu): "Furthermore, why do you not execute a power of attorney in favor of the Lord? Let all your cares and responsibilities rest on Him. If anyone trust an honest man, will that man do any wrong? God alone knows whether He will punish sinful acts or not."

Doctor: "He alone knows what is in His mind. How can man surmise it? He is beyond all human calculation."

Shrī Rāmakrishna (to Shyam Bābu): "You people of Calcutta always find fault with divine justice. You often complain that God is partial because He makes one happy and another unhappy. You foolish people see in God the same nature as your own. Hem used to come to Dakshineshwar with his friends. Whenever he saw me he would say: 'Sir, there is only one thing worth having in this world and that is honor, is it not so?' Very few understand that the end of human life is to attain God."

Shyam Bābu: "Sir, is it possible for anyone to show the subtle body? Can anyone show that the subtle body goes out of the gross body?"

Subtle Body

Shrī Rāmakrishna: "Those who are true *bhaktas* will not care to show you all this. They do not care in the least whether fools will respect them or not. They do not seek the favor of rich people."

Shyam Bābu: "Well, sir, what is the difference between the gross body and the subtle body?"

Shrī Rāmakrishna: "This physical body made of gross elements is called the gross body. *Manas* (mind), *buddhi* (intellect), *ahamkāra* (egoism), and *chitta* (mind-stuff, the subconscious mind), all these are in the subtle body. The inner body which feels the joy of the Lord and divine ecstasy is called the *kārana-sharīra* (causal body). The *Tantras* call it the *bhāgavati-tanu*, or the body derived from the Divine Mother. Beyond these is the *Mahākārana*, the first Great Cause. It is the fourth state. It cannot be expressed by words."

The Importance of Practice

"What is the use of hearing all this? Practice and you will know. You repeat the words '*siddhi, siddhi*' (hemp-leaves). Will that make you drunk? No, you must swallow some. There are threads of various numbers, No. 40, No. 41, and so on; but you do not know one number from another unless you are in the trade. It is by no means hard for those in the trade to know a particular number from that of another number. That being so, I say, practice a little. That done, it will be easy for you to have correct ideas as to the gross body, the subtle body, the *kārana* (the causal body made of joy), and the *Mahākārana* (the Great Cause or the Unconditioned).

"When you pray, ask for *bhakti*, devotion to His lotus feet. After Ahalyā[3] was made free from the curse called down upon her by her husband, Rāmachandra said: 'Ask for a boon from me.' Ahalyā replied: 'O Rāma, if Thou wilt give me a boon, do Thou grant that my mind may ever be on Thy feet beautiful like the lotus. O, I may be born among swine, but that will not matter.'"

Prayer for Bhakti

"For my part, I pray for love (*bhakti*) alone to my Divine Mother. Putting flowers upon Her lotus feet, with folded hands I prayed: 'Mother,

3 Ahalyā the wife of the great logician, the sage Gautama. She was a devoted wife, but the villainy of her seducer, who personated her husband, made her unchaste. Hence the curse, the effect of which was, it is said, that she was turned into stone. The touch of Rāmachandra made her human once more.

here is ignorance, here is knowledge. Oh! Take them; I want them not. Grant that I may have pure love alone. Here is cleanliness (of the mind and body), here is uncleanliness; what shall I do with them? Let me have pure love alone. Oh! Here is sin, here is merit; I want neither the one nor the other. Let me have pure love alone. Here is good, here is evil. Oh! Take them; I want them not. Let me have pure love alone. Here are good works, here are bad works. Oh! Place me above them; I want them not. Grant that I may have pure love alone.'"

Dual Existence

"If you take the fruit of good works, like charity, you must take the fruit of bad works also. If you take the fruit of merit, you must take the fruit of sin also. Knowledge of the One (*jnāna*) implies knowledge of the many (*ajnāna*). Taking cleanliness, you cannot get rid of its opposite, uncleanliness. Thus a knowledge of light implies a knowledge of darkness, its opposite. A knowledge of unity implies a knowledge of diversity."

Animal Food and Vegetarianism

"Blessed is the man who loves God. What matters it if he eats the flesh of swine? On the other hand, if a man lives upon vegetables but is attached to the world and does not love God, what good shall he gain?"

Work with the Mind Fixed on God

(To Shyam Bābu) "To live the life of a householder is by no means wrong. But take care that you work without attachment, with your mind always pointing to the feet of the Lord. Suppose a person has a carbuncle on the back. Now this man talks as usual. Perhaps he attends to his daily work. But pain constantly puts him in mind of the carbuncle. In the same way, although you are in the world, you should turn your mind constantly to God. A woman carrying on an intrigue with a lover thinks of this lover all the time that she is attending to her household duties. Live in the world like such a woman, doing your many duties with your soul secretly yearning for the Lord."

Shyam Bābu: "Sir, what do you think of Theosophy?"

Theosophy

Shrī Rāmakrishna: "The long and the short of the matter is that people who make disciples belong to an inferior order of men. Again, those who seek for powers also belong to an inferior class, such powers, for example, as the power of getting across the Ganges or the power of reporting here what a person is talking about in a far country, and other psychic powers. It is by no means easy for such people to get pure *bhakti* (love) for the Lord."

Shyam Bābu: "But, sir, the Theosophists seek to put Hinduism once more on a firm basis."

Shrī Rāmakrishna: "That may be. I am not well posted as to their views or doings."

Shyam Bābu: "Questions like the following are dealt with in Theosophy. What region is the soul bound for after death—the lunar sphere or the stellar mansions?"

Shrī Rāmakrishna: "I dare say. But let me give you an idea of my way of thinking. Somebody put it to Hanumān, the great lover of God, 'What day of the lunar fortnight is it?' Hanumān replied: 'My dear sir, excuse me. I know nothing about the days of the week, the day of the lunar fortnight, or the stars telling of the destiny on a particular day. That is not my concern. I meditate on Rāma and on Rāma alone.'"

Shyam Bābu: "Sir, the Theosophists believe in *mahātmās*. May I ask whether you hold that these *mahātmās* are real beings?"

Shrī Rāmakrishna: "If you care to take my word for truth, I say 'Yes.' But will you be good enough to let these matters alone? Come when I am better. Do but put faith in my words and I shall see that you find peace. Do you not observe that I do not take either money or clothes or any other thing? In some theatrical representations well-to-do visitors are expected to encourage the actors by gifts of money during the performance. Here people are not called upon to make such gifts. This is why so many come here."

(To the doctor) "What I have to say to you is this—but do not take offence! You have had enough of the things of the world, money, fame, lectures, and so on. Now give your mind a little to God, and come here now and then. It is good to listen to words relating to God. Such words enlighten the soul and turn it to the Lord."

A short while after, the doctor stood up to say goodbye. But just then Girish came in, and the doctor was so glad to see him that he took his seat again. Girish, stepping forward, saluted the Bhagavān and kissed the dust of his hallowed feet. The doctor watched all this in silence.

Doctor: "So long as I was here, Girish Bābu was not good enough to come. He must come just as I am about to go. (To Girish) Do everything else, but pray do not worship him as God. By doing so, you are only bringing ruin on such a holy man."

Worship of the Spiritual Preceptor

Girish: "Sir, there is, I fear, no help for it. He who has enabled me to get across this terrible sea of the world and the no less terrible sea of skepticism—how else shall I serve such a person? There is nothing in him I cannot worship."

Doctor: "I myself hold that all men are equal. As to this holy man, do you think I cannot salute and kiss the dust of his feet? Look here!" (The doctor saluted and kissed the dust of the Bhagavān's feet.)

Girish: "Oh, sir, the angels in heaven are saying: 'Blessed, blessed be this auspicious moment!'"

Doctor: "You seem to think that saluting anyone's feet is something like a marvel! You do not see that I can do the same in the case of everybody. (To a gentleman seated near) Now, sir, oblige me by allowing me to salute your feet. (To another) And you, sir. (To a third) And you, sir. (The doctor saluted at the feet of many)."

Vivekānanda (to the doctor): "Sir, we look upon the Bhagavān as a person who is like God. Let me make my idea clear to you. There is a point somewhere between the vegetable creation and the animal creation where it is difficult to say whether a particular thing is a vegetable or an animal. Much in the same way there is a point somewhere between the man-world and the God-world where you cannot say with certainty whether a person is a human being or God."

Doctor: "Well, my friend, matters relating to God cannot be explained by analogy."

Vivekānanda: "I say, not God, but Godlike man."

Doctor: "You should not give vent to the feelings of reverence like that. Speaking for myself, no one has been able, I am sorry to say, to judge my inward feelings. My best friends often regard me as stern and cruel. Even you, my good friends, may beat me some day with shoes and turn me out."

Shrī Rāmakrishna (to the doctor): "Do not say that, doctor. These people love you so much! They watch and look for you like ladies come together in the bride-chamber looking for the coming bridegroom."

Girish: "Everyone here has the greatest respect for you."

Doctor (sorrowfully): "My son—even my wife looks upon me as hard-hearted, and for the simple reason that I am by nature loath to show my feelings."

Girish: "In that case, sir, do you not think it would be better to throw open the door of your mind, at least out of pity for your friends? You well see that your friends do not understand you."

Doctor: "Shall I say it? Well, my feelings are worked up even more than yours. (To Vivekānanda) I shed tears in solitude."

Doctor (to Shrī Rāmakrishna): "Sir, may I say that it is not good that you allow people to touch your feet with their body while you are in *samādhi*?"

Shrī Rāmakrishna: "You do not mean that I am conscious of this?"

Doctor: "You feel that it is not a right thing to do, do you not?"

Shrī Rāmakrishna: "What shall I say as regards the state of my mind during *samādhi*? After the *samādhi* is over I often go so far as to ask myself: May not this be the cause of the disease that I have got? The thing is, the thought of God makes me mad. All this is the result of divine madness. There is no help for it."

Doctor (to the disciples): "He expresses regret for what he does. He feels that the act is wrong."

Shrī Rāmakrishna (to Girish): "You have great penetration. You explain it all to him, will you not?"

Girish (to the doctor): "Sir, you are quite mistaken. He is by no means sorry that his feet touch the persons of the devotees. No, it is not that. His body is pure, sinless; it is purity itself. He is good enough, in his anxiety for their spiritual welfare, to allow his hallowed feet to touch the bodies of the devotees. As a result of his taking their sins upon himself, his own body, he thinks, may be suffering from disease. Think of your own case. You were once taken ill, so you have told us, as the result of hard study. Well, did you not at that time express regret that you had sat up reading until very late at night? Does that prove that reading until the late hours of night is bad? The Bhagavān may be sorry from the point of view of the patient; he is by no means sorry from the point of view of a teacher from God anxious for the welfare of humanity."

Doctor (somewhat disconcerted): "I confess I am beaten. Now give me the dust of your feet. (To Vivekānanda) This matter apart, I must admit the acuteness of Girish's intellectual powers."

Vivekānanda (to the doctor): "You may view the question in another way. You sometimes devote your life to the task of making a scientific discovery, and then you do not look after your body, your health, or anything. Now the knowledge of God is the grandest of all sciences; is it not natural that the Bhagavān has risked his health for this end, and, it may be, sacrificed it? We offer to him worship equal to divine worship."

The doctor then saluted the Bhagavān and took his leave. At that moment Bijoy entered and prostrated himself at the feet of Shrī Rāmakrishna. He had been making pilgrimages to various holy places, and Mahima said to him: "Sir, you have just returned from a pilgrimage; you have seen many things, kindly tell us about them."

Pilgrimage Useless

Bijoy: "What shall I say? I see now that here I find everything. To go on pilgrimages is useless traveling. There are some places where you will find one-sixteenth, or at the utmost one-fourth, of what you see here. In the Bhagavān I find everything in full complement. I have not found anyone who possesses anything more than our Bhagavān."

Rāmakrishna (to Vivekānanda): "Look what a wonderful change has taken place in Bijoy. His character has become entirely different, as if the milk has been boiled and thickened. By seeing the neck and forehead I can recognize the state of *paramahamsa*."

Mahima (to Bijoy): "Sir, you take very little food, do you not?"

Bijoy: "Yes, I believe I do. (To Rāmakrishna) Revered sir, hearing of thy illness I have come to see thee."

Rāmakrishna: "What?"

Bijoy kept silent for a while and then said: "No one can understand thy perfection unless thou givest the power."

Rāmakrishna: "Kedār said to me that when he went to other places he starved, but that here he always found food in abundance."

Bijoy (clasping his hands before Rāmakrishna): "Lord, I know thee now. I understand thy glory. Thou needest not tell me of it."

Thereupon Rāmakrishna went into *samādhi*. When he returned, he said: "If that be so, let it be so."

Bijoy: "Yes Lord, now I know thee."

Saying this, Bijoy prostrated himself before Rāmakrishna and pressed to his breast the hallowed feet of the Lord. Bhagavān Shrī Rāmakrishna, again losing all sense-consciousness, entered into God-consciousness and remained motionless like a carven image. Seeing this wonderful sight, some of the devotees shed tears of joy and happiness, while others kneeled and began to pray to the Bhagavān. Each one fixed his eyes upon Shrī Rāmakrishna and, according to the innermost feeling of his heart, realized his ideal in him. Some saw in him the ideal devotee, while others recognized the Divine Incarnation in a human form. Mahima with tears of joy in his eyes chanted: "Behold, behold, the embodiment of divine love!" And after a few minutes, as if catching a glimpse of the Absolute *Brahman* in Rāmakrishna, he exclaimed: "Infinite Existence, Intelligence, and Love, beyond unity and diversity!"

Avatāra

After remaining in this state for a long time, Bhagavān Rāmakrishna came down once more on the human plane and said: "God incarnates Himself in a human form. It is true that He dwells everywhere, in all living creatures, but the desires of the human soul cannot be fulfilled except by an *Avatāra* or Divine Incarnation. The human being longs to see Him, touch Him, be with Him, and enjoy His divine company. In order to fulfill such desires, the Incarnation of God is necessary.

"When an *Avatāra* or Divine Incarnation descends, however, the people at large do not know it. It is known only to a few chosen disciples. Can everyone comprehend the indivisible Absolute *Brahman*, Existence-Intelligence-Bliss Absolute?"

Rāma

"When the supreme Lord incarnated Himself as Rāma, only twelve sages knew it. The other saints and sages knew Him as the prince of the Rājā Dasharatha. But those twelve sages prayed to Him, saying: 'O Rāma, thou art the indivisible Existence-Intelligence-Bliss Absolute. Thou hast incarnated in this human form. By Thine own power of *māyā* Thou appearest as a human being, but in reality Thou art the Lord of the universe.'"

CHAPTER 14

Cossipur Garden-House

Bhagavān Rāmakrishna resided for a few months in a large and beautiful garden at Cossipur, about two miles north of Calcutta. Here he was constantly surrounded by his most beloved *sannyāsī* disciples and by those women disciples who were especially devoted to him.

The *sannyāsī* disciples were twelve in number.[1] Most of them were young men of noble families and were graduates of the University of Calcutta. They had left their homes and relatives for his sake. Their one aim in life was to serve their Master, the living God on earth and the Incarnation of Divinity in a human form. The love of Shrī Rāmakrishna captivated their hearts and souls. Indeed these earnest and sincere disciples were the pillars upon which the divine Manifestation was about to build the structure of his universal mission. The illness which the Bhagavān had assumed upon his physical form was the means by which he gathered his beloved ones around him and gave them the opportunity to nurse and wait upon their divine Master. They sacrificed their personal comfort upon the altar of true devotion and served their Lord with whole heart and soul day after day and night after night. Their devotion was unique and unparalleled in the religious history of modern India. It was these young disciples who afterwards became the world-renowned Swāmīs of the Order of Shrī Rāmakrishna. There were also householder disciples, like Shuresh, Balarām, Girish, Rām, Mahendra, and others, who used to come frequently to see Shrī Rāmakrishna and to serve him by supplying the household with all necessary things.

1 Narendra (Vivekānanda), Rākhāl (Brahmānanda), Niranjan (Niranjānananda), Shashi (Rāmakrishnānanda), Sarat (Sāradānanda), Bāburām (Premānanda), Kālī (Abhedānanda), Jogin (Yogānanda), Lātu (Adbhutānanda), Gopāl (Advaitānanda), Tārak (Shivānanda), Subodh (Subodhānanda).

Rāmakrishna occupied the large room on the second floor of the beautiful house situated in the center of the spacious garden. He was seated on his bed, which was spread on the floor, and was surrounded by his *sannyāsī* and householder disciples. Conversation arose concerning *sannyāsa* (renunciation) and a householder's life, and Girish asked: "Bhagavan, which is right—to renounce the world with a view to avoid worldly cares and suffering or to worship God living with one's family?"

To Live in the World or to Renounce It

Bhagavān referred to the teaching of the *Bhagavad Gītā* and said: "He who lives with his family but is unattached to the relations and things of the world, who performs his duties without seeking the result of his works, attains to God in the same manner as one who has renounced the world after realizing that earthly relations and objects are transitory and unreal. Those who renounce the world merely to avoid worldly cares and suffering belong to the lowest class of *sannyāsīs*. He who has attained to God living in the world is like the man who resides in a crystal palace and sees everything of the outside as well as of the inside of the palace."

Girish: "Bhagavan, why is it that mind after reaching a very high plane comes down to the world?"

Fickleness of Mind

Bhagavān: "It is natural with the mind of one who lives in the world. Sometimes it is on a high plane and sometimes on a low. Sometimes there is a great upheaval of devotional feeling, then again it subsides, because the attraction of lust and wealth is very strong. A devotee who lives in the world may meditate on God and repeat His holy name, but again his mind is attracted by the power of lust and wealth, just as a fly sometimes lights on the most delicious sweetmeat and sometimes relishes the taste of filth or of a rotten carcass."

A True Sannyāsī

"It is different, however, with those who have renounced the world. They have detached their mind entirely from lust and wealth and have fixed it upon the Supreme. They constantly drink the nectar of divine love. The mind of a true *sannyāsī* does not care for anything other than the Supreme. He leaves the place where worldly talk prevails. He listens to discourses about the highest spiritual truth alone. A true *sannyāsī* does not speak of worldly matters, he utters no word which has not bearing upon the spiritual ideal. A bee sits on flowers only to drink honey. He does not care for any other object." Then, referring to Rākhāl (Swāmī Brahmānanda), who had a wife and a child before he renounced the world, Rāmakrishna said: "Rākhāl and others like him have now understood which is good and which is evil, which is real and which is unreal. They have realized that earthly relations are transitory and ephemeral. They will never again be attached to the world. They are like eels which live in the mud but remain untouched by it."

Girish: "I do not understand all that. Thou hast the power to make everyone unattached to the world and free from bondage. Thou hast the power to make everyone perfect whether a *sannyāsī* or a householder. When the Malaya breeze[2] blows it can transform all trees into sandalwood trees."

The Worthy Will Become Perfect

Bhagavān: "But pithless trees like the banana- and the cotton-tree are not transformed into sandalwood. Similarly those who are worthy will become perfect. Worldliness means attachment to lust and wealth. Many worldly people consider wealth as their heart's blood. But if you take too much care of wealth, perhaps one day it will go entirely out of your possession. In our country farmers build earthen embankments round their fields. Those who do not leave open any passage for water and take too much care of their embankments, invariably have theirs washed off first by the tremendous current of the water; but those who keep one side open, find that their fields become enriched with alluvial deposits and more fertile in the end. They make the best use of their riches who spend them in the service of the Lord and of holy sages. They reap good fruits of their wealth who give freely to the poor and needy and for the good of humanity."

2 A breeze from the Malaya mountains mentioned in the *Rāmāyana* and *Mahābhārata*.

The Bhagavān continued: "I cannot use any object that is given to me by physicians and medical practitioners who live upon the painful diseases of other people. However, it is different with those physicians who are kind-hearted, charitable, and unselfish."

Taught His Disciples Renunciation

To destroy the pride and egotism of his disciples, Shrī Rāmakrishna told them to wear the seamless ocher robe of the *sannyāsī* and to take up the begging-bowl. Being himself a perfect *sannyāsī*, he loved to see his disciples following him in the path of renunciation. On different occasions he sent them out, as Buddha and Shankara had done with their disciples, to beg food from door to door. One morning he called certain among his beloved ones—Narendra, Sarat, Jogin, Niranjan, Kālī—and asked them whether they could go forth with the *sannyāsī's* begging-bowl and beg uncooked food for him. It was indeed a great blow to the caste pride as well as to the sense of self-respect of these young disciples. Obeying the Master's wish, however, they took the begging-bowl in their hands, walked from door to door in the neighborhood, collected various articles of food, brought them before their Master, and offered them at his holy feet. Bhagavān Rāmakrishna blessed them and rejoiced at their sincere and earnest devotion. This was the manner in which the Bhagavān initiated his disciples in the life of absolute renunciation.

Meaning of His Illness

One evening Shrī Rāmakrishna was attended by his faithful servants Shashi (Rāmakrishnānanda) and Kālī (Abhedānanda), who were waiting upon him. The Bhagavān opened his mouth and inspired them by saying: "The illness of my body is caused by the sins of those who come and touch my feet. I purify the sinners by taking their sins upon myself and suffering for them. He who was Rāma, who was Krishna, Buddha, Christ, and Chaitanya, has now become Rāmakrishna. Blessed are those who know this truth. My

Divine Mother has shown me that the photograph of this body will be kept upon altars and be worshipped in different houses as the pictures of other *Avatāras* are worshipped. My Divine Mother has also shown me that I shall have to come back again and that my next incarnation will be in the West."

Narendra (Vivekānanda) had extreme longing for the realization of the *Brahman* the Absolute. One day Bhagavān Rāmakrishna, addressing Narendra in the presence of other disciples, said: "I hold the key of the chest which contains the treasure of the highest realization. I shall not unlock that chest until you have finished my work which I wish you to do."

Cure of His Illness

Pandit Sashadhar came one day to pay his respects to Bhagavān Rāmakrishna. Seeing his illness, he asked him: "Bhagavan, why dost thou not concentrate thy mind upon the diseased part and thus cure thyself?"

The Bhagavān replied: "How can I fix my mind, which I have given to God, upon this cage of flesh and blood?"

Sashadhar said: "Why dost thou not pray to thy Divine Mother for cure of thy illness?"

The Bhagavān answered: "When I think of my Mother the physical body vanishes and I am entirely out of it, so it is impossible for me to pray for anything concerning the body."

Hearing this, Sashadhar bowed at his holy feet and asked for his blessing.

His Love for Humanity

The news of Shrī Rāmakrishna's illness spread like wild-fire among all those who had known him or heard of his divine personality. Hundreds of people came every day to see him and to pay reverent homage to him. Some came to receive his blessing, some to kiss the dust of his holy feet, some to hear a few words uttered by him, and others to clear the doubts of their minds. Among these were a few more devoted ones, like Harī, Gangādhar, Sāradā, Tulsī, who afterwards joined the Order and were known as Turīyānanda, Akhandānanda, Trigunātīta, and Nirmalānanda. Bhagavān Rāmakrishna received them all with equal kindness and was ever ready to help them. Although his physical body was weakened and exhausted, still his desire to help mankind was so great that he often exclaimed: "I would give twenty thousand bodies like this if by that I could help one single soul in the path of righteousness and God-consciousness!"

Dr. Sircar and other physicians gave strict orders to the *sannyāsī* disciples to allow no one to come near the Bhagavān, as he needed absolute rest and must have no excitement of any kind. The *sannyāsī* disciples followed this advice to the letter and would not allow even the householder disciples to come near him or touch his holy body. But Shrī Rāmakrishna could not bear this bondage. He burst into tears when he heard of this restriction. His heart melted with divine love and he declared that his suffering was infinitely less than that of the worldly people who were groaning under the burden of their worldly cares and anxieties and who had no one to lift them above this mundane existence. His love for humanity was so great that, disregarding his bodily welfare, he called everyone near unto him in the same manner as Jesus the Christ called all those who were heavily laden and who sought for peace and rest.

Many a time the Bhagavān declared before his beloved *sannyāsī* children: "Divine Mother is working through this form. She has kept it so long because Her work is not yet finished."

His Oneness with All

When he could scarcely speak or swallow any food, the Bhagavān said: "I am now speaking and eating through so many mouths. I am the Soul of all individual souls. I have infinite mouths, infinite heads, infinite hands and feet. My pure form is spiritual. It is Absolute Existence, Intelligence, and Bliss condensed, as it were. It has neither birth nor death, neither sorrow, disease, nor suffering.

It is immortal and perfect. I see the indivisible Absolute *Brahman* (*Sat-Chit-Ānanda*) within me as well as all around me. You are all like my own parts. The Infinite *Brahman* is manifesting Itself through so many human forms. Human bodies are like pillow-cases of different shapes and various colors, but the cotton wool of the internal Spirit is one. When *jīva* (ego) enters into that Spirit and becomes one with it, there is neither pain nor suffering. I am the Infinite Spirit covered by a human skin which has a wound somewhere near the throat. Mind affects the body and is in turn affected by the body. When the body is ill, that illness reacts upon the mind. When one is burned by hot water one says: 'This water has burned me,' but the truth is that heat burns and not the water. All pain is in the body, all disease is in the body, but the Spirit is above pain and beyond the reach of disease."

Purpose of His Illness

"My illness is to teach mankind how to think of the Spirit and how to live in God-consciousness even when there is extreme pain in the body; when the body is suffering from the agony of pain and starvation, when there is no remedy within human power, even then the Mother shows that Spirit is the master of the body. My illness is to set an example of absolute mastery of the Spirit over matter in this age of materialism and skepticism. My Divine Mother has brought this illness upon this body to convince the skeptics of the present age that *Ātman* is divine, that God-consciousness is as true and practical today as it was in the Vedic period, that when one reaches perfection, freedom from all bondage is attained. My Divine Mother has shown through Her child what is meant by the various kinds of *yoga* and how people of this age can attain to it. She has also shown that all scriptures are true, that all religions are like paths which lead to the same common goal of the one Infinite Divinity. All of my religious practices, *yoga* practices, devotional exercises have been for the good of others and not for my own good. My Mother has set through this form a living example in this age.

"Whosoever will practice one-sixteenth part of what I have said and done will surely attain to God-consciousness in this life."

Glossary of Common Foreign Terms

āchārya: a religious teacher; preceptor.
ādesha: Divine commission (to teach).
Advaita: non-dualism; a form of *Vedānta* advocated by Shankara; see *Vedānta*
ahamkāra: egoism.
ajnāna: ignorance; knowledge of the many.
ākāsha: infinite space
ānnās: a small Indian coin; one-sixteenth of one *rupee.*
āratī: a ceremonial means of worship accompanied by the waving of lights.
āsana: yogic posture or physical pose.
Ātman: the true Self; the one permanent Reality.
avidyā: ignorance; attachment to worldly things.
avadhuta: a title for one who has realized God and is the master of nature.

Bābā: Father; a wise or aged person.
bābu: gentleman; also the equivalent of Mr. or Sir.
baddha: a bond; a soul bound to the world.
Bhagavad Gītā: a portion of the *Mahābhārata* in which Krishna converses with Arjuna.
Bhagavān (Bhagavan): Lord.
Bhāgavatam. See *Shrīmad Bhāgavatam*
bhakta: a devotee; one who loves God.
bhakti: devotion; the love of God.
bhakti yoga: the path to God by means of love.
Brahma jnāna: knowledge of *Brahman*.
Brahman: the Absolute; Ultimate Reality.
brāhmin: a member of the highest of the four Hindu castes.
Brāhmo Samāj: a Hindu unitarian church founded by Rājā Rāmmohan Roy in 1830 A.D.
buddhi: intellect; understanding.

chitta: mind-stuff; the subconscious mind.
Chitshakti: the Self-Conscious Power that rules the universe.

dayā: compassion.
deva: a male deity.
devī: a female deity.
dhāranā: concentration.
dhyāna: meditation.

Gāyatrī: the most sacred and the most universally used of all Vedic prayers: "Let us meditate on that glorious self-effulgent light of the Divine Sun; may He enlighten our *buddhi* or understanding."
ghāt: a series of steps leading to a body of water.
ghee: clarified butter.
gopī: cowherdess, milkmaid; in the forest of Brindāvan, a lover of Shrī Krishna.
gunas: the three qualities of nature—*sattva*, *rajas*, and *tamas*.
guru: a spiritual master.

hatha yoga: the branch of *yoga* dealing with the physical body.
hatha yogī: one who practices *hatha yoga*.

Īshvara: the Personal God.

jīva: the individual soul.
jnāna: true philosophy; knowledge of the Absolute;.
jnāna yoga: the path to God, the Absolute, by means of knowledge.
jnāni: a true philosopher; one who knows or attempts to know the Absolute.

Kālī: the Divine Mother of the universe.
Kali yuga: the last of four cycles of manifestation; the present materialistic age.
kāmini: woman, in the sense of a seductress; lust.
kānchan: gold; attachment to wealth; worldliness.
karma: action and its results; works and duties.
karma yoga: the path of *karma* or good works.
karma yogī: one who follows the path of *karma yoga*.
kārana: the causal body made of joy.
kartā: the doer.
kha: empty space.

līlā: Divine sport or play.

Mahābhārata: one of the two great Hindu epics.
mahābhāva: the most intense form of ecstatic devotion.
Mahākārana: the Great Cause or the Unconditioned.
Mahārāj: great king; an eminent spiritual person.
mahātmā: a holy man.
māhut: an elephant driver.
manas: mind.
mantram: a name of God, or sacred formula, that is ritually repeated.
māyā: the enchanting powers of the Divine Mother; the realm of qualities; worldliness.
mukta: the free or emancipated soul.
mumukshu: the soul seeking after freedom.

nāda: the sound of *Om*.
namaskār: salutation; a reverential greeting with palms touching and raised to the forehead.
nirguna: without qualities (*gunas*); impersonal and beyond all attributes.
nirvikalpa samādhi: the highest state of ecstasy (*samādhi*) in which the soul rises above the sense of "I" and reaches the realm of the Absolute.
nitya-mukta: the eternally free soul.
nitya-siddha: a perfected soul from birth.

Om: the eternal and all-pervading sacred sound, identified with *Brahman* (the Absolute), from which the universe arises and into which it dissolves.
Om tat sat: a sacred formula meaning *Brahman* is the only Reality.

Panchavati: five sacred trees forming a grove that has been set aside for contemplation.
pandit: a scholar.
paramahamsa: a perfected soul; also an honorific title for gurus.
prakriti: cosmic energy; nature.
prāna: vital force.
pranāma: salutation.

prema: intense devotion; the ecstatic love of God.
Purānas: the sacred scriptures of the Hindus, next in authority to the *Vedas*.
Purusha: cosmic Man; the all-pervading Self.

rājā: a king.
rājā yoga: the path to God by means of concentration and meditation.
rajas: one of the three qualities (*gunas*) of nature; worldly and creative activity.
rājasika: of the nature of *rajas*.
Rāmāyana: one of the two great Hindu epics.
rishi: one of the holy sages or seers to whom the *Vedas* were revealed.
rudrāksha: a species of tree whose seeds are used as beads in a rosary.
rupee: an Indian monetary unit.

sādhana: spiritual practice.
sādhu: a religious ascetic; an anchorite.
samādhi: ecstasy; the state of God-consciousness.
samsāra: the cycle of birth, life, death, and rebirth.
samskāras: impressions of previous lives.
sandhyā: rituals; evening service.
Sānkhya: one of the six schools of classical Indian philosophy.
sankīrtan: devotional singing.
sannyāsa: renunciation.
sannyāsī: one who has renounced the world for the sake of the Lord.
Sat-Chit-Ānanda: Existence-Intelligence-Bliss.
sattva: one of the three qualities (*gunas*) of nature; spiritual and unattached activity.
Shāktas: devotees of the Divine Mother.
Shakti: the Eternal Energy; the Divine Mother;
Shaiva: a devotee of Shiva, a central form of the Divinity.
Shāstras: post-Vedic lawbooks.
Shrī: an honorific often prefixed to names of Gods and saints.
Shrīmad Bhāgavatam: the most famous of the *Purānas*.
siddha: perfected; one who has absolute control over psychic

phenomena.
siddhis: yogic powers.
sircar: a steward.

tamas: one of the three qualities (*gunas*) of nature; negatively, destructive and passionate activity; positively, the resistance of evil.
Tantras: sacred writings of the Shaiva and Shākta sects.
tapasyā: ascetic exercises.

vairāgya: dispassion and non-attachment.
Vaishnava: a devotee of Vishnu, a central form of the Divinity.
vāk-siddhi: power of speech; the ability, by saying a thing, to make it come to pass.
Vedānta: one of the six schools of Hindu philosophy; see also *Advaita*; *Visishtādvaita*
Vedas: the most ancient Hindu scriptures.
vichāra: discussion and argumentations meant to actualize *viveka* (right discrimination).
vidyā: true knowledge that leads Godward.
vijnāna: complete knowledge or realization.
vijnāni: a fully realized *jnāni*; one who recognizes that the same Absolute *Brahman* appears as the Personal God (*Īshvara*).
Visishtādvaita: qualified non-dualism; a form of *Vedānta* advocated by Rāmānuja; see also *Vedānta*.
viveka: right discrimination (of the Real from the unreal).

yoga: union; various means of communion with God.
yogī: one who practices *yoga* or has mastered it.
yuga: one of four cycles of manifestation.

zamindār: a landlord.

For a glossary of all key foreign words used in books published by World Wisdom, including metaphysical terms in English, consult: www.DictionaryofSpiritualTerms.org.
This on-line Dictionary of Spiritual Terms provides extensive definitions, examples, and related terms in other languages.

Index

Biographical Notes

M or **Mahendranāth Gupta** (1854-1932) was a devoted householder disciple of Shrī Rāmakrishna. He was the headmaster of various schools, where he also taught English, philosophy, economics, and other subjects. Following Rāmakrishna's death in 1886, he dedicated the rest of his non-professional life to the completion of his master work, *The Gospel of Rāmakrishna*.

Swāmī Abhedānanda (1866-1939) was a direct disciple of Shrī Rāmakrishna. In 1897 he traveled to America to become the head of the Vedanta Society in New York. He stayed in America until 1921 teaching and lecturing. In addition to his work on *The Gospel of Rāmakrishna*, he was the author of several books on Indian philosophy and religion.

Joseph A. Fitzgerald studied Comparative Religion at Indiana University, where he also earned a Doctor of Jurisprudence degree. He is an award-winning editor whose previous publications include *Honen the Buddhist Saint: Essential Writings and Official Biography*, *The Essential Śrī Ānandamayī Mā: Life and Teachings of a 20th Century Saint from India*, *The Way and the Mountain: Tibet, Buddhism, and Tradition*, *An Illustrated Introduction to Taoism: The Wisdom of the Sages*, and *The Wisdom of Ananda Coomaraswamy* (with S.D.R. Singam). He lives with his wife and daughters in Bloomington, Indiana.

Alexander Lipski (1919-2009) was Professor of History and Religious Studies at California State University, Long Beach from 1958 to 1984. He was a Professor Emeritus from 1984 until his passing. He is the author of *Thomas Merton and Asia: His Quest for Utopia*, and is the editor of *Bengal: East and West*. His classic *Life and Teaching of Śrī Ānandamayī Mā* was recently incorporated into *The Essential Śrī Ānandamayī Mā: Life and Teachings of a 20th Century Saint from India*.

Swāmī Vivekānanda (1863-1902) was the closest and most famous disciple of Shrī Rāmakrishna. He was one of the first Indians to introduce and popularize Hindu philosophy, especially the *Vedānta*, to a Western audience. A speaker at the Parliament of the World's Religions in Chicago in 1893, he also delivered many other addresses in America and Europe. He founded both the Ramakrishna Mission and the Ramakrishna Order, which in America is known as the Vedanta Society.

Titles in the Spiritual Masters: East & West Series by World Wisdom

The Essential Shinran: A Buddhist Path of True Entrusting,
edited by Alfred Bloom, 2007

The Essential Sri Anandamayi Ma: Illustrated,
by Alexander Lipski and Anandamayi Ma, 2007

The Essential Swami Ramdas: Commemorative Edition,
compiled by Susunaga Weeraperuma, 2005

Frithjof Schuon: Messenger of the Perennial Philosophy,
by Michael Oren Fitzgerald, 2010

The Golden Age of Zen: Zen Masters of the T'ang Dynasty,
by John C.H. Wu, 2003

Honen the Buddhist Saint: Essential Writings and Official Biography,
edited by Joseph A. Fitzgerald, 2006

Introduction to Hindu Dharma: Illustrated
by Jagadguru His Holiness Sri Chandrasekharendra Saraswati Swamigal, Sankaracharya of Kanchi,
edited by Michael Oren Fitzgerald, 2008

The Laughing Buddha of Tofukuji: The Life of Zen Master Keido Fukushima,
by Ishwar C. Harris, 2004

Messenger of the Heart: The Book of Angelus Silesius,
by Frederick Franck, 2005

The Original Gospel of Ramakrishna: Based on M.'s English Text, Abridged,
revised by Swami Abhedananda,
edited and abridged by Joseph A. Fitzgerald, 2011

Paths to Transcendence: According to Shankara, Ibn Arabi, and Meister Eckhart,
by Reza Shah-Kazemi, 2006

Samdhong Rinpoche: Uncompromising Truth for a Compromised World: Tibetan Buddhism and Today's World,
edited by Donovan Roebert, 2006

A Spirit of Tolerance: The Inspiring Life of Tierno Bokar,
by Amadou Hampaté Bâ, edited by Roger Gaetani, 2008

The Sufi Doctrine of Rumi: Illustrated Edition,
by William C. Chittick, 2005

Timeless in Time: Sri Ramana Maharshi,
by A. R. Natarajan, 2006

Other Titles on Hinduism by World Wisdom

A Christian Pilgrim in India: The Spiritual Journey of Swami Abhishiktananda (Henri Le Saux),
by Harry Oldmeadow, 2008

The Essential Sri Anandamayi Ma: Life and Teachings of a 20th Century Indian Saint,
by Alexander Lipski and Sri Anandamayi Ma, 2007

The Essential Swami Ramdas: Commemorative Edition,
compiled by Susunaga Weeraperuma, 2005

The Essential Vedanta: A New Source Book of Advaita Vedanta,
edited by Eliot Deutsch and Rohit Dalvi, 2004

A Guide to Hindu Spirituality,
by Arvind Sharma, 2006

Introduction to Hindu Dharma: Illustrated
by Jagadguru His Holiness Sri Chandrasekharendra Saraswati Swamigal, Sankaracharya of Kanchi,
edited by Michael Oren Fitzgerald, 2008

Lamp of Non-Dual Knowledge & Cream of Liberation: Two Jewels of Indian Wisdom,
translated by Swami Sri Ramanananda Saraswathi, 2003

Paths to Transcendence: According to Shankara, Ibn Arabi & Meister Eckhart,
by Reza Shah-Kazemi, 2006

The Power of the Sacred Name: Indian Spirituality Inspired by Mantras,
by V. Raghavan, edited by William J. Jackson, 2011

Timeless in Time: Sri Ramana Maharshi,
by A.R. Natarajan, 2006

Tripura Rahasya: The Secret of the Supreme Goddess,
translated by Swami Sri Ramanananda Saraswathi, 2002

Unveiling the Garden of Love: Mystical Symbolism in Layla Majnun & Gitagovinda,
by Lalita Sinha, 2009

The Wisdom of Ananda Coomaraswamy: Reflections on Indian Art, Life, and Religion,
edited by S.D.R. Singam and Joseph A. Fitzgerald, 2011